GAIL S. HALVORSEN

To Daryl —

Gail W Halvorsen

29 Nov 04

THE BERLIN C·A·N·D·Y BOMBER

HORIZON PUBLISHERS
SPRINGVILLE, UTAH

ISBN 13: 978-0-88290-616-4

Published by Horizon Publishers, an imprint of
Cedar Fort, Inc., 2373 West 700 South, Springville, UT, 84663
Distributed by Cedar Fort, Inc., www.cedarfort.com

Cover design by Angela Olsen
Cover design © 2010 by Lyle Mortimer

Printed in the United States of America

10   9   8   7   6   5   4

Printed on acid-free paper

Contents

This book is dedicated to:

- Alta for her inspiration;
- our children: Brad, Denise, Marilyn, Bob, Mike, and their wonderful spouses;
- our cherished grandchildren;
- young people everywhere with their hopes for a better world.

Author's note:

The crew members, Captain Pickering and Sergeant Elkins, were with the author on many flights, but not on all the flights indicated in the book. Conversations represented as being with them also portray conversations with other crew members whose names are not available.

1

Survival

Mercedes put down the partially filled bucket of water that she had drawn from the public water supply. The water pressure to the upper floors of the apartment building at 15 Hahnelstrasse, Berlin, was insufficient for the second time that week. Although not full, the large bucket was a challenge for a seven-year-old girl navigating the bomb-splintered stairs to the apartment above. Her thin legs needed a rest before the climb. Rations were meager after the war, and now there was even less food available. The city was under siege by the Soviets. They had cut off all the supplies coming over the land routes to West Berlin.

She paused to glance at the threatening sky before she began to climb. How different this place was from just a few years ago. A pile of bricks and jagged cement blocks smothered the space on both sides of the walk where roses once bloomed. A piece of railing from the balcony still had evidence of spilled water colors from happier times. She hurried past these stark reminders of civilization gone berserk. The once-elegant entryway was now a shambles. She stopped for a short rest here, then went on up the stairs.

"Mercedes, where in the world is that water?" her mother called. Compared to what Frau Simon had been through, this was a very minor irritant, but the water was an essential ingredient to go with the few ounces of flour she had received that morning from the distribution center.

It wasn't long before dark and there would be no lights available until 2 A.M. Some wood splinters and limbs from the once-majestic

7

shade tree in the courtyard below were carefully rationed and neatly placed next to the tiny wood-burning stove. All was in readiness for some chicken broth and hot bread. There was promise of more flour but the stock for the broth was all that was left from the white chickens that were not laying eggs. The egg producers had at least a temporary promise of life unless things got worse. Eggs were nice to have during a siege where food was the ultimate weapon. In any case, the producing chickens would be there for a subsequent meal barring an unwelcome intruder.

Mercedes put down the bucket on the kitchen stool and stooped over to slide the wooden block under the table leg to adjust for the sagging floor. The kitchen had fared better than some of the other rooms in the apartment, but even it needed some major repair. For that matter, there was little of 15 Hahnelstrasse that resembled its old self. What the British and the American bombers had missed the Russians had just about finished off.

The look on her daughter's face was enough to cause her mother to inquire, "Mercedes, what is the problem?" Mercedes stepped toward the kitchen window which was partially obscured by a piece of canvas used to replace the broken glass. She pulled back a corner and pointed toward the heavy black clouds that completely covered the city.

"There's something wrong up there," she said. "Listen to the sound of those engines."

It was 12 August 1948. The steady drone of one aircraft right behind another bringing desperately needed supplies for the two million survivors was no longer steady. The usual rhythmic sound of aircraft approaching for a landing at nearby Tempelhof airport was now replaced with the pulsating, irregular roar from 120 Pratt and Whitney R-2000 Twin Wasp engines. These magnificent power plants were securely fastened to aluminum shells full to the brim with flour, medicine, coal, and milk. Few of the aircraft were getting onto the ground.

The air was vibrating with the force of three-bladed Hamilton Standard propellers placed in near flat-pitch, driven by advanced throttles in response to the pilot's request for an emergency go-around or climb to a holding altitude. The visibility was too low to allow enough landings to accommodate the string of Douglas C-54's coming through the air corridors from the west. The cumbersome and slow let-down procedures using the low-frequency radio range were no match for the Berlin weather. Effective radar aids for the approach and landing were yet to come.

The dark clouds had joined the scarred surface of the city to deny it what it needed most. The pilots were circling in the murk, awaiting a clearance for another approach, while desperately trying to stay out of each other's way.

Frau Simon never took Mercede's concerns lightly. She had been father and mother to Mercedes almost from birth. The steady, loving nature of this good woman had provided a secure haven for the little girl growing up in such perilous times. Still, Mercedes longed to meet the father she never remembered seeing. Each day she hoped to hear something of his demise or, more hopefully, of his capture or release. He had held some very important positions. Mystery still surrounded his whereabouts and status. "Your father may be a prisoner in Russia for all I know," Frau Simon would answer in resignation to Mercede's frequent requests for information.

The sense of anxiety Mercedes felt was borne of many years listening to the roar of aircraft engines overhead. Not long ago that sound meant death and destruction and was a warning to find the best shelter as quickly as possible, for bombs were about to rain down all around her old apartment house. The anxiety now was because those engines overhead were not making their usual rhythmic sound.

There was anxiety in the faces of the pilots in that milling mass of metal and men. Their concern was reflected in their voice communications with traffic control. The radio traffic was mostly emergency go-around instructions and clearances for changes in altitude and holding locations as the airspace became saturated.

One C-54 had just landed long, skidded off the runway, collapsed the nose gear, ruptured a gas tank, and was burning furiously on the end of the runway. Heroic efforts by volunteer Berliner flour unloaders were underway to extract the aircrew, one of whom was engulfed in flames. Any moment the whole aircraft could explode. Control procedures were rapidly breaking down in an atmosphere of impending and expanding disaster.

I found myself in the middle of this chaos carrying 138 very large sacks of flour. My immediate instructions from control were to climb to 10,000 feet and to hold in a standard pattern on Wedding beacon.

Burning C-54 aircraft. Bad weather conditions, pierced steel plank runway, and landing long contributed to the crash.

On arrival over Wedding at 10,000 feet we were still in heavy cloud. I couldn't make a position report to control because of the constant radio interference. I leaned over to Capt. John Pickering and said, "I don't like this, John. Try and get to traffic control for a different altitude or holding fix."

John replied, "I don't think we can get through, and if we did I don't think they know where half the people are up here."

I turned to the crew chief, Sgt. Elkins and said, "Sergeant, we will watch the gauges and keep track of the temperatures. You keep a look out the windshield for a break in the clouds. If possible I intend to climb out of this mess."

About that time I completed our holding pattern turn and was inbound to Wedding beacon at 10,000 feet when I suddenly became aware of an outside threat. I glanced up just in time to hear Elkins shout, "Push forward!"

We were suddenly eyeball to wide eyeball with two other pilots and a crew chief headed the opposite direction at the same altitude. Through some miracle our wings were parallel with each other at the moment we passed. By the time it took to blink, they were gone.

I still remember the look on their faces and our mad scramble to see if we had lost anything. Then, almost as quickly, a break in the clouds appeared before us. What a welcome but sobering sight! Revealed below and about us were grey swarming hulks, like spawning salmon in a shallow pool. Some of the aircraft were at the same altitude and in the same air space. We realized then that we must have had a guardian angel as the third pilot that day. It seemed an eternity before we got our load of flour onto the ground at Tempelhof.

That night in the snack bar at Rhein-Main I had two double orange juices. Pickering and Elkins outdid me. Then we made our way through the rain to our beds in the barn at Zeppelinheim.

The next day, as the traffic was again increased, General Tunner boarded one of the C-54's with his crew for Berlin. His trip had two purposes: to award a gold watch to an airlift pilot from an old and grateful Berliner, and to observe for himself the problems posed by the approach to Tempelhof in deteriorating weather situations.

The weather went from bad to worse. By the time the General arrived over Berlin he found himself in the same situation that I had encountered the previous day. Aircraft were stacked up, and command and control capabilities were unable to cope with the ever-increasing demands.

General Tunner, in frustration over the system's inability to cope with the demands, picked up the

General William H. Tunner Commander of the Combined Airlift Task Force, (CALTF).

mike and said in a voice that came through with authority, "This is 5549, Tunner talking, and you listen. Send every plane in the stack back to its home base." A completely surprised controller asked for the message to be repeated.

"I said: Send everybody in the stack below and above me home. Then tell me when it's O.K. to come down." The reply came back immediately, "Roger sir!"[1]

On the ground, the ten tons of coal were quickly unloaded while General Tunner presented the Berliner's gold watch to Lieutenant Paul O. Lykins, the pilot with the greatest number of Vittles flights to that date.

The pilots that flew in with General Tunner, Colonel Red Forman and Lieutenant Colonel Sterling P. Bettinger, flew with the General on the Hump operation into China during the war. The flight engineer was an old pro, T/Sgt. Earl Morrison out of Hamilton Field, California. General Tunner left the two Colonels in Berlin to establish flight control procedures that would preclude "this mess ever happening again—ever!"[2]

General Tunner pressed for safety first and foremost. He earned the nickname of "Tonnage Tunner" but there was a warm spot in the hearts of the air and ground crew members for him because of his concern for them operating in a somewhat hostile environment.

After "Black Friday," 13 August 1948, the day that the General flew to Berlin, there were new procedures established. From that time on if a pilot was unable to get on the runway on his first attempt to land, it was required that he would exit Berlin and take the load back to his departure base in West Germany.[3]

The pilots had mixed emotions. They hated to take back a load of supplies that the people so desperately needed, yet without that precaution safety would be sacrificed and effectiveness compromised.

Even though the air traffic into Berlin was to greatly increase in the months ahead, the confusion and roar of stacked aircraft over the city experienced during those days in August were not to be heard in the same way again.

The next few days the weather cleared and the sight of Berlin from the air with the vacant, bombed-out buildings stretching their uneven, broken fingers to the sky was easily seen. As I looked down below I wondered to myself how we were bitter enemies, these Germans and and ourselves, such a short time ago, trying to exterminate each other. Now, through the greatest air transportation effort in history, we were risking whatever it took to keep the Berliners alive.

I wondered, not only on these clear days, when the whole panorama shouted from below of the futility of war, but also in the middle of the night, in thunder storms over East Germany, why it was that these

Berliners seemed to know what freedom really was and what it was worth, even more than I did.

Destroyed bunker and buildings in Berlin.

My thoughts also dwelt on the green and fertile valleys nestled in the mountains of Utah where I was born, and on the peace and contentment I had found there close to mother nature, digging the earth for the basic necessities of life.

What would cause someone like me to be removed out of such a place to the congested sky over this city? Thoughts flooded back over decision points in my life, some forced by happenings like Pearl Harbor. What thread of events led me to being here in the cockpit of this marvelous C-54 Douglas Skymaster, over the bones of a once magnificent city?

2

The Quest For Flight

It was a beautiful spring day in Bear River Valley nestled in the Wasatch mountains of Utah. If anything it was hot for the time of year. I straightened up my aching back to wipe the sweat from my brow with an old red bandanna handkerchief. I gazed out over the ten acres of sugar beets.

It was best not to look at the whole field at once because the job of thinning out those solid rows of sugar beet plants to a single skinny root every eight inches would become overwhelming. There had been enough moisture that spring to sprout every one of the seeds that had been planted. They were so thick that it was difficult to make very good time going down the row. At least two chops of the hoe with the right hand were required between each remaining plant while the left hand was concurrently separating the little clump of plants down to a single unit. Perpetual motion with both hands was the goal.

Because it was necessary to always have the left hand at ground level a long handle in the hoe would be terribly awkward. Thus the 12-inch handle. The posture dictated by these physical arrangements kept my nose in the dust cloud generated by my right hand. When the strain on my back got too much, I would occasionally move along on my knees, but that was slow and it placed the nose even closer to the hoe.

Thinning sugar beets was about the only job one could get cash for in farm work during the tough times of Spring 1939. Doing a fast job efficiently was important to an 18-year-old young man who had a serious need for cash. The job was a real taskmaster and professor of discipline for the 10 hours a day, six days a week that it required.

The demands associated with this job were enough to stimulate some serious thinking about career opportunities in the years ahead. There was one thing the task demonstrated to me conclusively. I had and was developing exceptional hand and eye coordination. Where would that pay off? With my hands busily engaged, my mind dwelt on many subjects including other lands, transportation, and deteriorating world conditions.

At that time I wasn't very fond of what I knew of the German people. Everyone in the United States had heard of the Lindberg kidnapping case and the assertion that a "typically hard" German was the culprit. Now, for over the last year, we had heard a steady stream of reports about German military activities. In four months Hitler would invade Poland.

I remembered Mr. Richards, the agriculture teacher at Bear River High School, explaining that it was the Germans who developed the sugar beet. That didn't do anything to improve my image of the Germans.

The prospects for an 18-year-old young man over the next few years looked more serious to the parents than to the young man. The older one becomes, the more effect history has on one's future outlook, for good or ill.

Combine parents' experience with World War I with their attitude towards the Germans for their role in that conflict, plus their concern for the well-being of a son or daughter, and also their need for help on the farm, and you have some of the salient reasons for the parent-child divergence in opinions of the future. The difference is commonly described as the generation gap, not a new phenomenon.

I stopped briefly and examined one of the deep-green crisp seedlings I had just cut from its bed. The plant's misfortune was that it had sprouted three inches beyond the last single plant that I had selected to leave for the sugar beet knife at harvest time. Marilyn, my little sister, was already gathering a bucket full of these succulent greens for supper.

The water bag hanging on the fence post caught my eye. The evaporation from the canvas bag kept the water delightfully cool. We had no refrigerator so the water temperature suffered nothing from comparison. The cool water rinsing my mouth and the next gulp washing the dust out of my throat was one of the few welcome sensations found in that business. Back to work.

Our field lay almost directly beneath the airway from Salt Lake City to Malad, Idaho. Every once in awhile the sound of an aircraft would come over that quiet valley and provide an occasion to straighten up and look.

The sight of a silver shaft against that beautiful blue western sky and the sound that kept it there sent a shiver down my spine each time the event was repeated. My mind would pick up where that graceful voyager in the sky left off. It wasn't just what I saw and heard that stirred my soul, but thoughts of the strange places far away that would nest this silver bird for the night. Up to this point I had scarcely been out of the area except in geography books which were like an irresistible magnet to me.

Up and down those endless rows of sugar beets my body flung itself hour after hour, day after day. But my mind was free, flying through the blue of the sky and around the white puffy clouds, stopping in faraway places with strange-sounding names, only to hurry on again. I was at the shiny controls with all the dials, changing fuel tanks, calling the ground stations, plotting my course, through good weather and foul, turning upside down, doing rolls, spins, and loops. Such fantasy kept me going.

Later that summer I was hoeing weeds in the beet field when I suddenly became aware of the sharp staccato beat of an increasing roar coming in from the west. The source was an aircraft not on the airway but headed straight for me at tree top level. I had no thought to hide, in my ignorance I wanted to get as close as I could. At the last possible second the sleek bi-plane pulled up vertically, the prop wash cooled my face but my heart was in my throat and my feet were off the ground. Too soon it was a tiny speck and then gone. I just had to learn to fly!

The following weekend a neighbor friend of mine, Arthur Hansen, who was attending Utah State University in Logan, Utah, came home for a visit. It was he who had flown over the farm and had given me that hair-raising demonstration.

"How did you like that, Seymour?" he queried with an expectant grin on his face. "Sure beats playing nursemaid to a sugar beet!" Art told me all about what it was like. What he said exceeded my fantasies, which admittedly were somewhat limited by a lack of knowledge.

"How do I get started?" I pleaded.

"All you have to do is go to college, qualify as a sophomore, pass a test and they will enroll you in the beginners' part of the flight program. If you pass that phase you will get a shot at that little Waco bi-plane jewel I dusted you off with last week."

My heart sank. "Two years?" That was the easy part. There was no way in the world that I could go to college. I was the only one that Dad had left to help on the farm and if that wasn't enough there just were not any resourses available. If there had been other funds, Dad would have gladly shared them. There certainly was no problem qualifying scholastically. My high school grades were excellent, especially in the sciences and geography.

The avenue used by Art Hansen to learn to fly just wasn't open to me. I began reading all the books on flight I could find. Something would somehow turn up.

The opportunity came in 1940, wrapped in the ominous shrouds of war. The German successes and lack of a credible pilot pool in the United States led Robert Hinckley, a fellow Utahn, to play a key role in the Federal Aeronautics Administration's decision to train more young men and women to be pilots. There were not enough pilots being turned out in the college program so they began a non-college program. That was my case! No two-year wait.

Ground school classes were established in community facilities around the country. In our area they were in Ogden, Brigham City, and Bear River High School in Garland, my home town. The material necessary to qualify for a private pilot licence was taught. At the end of the course the private pilot written test was administered and ten flight scholarships were to be awarded between the three locations.

I was the first of many to sign up in our area. My determination to get one of those scholarships was only occasionally dampened by thoughts of the other 120 contestants for those 10 slots. The sugar beet was a powerful motivator. I received the sixth scholarship. I had unwittingly taken the first step on the way to Berlin.

I began flying lessons at the Brigham City Airport in instructor Johnny Weir's first class. The aircraft was a 65-horsepower Lycoming-powered Piper Cub. Johnny was a great instructor, just beginning what

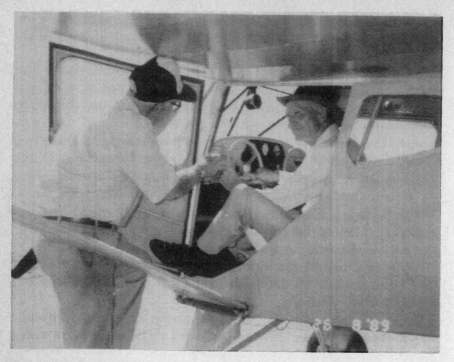

Johnny Weir, my first instructor (left) with a plane like the first one. Johnny is still instructing,
has 36,000 hours and is 76 years old. Brigham City, Utah. (1989)

would be his fabulous career in aviation. From up close that flying
machine looked every bit as good to me as anything I had seen fly
over the farm. There were times when I was too eager, forgetful, or
just plain stupid. But John was always patient, understanding, and
enthusiastic about teaching the subject that I had fallen in love with.

I put my heart and soul into that airplane, the program and into
the theory that made it fly. The loops and spins were especially exciting.
When I had completed that phase and was scheduled
for my first solo cross country it was an instant thrill to discover that
one leg of the route went right up Bear River Valley, over the farm!

The flight would put me over our house just about the time that
Dad would be out in the field and Mom would be in the garden. As
I took the runway and eased the throttle up on that 65-horsepower
engine, it was a thrill to sense the "surge" of power, compared to the
two-horse beet cultivator, and anticipate the eagerness of the tail wheel
to get off the ground. The stiffening feel of the stick in my hand and

at the right moment the gentle pressure it took to lift her into the air was a physical-neural sensation that bordered on the addictive.

Breaking free of the ground, the old hanger dropping out of sight behind the wing, the first turn out, all gave me a feeling of freedom that was never to grow old. That break in contact with mother earth seemed to cut all lines to daily drudgeries and boredom. The nose swung around gently to the north and upward in a climb that would insure enough altitude for a spin by the time I reached the farm. That was my plan.

On the farm, Garland, Utah, 1939. The black dog chased aircraft rather than cars. The car is a 1924 Maxwell.

It seemed important to demonstrate that I had truly learned to master that fabric-covered mass of tubing and cables. Old Shep, my cattle dog buddy, would also enjoy it. Some dogs chased cars but Shep was in a class of his own. He chased airplanes!

In ten minutes I could see the sugar beet factory smoke stack and the little town of Garland to the west of it. The farm was just beyond. It was necessary to circle once over the farm to get the full 9000 feet above sea level that I thought I needed for a two-turn spin. That altitude would give me 4800 feet above the ground.

Sure enough, Dad and Mom were down there with Shep watching me circle. My altitude would give me plenty of room to make at least a couple of mistakes and still pull out. They had an idea that it was probably me up there but they didn't have the foggiest idea about what I was planning to pull off. During my circle I checked below for any other airplanes that might be around and then made another circle in the opposite direction just to make sure. By this time Shep was running in circles, barking his fool head off.

When the nose swung through 270 degrees I continued the turn, pulled the carburetor heat out, and eased the throttle all the way off. Responding to steady back pressure on the stick, the nose came up enough to maintain my altitude as the airspeed progressively dropped off. By the time we reached North we were about through flying. I leveled her out briefly, held the nose up to that first full shudder, then shoved in full left rudder and jerked the stick all the way back into my stomach and held it there.

Just like before, the nose rose a bit and then plunged almost straight down; mountains, sky, fields, Mom, Dad, and Shep spun around crazily in a characteristic blur.

I counted the turns, one, one-and-a-quarter, one-and-a-half, one-and-three-quarters. The altimeter was unwinding, time to feed in right rudder and push the stick forward. There was a brief hesitation, a shudder, and then out she came, a little sloppy, but safe none the less.

On setting course for Logan, I noticed that Dad and Mom were not waving but Shep was still doing his duty.

That night when I came home still excited and exhilarated from the cross country, I was met by a set of very stern parents.

"You are through flying" Dad announced in a tone of voice reserved for the most serious of occasions. That and the look in Mom's face returned me to earth in a hurry.

"You almost did Mom in with your foolhardy shenanigans. She's still not herself." Dad glowered at me from close range.

I had totally misjudged the results of my demonstration. Both were convinced that I was going to crash. I had forgotten the crash in a field two miles north of us that took the life of Mr. Keller and his passenger.

It took some earnest explaining and a firm promise that I wouldn't do it again, at least over the farm, to get me back on flying status.

That night my spirits were boosted somewhat with a visit from my neighbor and best friend, Bill Capener. "Wow, that was great! I didn't know you could fly that well already" he exclaimed with undisguised admiration.

My flight training continued, and when a flight took me over the farm the spins were replaced by a friendly wiggling back and forth of the Piper's wings. Dad and Mom would wave back and old Shep would go into his routine. I would leave the area wiggling the wings back and forth until I was just about out of sight.

It wasn't long before the course was completed and the final check ride with the examiner, Art Mortensen, cleared me to receive my long-nurtured dream of becoming a licensed pilot. The date was 1 September 1941. In spite of the war in Europe, I was happy and at peace with my new-found adventure in life.

The rosy glow of things as they were for me at that moment would be irreversibly altered in a few months on a sleepy Sunday morning at a place called Pearl Harbor. Most of us in the United States were in a condition of bliss through ignorance for those few months.

The past impressions I had internalized about the Germans was about to receive double reinforcement from every facet of the media. On top of that was added "The day that would live in infamy," contributed by the Japanese. This time it was not some country far away that was being attacked but it was a strike that killed friends in families that I knew. On the very next farm to the north lived a family with two wonderful friends of mine, Jim and Touch. Their last name was Tazoi. Japanese.

They thought pretty much like I did, they liked many of the things I did, they were hard workers and great neighbors, they were honorable, and their word was their bond. A Christmas or Thanksgiving didn't go by without some special gift from their farm, usually a supply of celery, something we couldn't seem to get to grow.

This next-door neighbor was of a race that was being represented as totally savage and uncivilized. The American reaction even to Japenese individuals was irrational, but at the moment and under the circumstances, it was too often accepted, even by myself. Somehow I didn't consider Jim and Touch and their family in the same category. They were Americans the same as I was. My Dad's roots were in Norway but he was American. Seeing Jim and Touch every day, while hearing people speak daily of the evils of the race whose outward characteristics they bore, was real cause for introspection and confusion in my young mind. What was truth? I was taught every Sunday and during the week that we are all brothers and sisters regardless of our national or political origins.

I feared that any moment the Tazois would be sent to a resettlement center and wondered how I would handle that eventuality. Thank goodness the family and community were spared that indignity.

Jim Tazoi was one of the first to volunteer for the Armed Forces. There was no question which country's Force that was. Jim was to give every measure of devotion except his life, and that but by the narrowest of margins. Jim still carries some of the metal that nearly finished him off. His pace on the farm was reduced by necessity but his quality as a neighbor was enhanced by his deeds.

Telephone calls started to come in from young men who wanted to get into the United States Army Air Corps. Shortly after Pearl Harbor a lot of decisions were being made. Some wanted to join early so they might have a better chance to get their service of preference instead of being drafted. Those who thought they wanted to fly, but weren't sure, wanted to see what it was like. Those who knew they wanted to fly needed to get a little experience to enhance their chances of success.

For help with buying the gas I flew young men in both categories, not as an instructor, but just to let them feel what it was like to do stalls, some aerobatics, and general air work. With the dual controls they could get some feel for what was going on. This arrangement also helped to build my flying time rapidly.

Some young men were encouraged by the experience and were accepted into the Army Air Corps. Others were discouraged by being a bit susceptible to air sickness. One such young man had filled a sack that I had in the aircraft for that purpose. The plain brown bag was about to dissolve so we opened the side window and dropped it out. We weren't very far from the Garland Elementary school. It happened to be recess time. The flying object was almost immediately investigated and as quickly abandoned.

The young man's name was Conrad Steffan from Tremonton, Utah. His desire to fly soon overcame his queasy stomach and he went on to become an outstanding fighter pilot in the Army Air Corps. It was with great sadness that I learned some years later that Conrad had been shot down in his P-47 Thunderbolt somewhere in Germany. He never survived.

One spring day a small note in the Garland Times caught my eye. The United States Army Air Corps would test applicants for Aviation Cadet appointments at Utah State University in Logan on 17 May 1942.

I passed the physical and the written exams and was sworn in that very day to become a military aviator. There was a backlog for the

Receiving my Royal Air Force wings from Wing Commander Roxborough, 17 June 1944.

Aviation Cadet program. It would be many months before I would have a chance to earn my military wings, but it was another step toward a rendezvous with Berlin.

While waiting for my call, I attended Utah State University where I met a wonderful young lady by the name of Alta Jolley from Zion National Park, Utah. She would play a crucial role in my future life. This state of bliss came to an end one day with the arrival of a long official envelope bearing the news that my short two quarters of University life would end and my active duty life would begin on 23 March 1943.

My pre-flight training was at the San Antonio, Texas, Aviation Cadet Training Center. My flight training was with the Royal Air Force Number 3, British Flying Training School in Miami, Oklahoma. I was awarded the coveted Royal Air Force cloth wings and the United States Army Air Corps silver wings on the 17th of June, 1944. The sugar beet field seemed far away and almost unreal. My dream had come true.

After pilot training graduation one of my flying assignments was in Natal, Brazil in foreign air transport operations. We were flying C-47 "Goonie Bird" passenger and cargo routes in the South Atlantic Theatre. Here I was introduced to and checked out by Captain John Hudson as an aircraft commander in that wonderful aircraft, the Douglas C-54 Skymaster. While in Natal I decided to stay in the Air Force and make it my career.

The war came to an end and I was sent back to the States. In 1947 I was assigned to Brookley Air Force Base in Mobile, Alabama.

3

Blockade Storm Clouds

The Military Air Transport Service foreign operations out of Brookley primarily used C-54 and C-74 aircraft.

The C-74 was a much larger aircraft than the C-54, with two-and-a-half times the C-54's 20,000-pound payload. Only twelve of these aircraft were delivered, and we had all of them at Brookley. I knew that the next challenge would be to check out in that huge aircraft. The opportunity came quickly, and I was transferred to the C-74 squadron.

One of my best friends at Brookley was Peter Sowa. He was married to a wonderful young lady who had just delivered a healthy set of twins. Peter and his wife often had my friend Don McCullouch and me over for a home-cooked Sunday dinner. We were two bachelors who really appreciated the Sowas' family environment.

On 8 July 1948, Peter was scheduled for a flight to Panama. News of the Russians blockading Berlin was already about twelve days old, and rumors were flying that our C-54s might be called on to fly supplies into Berlin. So far, no word. At any rate, I didn't think it would affect me because I was now in the C-74 squadron.

Two days later, Colonel George Cassady, our commander, called an emergency meeting of all the C-54 pilots. My flight to Borinqen (Ramey) Field, Puerto Rico in a C-74 was delayed for aircraft maintenance. There was nothing better to do than see what the meeting was all about.

This was it. Four C-54's were to leave almost immediately for Rhein-Main near Frankfurt, Germany. There would be three or four crews on each aircraft. There would be no crew rest on the way and stops would be for fuel and food only. There would be only one navigator on each aircraft. It was recommended that he be rested in preparation for the 1450 mile overwater leg from Newfoundland to the Azores. The rest could be handled with radio navigation by the pilots.

The names of those selected to go were read out. There were a few gasps from those who had other plans for the immediate future. Some of the men were single, and many of them had reasons why they would rather not go, but generally they were manageable. Others were married with young families, a few with serious health problems in the family. My heart went out to them.

Most of the pilots had been overseas during the war and were not expecting or hoping to return this soon. A similar situation existed with the crew chiefs and ground personnel. The call to leave home again so soon on behalf of a former mortal enemy was not a popular one.

As the names continued to be called out one person didn't respond. It was Peter Sowa, now on his way back from Panama, totally unaware that he had been selected to leave for Germany shortly after his arrival at Brookley.

Things were not progressing all that well between Alta and me. The long-range courtship between Utah and Alabama just wasn't getting anywhere. Letters were a little sparse and not all that warm.

Peter's case came back to me in cold reality. He had twins and a wife that needed his help. I knew that under the present circumstances he would much prefer not to go. His wife ought to know. I picked up the phone and the sound of her response convinced me that an alternate solution would be more than welcome, but what could that be?

"Why not you?" came a prompting that had to be dealt with.   "But I'm not even in the right Squadron," came back just as promptly.

There were no additional reasons, besides my new car, why I shouldn't volunteer. Like in a dream I found myself talking to Lt. Col. Gilbert, Commander of the C-74 squadron. "Could I be transferred back to the C-54 Squadron and take Capt. Peter Sowa's place?"

"It's alright with me, but you will have to take the replacement issue up with Sowa's Commander, Lt. Col. James R. Haun. I'll transfer you if he will agree to the switch," he said.

My transfer was accomplished before Peter Sowa landed at Brookley. As he pulled onto the ramp there were feverish preparations on the four aircraft about to depart. The area was littered with special equipment being sorted out for loading. Capt. John M. Kelly, Lt. Guy B. Dunn Jr., Lt. James L. Hunt, Capt. Lawrence L. Caskey, Lt. Everett E. Peyton, Capt. John H. Pickering, T/Sgt. Herschel C. Elkins and myself were some of those on C-54 number 45-548 which was about to depart.

"What in the world is going on here?" queried Peter as he came down out of his aircraft. After a quick explanation and a thank you he helped us get the gear together.

About a month before I had managed to buy a beautiful new, red, four-door Chevrolet through a dealer on the island of St. Croix in the Caribbean. Delivery had been arranged through a dealer in the States. How hard cars were to come by, and how sweet it was to drive on a date! That beauty compensated for my sparse hair line.

I just had time to drive my dream boat under a heavy growth of pine trees for protection, pocket the keys and head for the aircraft. Looking back over my shoulder I experienced a few pangs of regret at my hasty decision. Then I remembered the briefing, "The blockade shouldn't last over 25 days," we were told. That wouldn't be so bad.

I had no idea how wrong that estimate would be, or what lay in store in the next few months ahead. I would never see that car again.

Even before the call came for support of the airlift operation there was a lot of information in the press about the rising tensions around the Berlin issue and the subsequent blockade.

After the call came for support we all had a much greater personal interest. Some even did a little serious library research that was shared in aircrew bull sessions. There was enough of an information gap that we all wanted to know more.

Some background briefings would be provided on arrival in Germany. By the time we completed a few missions there were some basic facts that helped us understand why we were in the cockpit in that far-away setting. These were the factors we discussed:

The blockade began on 24 June 1948 with Stalin's order to close all the land and water access routes to Berlin from the west. The air corridors could not be closed because access by air was guaranteed by treaty. Not so for the surface routes.[4]

At that time there were no C-54s available except a few commercial DC-4s employed by American Overseas Airlines. The first flights of the blockade were flown by the Troop Carrier pilots in some of the 80 to 100 C-47s that were available in the European Theatre at that time. The first official blockade flights were dispatched to Berlin on 26 June 1948.[5] It must be remembered that the British were full partners in the operation and were moving ahead as fast as we were.

The American effort was first named, "The LeMay Coal And Feed Delivery Service," after the Commander of the United States Air Forces in Europe, Major General Curtis LeMay. The name would soon be changed to, "Operation Vittles." The British effort was named, "Operation Plainfare." [6]

The C-47s carried three to four tons and the C-54s carried about ten tons. Capacities varied with the individual aircraft configuration and the fuel requirements from the point of departure to Berlin. Over water gear, extra tanks, and some navigaton equipment were removed in the interest of reduced weight. The C-47s would be completely phased out by the end of September, 1948.[7]

It was some time before I realized the extent of political infighting that had taken place before the blockade began. In Berlin the Russians had a very real problem. It was the first time in history that an island of capitalism was located behind the Iron Curtain.

In the Russian's attempt to convince the East Berliners and East Germans that the Soviet five-year plan and their idea of the State being supreme were the ideal way to go, the Russians were coming face to face with questions from their own troops.

It was simple, and certainly of interest to Russian soldiers and civilian employees, to walk across the border into capitalist free Berlin and see what was going on. They had their free agency to choose what they would be and what they would do. Their economic future was in their own hands.

Some of the statements being made by the Russians who had visited the free part of the city were to the effect that, "I don't see what is so terrible about the capitalists' system. The stores have more food of greater variety than we do. There are more clothes and shoes and some other goods that are not available at all in our part of the city. Why is that so?"

Free enterprise was taking the shape of a huge thorn in the side of the Russian Bear and the ideology that was being preached as gospel to the East Berliners and East Germans. Political freedom was the spawning ground for economic freedom. Performance was a much more powerful spokesman than words. This was becoming a problem of major proportions. The only difference between the East Germans and the West Berliners was an arbitrary mark on the ground.

Other books contain the details and the politics that led up to the final imposition of the blockade on all the ground access routes into the city. Suffice it to recognize that there were written provisions made for air access to West Berlin through three air corridors, each 20 statute miles wide, from West Germany, 24 hours a day. No such provision was written for surface access. The Western allies believed that they had a gentleman's agreement for free access to West Berlin but didn't press the Russians for the understanding in writing. There were at least two possible reasons. One was the desire not to appear distrustful of a comrade in arms at the conclusion of a war jointly won. Why upset working relationships by insisting that gentlemen had to reduce an agreement to hard copy? The second possible reason was that if specific access agreements were spelled out, travel would be limited to just those routes. The desire of the British, French, and Americans was for unrestricted access to West Berlin.[8]

Unfortunately, the lack of the understanding in writing resulted in the Russians doing as they pleased with surface routes into West Berlin. Monday-morning quarterbacks have said we could have had a written agreement providing unrestricted access. They say we should have made the removal of the British and American forces from the territory that was to become East Germany conditional on the signing of such an agreement. That is probably true.[9]

West Berlin is located 110 miles deep inside East Germany and depends on traffic from West Germany over one autobahn, one rail line, one canal system from the river Elbe, an electrical power plant located in East Berlin, and the three air corridors for its life blood. These are tenous, fragile, and vulnurable supply lines upon which to base a city's every breath.

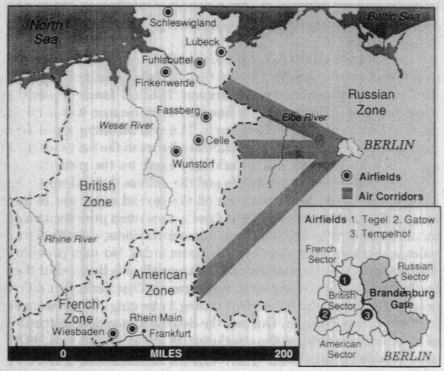

Newsday/Joe Calviello

Representation of the two major zones of Germany and the Berlin access situation. Reprinted by permission, Newsday, Inc. Copyright 1989, Artist Joe Calviello.

The difference in the recovery rate between East and West Berlin, even at that early date, was so startling that it was a major topic of discussion on both sides of the border. The people in East Germany and East Berlin were talking about how fast their Aunts, Uncles, Cousins and friends in West Berlin were going about cleaning up the mess on their side of the border. Paint was scarce in West Berlin but used whenever it could be found. Window boxes filled with flowers began to appear in partially bombed-out apartment houses. All this was because of individual free agency and responsibility for self, factors that are associated with capitalism.

The philosophy of "You have your political and economic destiny in your own hands," rather than, "We'll tell you how you fit into our five year plan," was an over-simplified quick explanation for the difference in the two systems. At that it was pretty close to the mark. For whatever reason the comparison in recovery rates was embarrassing.

The Russians reasoned that with little or no food reserves in West Berlin, if the Russians withdrew the substantial food and coal supplies that were being provided from East Germany, and if supplies from the West could be blocked, food riots would ensue. If the West Berliners or East German "plants" were to disturb the tranquility and threaten the peace, the Soviets were in an excellent position to restore "permanent" peace to this troublesome capitalist island. At least 300,000 Soviet troops were in close proximity to West Berlin.[10]

By this time the only thing that the four governing nations had in common was the super inflation under way with the old German Reichsmark which was the currency used in the East and West Berlin and also in the British and American Western Zones of Germany.

Major economic changes had been proposed for Germany by the Western Allies but the Russians would not cooperate. It was time for action. On Friday 18 June 1948, in Frankfurt, the British and the Americans announced that they were issuing a new currency, the Deutschemark, to replace the Reichsmark in the Western Zones and in West Berlin. The currency would be backed by "the German people's industry, their tradition of hard work, and the promise of Marshall Aid."[11]

This act was tantamount to an acknowledgment by the Western Powers that the division of Germany was complete and signalled the end of four-power government for West Berlin. In practice it had ceased long before. For months the Russians had done everything possible to sabotage progress on both the overall German post war recovery issue and also the solution of day-to-day management problems for Berlin generally.

Although the currency change was a real surprise and a blow to the Russians, it was most convenient and timely to be used as an excuse for the blockade of Berlin. Soviet retaliation began immediately with increased harassment and increased intervention in Berlin traffic. Finally, on 24 June 1948, all road and rail links between Berlin and the West were severed.

Part of the rails were removed from their tracks, the autobahn bridge over the river Elbe was closed as unsafe, and the locks in the canal serving Berlin from the Elbe were blocked. The switch that shunted electrical power to West Berlin from the principle power plant located in East Berlin was thrown open. The struggle was joined.

The Russians announced that "Due to technical difficulties there would be a delay in access to Berlin." President Truman clearly understood the threat and was unshakable in his determination that the Western powers stay in the city.[12] Lt. General Albert C. Wedemeyer, Director of Plans and Operations for the Army, had been the principle source of confidence for the Aministration's decision to consider the feasibility of airlift to save Berlin.

On 25 June President Truman directed James Forrestal, Secretary of Defense; Kenneth Royall, Secretary of the Army; and Robert Lovett, Under Secretary of State to channel all necessary resources into forming an airlift capable of feeding the over two-million people of West Berlin. These actions were taken in closest coordination with our most trusted ally, Great Britain. Prime Minister Clement Attlee and Foreign Secretary Ernest Bevin were of like mind.[13]

For weeks before the blockade there had been increased flights into Berlin by the Royal Air Force and the United States Air Force to give added support to the American and British elements in the city. However, 26 June was the beginning of the military air lift to the civil population in West Berlin. Because of their previous occupation by the Germans the French had few resources, no aircraft, and some reservations about embarking on a full-scale airlift to Berlin. But committed, the three Western Allies spoke with one voice.

Enough can not be said for the pivotal role that General Lucius D. Clay, United States Military Governor in Germany, played during these critical years in shaping policy, programs, diplomacy, and the establishment of the airlift to keep West Berlin free. At the same time he took extraordinary steps to prepare for a hot war to save Berlin in case negotiations or the airlift failed. The spector of World War three was ever present in the early deliberations.[14]

The United States Air Force officers in Europe in key roles at the inception were: Major General Curtis LeMay, the Commander of the United States Air Forces in Europe [USAFE], who later became a legend for his role in airpower; Brigadier General Joseph Smith, Commander of the Military Post in Wiesbaden, who is given credit for naming the American supply effort to Berlin "Operation

General Joseph Smith (left) briefly commanded the Airlift before General Tunner arrived. (Smithsonian Air and Space Museum, 1989)

Vittles," and was the designated American airlift commander in the earliest phase; and Major General William H. Tunner, who arrived on 28 July 1948 and assumed command of the airlift on 29 July through General Order 61, Headquarters USAFE. On 14 October 1948 General Tunner was also named the Commander of the Combined USAF-RAF Airlift Task Force. He was the world's genius in airlift operations.[15]

The backbone of airlift capability on 26 June 1948 resided in the 60th Troop Carrier Group, under the command of Colonel Bertron C. Harrison at Wiesbaden AB, and in the 61st Troop Carrier Group, under the command of Colonel Walter S. Lee, at RheinMain AB. Both of these excellent Groups gave the initial leadership and direction to get the airlift off the ground. The only aircraft available to them at the time was about 100 old faithful C-47 "Goonie" birds.[16]

As good as this workhorse was, it would not be up to the task of supplying the minimum requirement of 4,500 tons a day to keep the Berliners from starvation. By 1 July 1948, two of what within a few months would be over 200, C-54's were added to the fleet.

The major cargo on the airlift was flour and coal.

Those in government and the military in Great Britain, France, and the United States who had strongly advised the use of armed force to open the supply routes to Berlin had finally given way to those who championed the more-peaceful approach of the airlift. Some Monday morning quarterbacks still argue the merits of that decision.

Because of these and many other factors we were engaged in the most massive use of airpower for humanitarian reasons that the world had ever known.

4

Off to Rhein-Main

With our preparations complete at Brookley we were eager to join the relief forces being marshalled for the support of Berlin. After fond farewells to sweethearts, wives, children, and cars, we were in the aircraft preparing to leave. On the takeoff roll I caught a short glimpse of a red ray of sunshine from the top of my Chevrolet underneath the pine trees.

We were soon in the air, nosing our way toward the Eastern Seaboard, then on to a fuel stop in Newfoundland. With the extra crews aboard and two full-length bunks it really wasn't a problem to fuel and go and fuel and go.

Our sole navigator was Lt. James Hunt. We kept him in one of the bunks and provided him first class service at his every waking moment. Navigation to Newfoundland over land using radio aids was no problem.

There was a message waiting for us in Harmon Field Base Operations: "Press on as fast as you can. Ignore minor maintenance."

We departed Newfoundland as soon as we got a bite to eat and had fueled the aircraft. We promptly pried Lt. Hunt out of the bunk for the 1450-statute-mile-over-water flight to the Azores. The flight went well and as daylight broke a puff of cloud could be seen dead ahead, perched like a floppy hat on the crown of the tallest visible peak. Jim had done a perfect job of splitting the main island. The cloud was visible first and is the usual sign of an island of any size surrounded by an ocean. A friendly cloud of this type has brought many a pilot to a safe haven when other means of navigation have

36

failed. Except right over the island there was bright sunshine. Beautiful bright blue waves pounded the shore in front of the windy cliffs that nestled the main runway.

"It's a good thing they have the runway cemented down," joked big John Kelly as he recounted some previous landings under near-hurricane-force winds that are all-too-common to that beautiful group of islands.

The tower responded to our call with a warning about high winds, turbulence over the cliffs on the approach, and livestock crossing the runway. "Standard day at the office," big John quipped.

That report poured a little more adrenalin into me as I was the pilot for this leg. The closer we got to the cliffs the more we were getting bounced around. The runway was now visible just beyond the rim. Sure enough, there was a string of cows crossing the runway about one-third of the way toward Base Operations. Looked like they would clear by the time we got there.

"Look out for strays coming across behind the others," I warned John Pickering, my co-pilot. Being an old farm boy, that was one

The crews on C-54 548 at Lages Field, The Azores, enroute to Frankfurt on 11 July 1948. From left to right: Capt. John H. Pickering, Lt. James L. Hunt, Jr., Capt. Lawrence L. Caskey, Lt. Everett E. Peyton, Lt. Gail S. Halvorsen, Lt. Guy B. Dunn, Jr., and Capt. John M. Kelly.

area where I considered myself an expert. We were over the cliff's edge now and taking a pretty good pushing around when we got hit by one tremendous updraft. In no time at all we had gained 200 feet just as the approach was looking pretty good. Just as quickly it dropped us. "Second floor, household goods; next, first floor, mens clothes, going down," chimed in Larry Caskey as we settled fast toward the runway. There was enough ground effect to help straighten things out before we made contact and the landing wasn't all that bad, given the circumstances. No stray cows.

Another message was waiting for us urging all prudent dispatch in refueling and getting airborne as soon as possible. We didn't feel left alone. The snack bar had lunch prepared for us and we were soon on our way, headed toward land fall at Brest, France. I could take it easy on this leg. Capt. Larry Caskey, Lt. Everett Peyton, and T/Sgt. Ellsworth Erickson Jr. were assigned to fly this segment.

I put on a set of head phones as we approached Frankfurt. There had been many airports with lots of ratio chatter in my experience but nothing to compare to what was struggling to get through that headset from aircraft trying to get in and depart from Rhein-Main at Frankfurt. This was going to be interesting.

Rhein-Main ramp early in the Airlift. The trucks belong to the Army 67th Transportation Truck Company.

Rhein-Main Status Board for daily posting of tonnage hauled to Berlin. Located on the old brick control tower.

There were a limited number of VHF communication channels in our aircraft and we were almost on top of Rhein-Main before we could contact traffic control for landing information. It took us 40 minutes more to get on the ground.

We arrived at Rhein-Main on 11 July 1948, adding our C-54 to the mixture of C-47s and C-54s that were scattered about in front of the old brick control tower. As we touched down we were immediately warned to expedite clearing the runway and to taxi toward Base Operations. The place was swarming with people and machines of all descriptions. Semi-trailer trucks loaded, unloaded and in the process were everywhere. Some snuggled up to the silver bellies of the big birds like piglets sucking the sow. In this case the nourishment was coming from the other way, being loaded into the gaping insides of the "mother" to be regurgitated intact in Berlin.

We were promptly met on the ramp by a harried 1st lieutenant toting a sheaf of papers attached to a clipboard that had seen better days.

His words of greeting were, "Welcome to Rhein-Main, who will be the first crew to Berlin?" Although we hadn't expected a brass band for our exhausting non-layover flight we had expected a little more of a "Glad you made it, must have been quite a trip," kind of greeting.

Not waiting for a reply the lieutenant continued, "Let's go, follow me." He abruptly turned and headed for the Operations building. We passed by a C-54 that was being loaded with sacks of flour. I noticed down below the cargo door, on the ground, mixed with dirt and gravel, was a small accumulation of flour over which was hovering a raggedly dressed man with a little sack and what appeared to be a small clothes brush. Even in the time it took us to pass he had the little treasure in the bag and with a furtive glance was back to work loading the aircraft. "If that flour is so valuable here, what in the world must it be like in Berlin?" I thought as we hurried on. Dodging a few mud holes, jeeps, and trucks we soon arrived in Base Operations.

Inside, the activity was even more accelerated. Pilots with animated gestures and excitement in their voices were milling about without apparent direction or purpose. My thoughts were on how soon we

Wiesbaden Air Base railhead. Unloading flour from railway cars for reloading into C-47 and C-54 aircraft. The aircraft tail is a B-17 assigned to the Commanding General of USAFE, General Curtis LeMay at first and then General John Cannon.

could get a hot shower and collapse into a decent bed. Certainly we thought that such professional pilots, grimy from a long trip, would have some quarters equal to the moment waiting for us.

I didn't have long to think about that before our 1st lieutenant broke in with, "Y'all didn't tell me who was going to be the first crew to Berlin."

John Kelly and crew were selected. They were to be on their way to Berlin in our plane within an hour and fifteen minutes. The lieutenant went on to explain, "Your airplane already has a truck load of coal backed up to it and it will be ready for pre-flight in 30 minutes."

The lieutenant waved to a tieless sergeant and told him who was taking the flight. "Take 'em by Intelligence, Weather, and the Clearance office for their briefings and materials. It's their first trip. Make sure they get a full set of maps and someone who has had first-hand experience on how to get to Berlin." Turning to John Kelly and without taking a breath he continued, "Sorry we haven't the luxury of a route check pilot but I'm sure with your experience you can find it O.K." Then the lieutenant was gone. The Sgt. smiled and motioned for John and crew to follow him. The rest of us wanted to talk to someone quick about that hot shower and a bed.

The dynamics of the moment temporarily overcame my fatigue and I began to marvel at the dedication and intensity of the American military people who had not long ago been bent on exterminating the Germans and now were dedicating their all to saving the Berliners.

I began to think of my own feelings about the German people. There was much in the media about the hardness of the Germans, the atrocities, and their claims of superiority. Some Americans had offered a defense by blaming the reported behavior on Hitler and his policies and not on the nature of people.

There were people of German decent in Garland, Utah that were wonderful members of the community. One of my best friends had been Gus Korth. His dad still had an accent. Their good example always came to mind when the worst of these stories were told. I also remembered from somewhere that the largest minority group in the United States was German. However, the media conditioning had been the more effective and even now I found myself expecting the "typical" behavior from the first Germans I would shortly come across on their home turf.

John Pickering had disappeared but now was back with a different lieutenant in tow. "This is our man," he announced with a flourish. "He has news of a shower and bed!"

The lieutenant didn't seem as enthusiastic about what he was going to say as John was in presenting him.

"The news isn't so good. All the regular quarters are saturated. You have a choice between tents and some tar-paper shacks." The lieutenant had his eyes on his shoes when he apologetically gave us the choice.

That certainly didn't sound like a bath with every room. Our minds began to go back to some of the inconveniences that we had experienced during the war period. The lieutenant continued, "The tar-paper shacks are in a barbed-wire compound at Zeppelinheim, across the autobahn. There is a nearby building with showers. Want to look?" A glance around the group was enough to tell that we wanted nothing to do with the tents. "We'll take Zeppelinheim," I replied with some resignation.

"There will be a few minutes delay in moving you in," continued the bad news bearer. "The shacks are currently occupied by displaced persons." We looked at each other with some concern and moved our flight bags and duffle off in one corner. In 45 minutes a weapons carrier was in front to pick us up. We awakened John Pickering, threw in our bags and piled in the back. Even as we loaded we noticed several new crews just coming in from a recently arrived aircraft.

Even though it was July a cold rain was falling and the brisk breeze, combined with the movement of the weapons carrier, chilled us to the bone.

It didn't take long to cross the autobahn. There was no traffic in any direction and parts of the autobahn were still showing bomb damage.

After the autobahn it was less than 10 minutes before we pulled into the compound through a barbed wire gate to witness a scene that could have been shot from the liberation of a prisoner of war camp. There were already several two-ton trucks in the compound loading nondescript belongings in a variety of bags and battered suit cases. The owners, by their haggard looks and disheveled mixed dress, had seen happier times. We were adding to their misery. The displaced persons were once more being displaced.

Some of them were left over from Nazi slave-labor and concentration camps. Millions had been placed in such camps by the Nazis during the war. At the end of the war there were 8,000,000 displaced persons in Western Europe—people who were out of their homeland due to war or political or religious persecution. Approximately 1,000,000 Russians had refused to return home. On 25 June 1948 the U.S. Congress passed the Displaced Persons Act which allowed 440,000 such persons to enter the United States between 1 July 1948 and 1 July 1952. Some of these had hopes of being in that allotment.[17]

This particular group was working for the Americans on various jobs before the airlift began, and now they were heavily involved with loading the aircraft for Berlin. Most of them were Serbs, Latvians, Estonians, Lithuanians, and Poles.

The compound area was without benefit of a hard surface and we sank in the mud to the tops of our low-cut oxfords. The occupants didn't have many belongings and it was amazing how fast the evacuation occurred.

As the last person left we began to explore the interior of the buildings. Because of the previous occupants' hasty departure the floors were covered with litter of all types. The prospects of a G.I. party before we got a shower were not pleasant.

Four walls were all that was there besides the black potbelly stove and metal cots covered with what had once been reasonably good G.I. issue mattresses. There were obviously no washing or toilet facilities inside the buildings.

Soon the low-frequency throb of the truck engines increased to a higher pitch and the sound of the tires, biting into the mud, changed as they made their way out of the compound gate and then ceased altogether. I wondered where they were taking those poor unfortunate souls. Certainly to nothing better than tents.

A captain with rubber overshoes was busily going back and forth directing not only our unloading efforts but the crews who had joined us in other weapons carriers. Several people who thought they needed a shower were trying to locate where such a luxury might be found.

"See that building over there? All the washing facilities are over there, including the showers," the captain announced with a gesture toward some pine trees on the other side of the compound. "I can't vouch for their condition. This place was just beginning to get some attention when the airlift started."

As he turned to leave I grasped his arm and asked, "What is that big building at the other end? It looks like a barn.

"That's exactly what it is," he replied.

"Well, is there any place in there I could put a cot?"

"I don't think so," he replied, "It's full of old machinery and junk downstairs and I don't know what is up above."

It was obvious he didn't know and he didn't care. I turned to John Pickering and said, "John, let's go over to that barn and see if there isn't a better place to stay than in these old shacks; they don't smell so good."

We slogged our way across the compound and found the first barn door locked. We proceeded along the side of the building with water dripping off the eves down our neck until we came to a small

The famous old barn and the more than muddy court yard. My room was at the window, far right, just above and to the right of the stove pipe. From left to right: Lt. Col. James Haun, Capt. Kline, and Capt. DeWitt who holds his shaving kit under his arm.

door which was open. The interior was pitch black and as we stumbled about, it was obvious that we needed a light. John soon produced one.

A quick inspection inside indicated that the downstairs was worse than the tar-paper shacks. As we turned to leave, our eyes caught sight of a ladder leading above.

We quickly climbed the ladder and opened the squeaking door that led into the loft above the barn. We were pleasantly surprised. There were a few cobwebs but the floor was cement and reasonably clean. It smelled a little musty but nothing like the shacks. In a moment we both agreed this was where we were going to bunk. The decision was kept to ourselves because we didn't want the whole Squadron trying to squeeze into that limited space.

Expeditious trips back to the tar-paper shack for two bunks and our baggage didn't go unnoticed. By the time we got set up by one of the few windows, there were three or four other guys coming up the ladder to take a look.

Where to hang our clothes? A quick foraging party downstairs in the barn was rewarded with a handful of large nails and a bolt heavy enough to drive them. Soon the rafters looked like the back of a porcupine and our thumbs were a little worse for wear from the makeshift hammer. The timing was just right as we heard someone down below shout out that a truck had just arrived with sheets and pillow cases.

It wasn't long until the limited space was filled up with other pilots of the same opinion. Little did I realize that fifteen years later our son, Bob, would be going to the first grade in this old barn where some broken down wagons were now in sad disarray.

Finally we grabbed our towels, soap, and clean clothes and rushed to get in line for the showers. "Hurry up and wait," wasn't the figment of someone's imagination.

Among some of the new occupants in the loft were pilots from Travis Air Force Base in California. In my discussion with one of them he shared his feelings about the Germans. He had been a B-17 bomber pilot and had flown a number of bombing missions over Berlin and other targets in Germany.

On one of his missions two of his crew members were killed as they limped back out of Germany to England. "How do you feel about coming back here and supplying food and medicine to these people?" I asked with sincere interest.

"When I was first assigned to the airlift and began getting my things together in California, I had some long thoughts about the situation. My first impression was that it was interfering with my plans to get on with my life after the war. I was downright resentful," he replied. "Being gone so long once was bad enough, but twice?"

He then went on to explain in a more deliberate voice the process that enabled him to leave without the bitterness that first swept over him.

He described how he came to the understanding that these people wanted to be free just like we in America were free. "You can't fault people for that," he said, looking me straight in the eye, "and I don't like to see people bullied."

"When defenseless women and children are involved it cancels out a lot of the past. Things during the war were based on a whole different set of rules. Somehow that faceless mass of two million people suddenly became individuals just like my mother and sister. From then on I could handle it," his voice trailed off as his throat tensed, "I didn't feel good about dropping the bombs. Now maybe I can do something about the food. I'm ready to go."

The cloud from the gas chambers and the ghosts of six million innocent victims were impossible to set aside, but the barely living called and begged a response.

5

The First Corridor Flight

Early on the first morning after our arrival at Rhein-Main I checked the brand new bulletin board which had been located near the makeshift mess hall.

My name jumped out at me from the scheduling sheet. Our crew, Capt. John Pickering, and Sgt. Herschel Elkins were listed for our first flight to Berlin at 13:00 hours.

The 11:00 weapons carrier shuttle arrived right on time in the middle of a receding mud puddle. We swung our flight gear in the back and followed it in. We had just finished lunch and stuffed a couple of good Washington apples from the mess hall into the ample pockets of our flight suits.

Our first stop was in operations where we received the details of the flight to Berlin. The materials contained in the pilot kit consisted of maps, let down charts, radio information, and flight procedures. We each were issued special Operation Vittles identification cards written in Russian, French, German, and English. We hoped we wouldn't need the Russian explanation of our status.

The briefing officer explained that due to the pilot shortage there would be no route check pilot available. "If you get lost, the maps you have extend from England on the West to Italy on the South, and to the Russian border on the East. Good luck! If you get out of the corridor over East Germany you will likely be forced down if it is daylight or a clear night," he intoned as he pointed the way to the Intelligence office.

The members of our Squadron averaged about 3,000 hours in the air, including a great deal of experience in weather and night operations. The Military Air Transport Service and Troop Carrier pilots that were joining the Lift were some of the best airlift pilots anywhere. It was only about 280 miles from Rhein-Main to Tempelhof. That was a pretty short haul compared to what most of us had been used to flying. Of course we hadn't been flying over hostile territory since the war.

The intelligence briefing officer was almost melodramatic and spoke as though he had a straight pipeline to the Kremlin. He gave us the latest reports of Russian fighter activity in and near the air corridors. "In the corridors? I thought they weren't supposed to be in the corridors," I interrupted.

"They aren't there all the time, but you can expect to get buzzed sooner or later. They aren't supposed to shoot" he replied with a wink as he reached for a small stack of Yak photos.

The fighter airfields at Kothern, Dessau, and Zerbst, in the Southern corridor and Briest and Mahlwinkel in the Center corridor were pointed out, and photos of the fighters at each base were identified. "If you see anything unusual enroute, stop in on your way back and give me a report," the Captain concluded with a meaningful look over his wire-framed reading glasses.

The next stop was the weather desk to learn current and forecasted weather conditions. I was particularly impressed with the extensive and detailed information they had assembled for the route and our destination at Tempelhof. "Our data for your flight over East Germany is mostly from pilot reports. The Russians stopped sending the East German data some time ago. Make sure you get a good wind check leaving West Germany at the Fulda beacon" he said as he handed me a written summary of the forecast. "The wind is often strong and blowing across the corridors, which could drift you out by Berlin if you don't crank in the drift. Sorry I can't give you better data for that segment."

There were no navigational aids over the 211 miles in the South corridor across East Germany, and it was important that we stayed within the 20 statute-mile-wide corridors unless we wanted to test the

Russian fighter intercept capability. The distance to Berlin through the Center and Northern corridors was much shorter.

From the operations building we went to the hardstand that had our assigned aircraft. It was in the final loading stage. We looked the aircraft over carefully and it seemed to be in reasonable condition. The automatic pilot and one of the rotating propeller synchronizing indicators were out of operation. We didn't appreciate it, but that would be the cleanest aircraft we would get for the rest of our time on Operation Vittles.

Sgt. Elkins, our crew chief, had already preceded us to the airplane. He greeted us with a big smile and said, "If we go down we are going to have plenty of pancakes. There are 138 sacks of flour on this bird but no skillet." We had about 30 minutes before takeoff and proceeded to strap ourselves in and run the check list.

Captain John Pickering and Sgt. Elkins were not strangers to me. We had flown together in foreign transport operations out of Mobile to many different destinations.

The crew from left: Lt. Gail S. Halvorsen, T/Sgt. Herschel C. Elkins, and Capt. John H. Pickering.

This flight, however was different. There was an extra measure of tension and excitement about the first time through the corridor and the attendant unknowns.

As I looked out my window at the two smooth-running engines

on my side, the confidence in that great bird was renewed and all seemed well with the world. Those friendly engines were Pratt and Whitney Twin Wasp radial R-2000s. Each one of those beauties had the capability of 1450 horsepower.[18] Three of them had got me back from the mid-Atlantic to Natal one day with no problem.

The horsepower generated in those air-cooled cylinders was transmitted to the air in front our wing's leading edge by a Hamilton Standard

The "Candy Bomber" on the first flight to Berlin.

Hydromatic three-bladed propeller. That propeller and that engine made one terrific team. They represented some of the highest component reliability in the United States Air Force at that time. We were all happy with what we had to work with. My joy at flying the airplane had not diminished any from that first flight in Natal.

There came a short break in radio traffic. "Call the tower, we're ready to taxi," I suggested to John. "This is Big Easy 548 taxi to takeoff instructions." The tower came back with "Big Easy 548 cleared to runway 07, altimeter 29.98, time is 12:50 hours, wind East at 15 gusts to 20, call when ready for takeoff." The identifier, "Easy" was given to aircraft east-bound to Berlin and "Willie" identified west-bound aircraft.

The run up was smooth and the Rhein-Main tower responded to our takeoff request with, "Big Easy 548, you are cleared to the Tempelhof range, cruise 6500 feet, your route and climb are as briefed, cleared for takeoff."

We pulled out on the runway and smoothly advanced the throttles all the way to the stops. Those 138 sacks of flour weighed within a few pounds of ten tons. That and enough fuel on board to get to Tempelhof and back plus to a reasonable alternate was enough to let us know that we were loaded to the hilt.

John called out, "We've got 49 inches of manifold pressure and 2700 RPM; everything looks good. With our existing dew point you can have another inch of mercury manifold when we get some ram pressure."

The aircraft accelerated slowly, lumbering down the runway. I made the transition from the nose wheel steering to rudder control at 50 MPH but kept the nose wheel on the ground until we reached 95 MPH. That speed is the minimum speed that full rudder could maintain directional control if we lost an outboard engine. The nose wheel soon came a few inches off the runway. We were doing 100 MPH. The speed increased more rapidly and the big silver bird soon gave indications that she was ready to fly. I applied a little back pressure on the control column and we were off at 118 MPH.[19]

The same old feelings of breaking loose from mother earth, even though ol' 548 was heavily burdened, still made my spine tingle. "Gear up!" I commanded, and with a sweep of his experienced hand, John had the gear on its way into the wheel wells.

At 140 MPH and 250 feet we began to milk the takeoff flaps up slowly. By this time we had brought the manifold pressure back to 41 inches of mercury and the RPM to 2550. We were close to 155 miles an hour and began our steady climb out. Our rate of climb indicator varied between 300 and 450 feet per minute. At 500 feet altitude I reduced the manifold pressure to 34 inches and the RPM to 2300. We turned to 180 degrees [South] and maintained that heading to 900 feet. At that point we turned left toward the Darmstadt beacon. A double check on the homer audio gave us, dah-dit-dit, dah, [DT] coming in clear on a frequency of 272 kilocycles. We were just under 3000 feet and crossing Darmstadt.

From there we tuned in Aschaffenburg beacon on a frequency of 380 kilocycles with an identificaiton of dit-dah, dah-dah-dit [AG]. After Aschaffenburg we soon reached our assigned altitude of 6500 feet and an air speed of 170 miles per hour which we were to maintain through the flight into Berlin. On leveling off I pulled the power back to 29 inches of mercury and 2050 RPM. It looked like that would hold our 170-miles-per-hour indicated air speed.

The next radio fix was Fulda on a heading of 033 degrees, 45 miles. It came in loud and clear on a frequency of 256 kilocycles with a call sign of dit-dit-dah-dit, dah-dit-dit, [FD]. At that time only the low frequency radio range was in service at Fulda. Later on an additional navigational aid in a higher frequency range, an Instrument Landing System [ILS] type leg was aimed from Fulda down the center of the corridor, across East Germany toward Berlin. It would be of limited range.

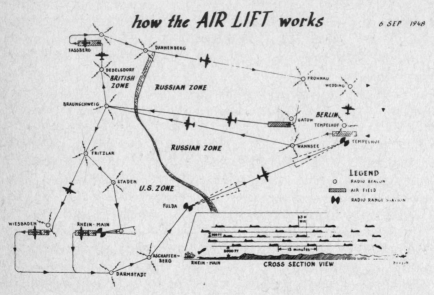

The diagram shows five flight altitudes which were later changed to two altitudes when better navigation and control equipment became available.

Approaching Fulda we listened carefully for the aircraft ahead of us to report crossing that radio fix. If the aircraft crossed Fulda less than three minutes before us we would have to slow down a bit. If he were more than that ahead of us we could pick up a few miles per hour. He would be either 1000 feet above us or 1000 feet below us. Then we were over Fulda range and Big Easy 571 was almost exactly three minutes ahead of us. We broadcast our call sign, altitude, and time over the fix and in short order we approached the East

German border. We looked at each other and wondered what the Yak activity would be for our inaugural run to Berlin. "A bottle of orange juice to the first one spotting a fighter," I announced as we crossed over into East Germany.   We established our outbound track from Fulda by using that facility as a bearing reference and taking up an initial heading of 057 degrees. As the wind would drift us off that course we would add or subtract the number of degrees needed to kill the wind drift and proceed to Templehof range. It would be some time before we could get a reliable signal from Tempelhof. We had no navigational aids in East Germany. Ten miles on each side of the center line didn't seem bad in the daylight on a good day but that far under other conditions could find us outside the corridor quite easily. Things would be improved later in the airlift with the addition of long-range radar. For now, pilotage and dead reckoning would have to do.

Fortunately the weather was quite good and we could see for miles of space that revealed the aircraft three minutes ahead and below us, plus others that were but specks disappearing in the distance. For the first time the enormity of the operation began to sink in. The silver skins of the big Skymasters reflecting back the suns rays were like a long string of pearls in a setting of deep azure blue. A feeling of pride to be involved in such an undertaking came over me and crowded out any misgivings that were hanging around the edges.

Forty minutes after passing Fulda John called Tempelhof airways and gave them our estimated position and received their altimeter setting and time hack.

In spite of straining our eyes no one had spotted a fighter in the corridor. We saw plenty of them on the ground and in the flight patterns at Dessau and Zerbst airfields. We were sitting ducks if they decided to terminate our flight.

By the time we reached Tempelhof range, airways gave us instructions to contact the tower if we were on VFR [visual flight rules], or to remain on their frequency for a range approach if we were on instruments. Later, when it was installed, we would be referred to GCA [ground controlled approach radar] whether we were VFR or IFR.

In some cases we would be routed by the Wedding beacon for spacing or to put us in the proper sequence for landing. By then we would have slowed our speed to 140 miles per hour and reduced our altitude to approximately 2000 feet. As we turned on our down-wind leg for the approach, control would have us descend to 1500 feet.

Approaching Berlin we had been in and out of fluffy balls of white clouds. Then suddenly, right over Berlin, we were in the clear. As we looked down it just about took our breath away. Nothing I had read, heard, or seen, prepared me for the desolate, ravaged sight below. The gaunt, broken outlines of once-majestic buildings, struggling toward the sky, supported by piles of rubble at their base, irregularly stretched from one end of the city to the other—a mottled mass of total destruction. The Anhalter train station was flattened with just part of the walls standing.

"Where in the world do the two million people live?" Sgt. Elkins asked as he stood up from his jump seat between John and me. There was no reply, just a shaking of heads.

The RAF and American bombers combined together almost completed the destruction. What wasn't destroyed from the air was finished off by thousands of artillery pieces manned by revenge-minded Soviet soldiers filled with vivid memories of the atrocities heaped upon their families by the Nazi invaders. This is what was left. Now there were RAF and USAF aircraft again over the city, in numbers, with a different purpose.

Most of the landings were to the west so we were positioned on a heading of 90 degrees for our down-wind leg and descended to 1500 feet for one minute. A turn to 180 degrees, for a right-hand base leg, brought us in position for a turn to the final approach, heading 270 degrees.

As we turned for the final approach Sgt. Elkins exclaimed, "There it is up ahead, that five-story apartment building on the end of the runway! How in the world did it escape with so little damage?" It was almost in the best condition of any building we had seen and it was right on the end of the short runway, just like we had been briefed.

"Remember, it's not a paved runway, and Hitler made it too short for a plane with this kind of load," John warned as we dropped full flaps and eased back on the power. "You need to pop it down just past the apartments, the little grass strip and the fence. Probably need some power on the flare to keep us from driving into the runway.

My C-54 Rosinen Bomber wing over one of the main aiming points for British and American bombers, the Anhalter Bahnhof, a crucial target in the center of Berlin. The subway tunnels under the Bahnhof became tombs for hundreds when the tunnels were flooded during the last battle.

The Kaiser Wilhelm Memorial Church stands as a reminder of the ravages of war. (Photo taken circa 1948.)

You'll have to get her down quick or we'll run off the end like some others have done."

The rational matched my intentions. The tower broke in with, "Big Easy 548, you are cleared to land after the C-54 ahead is off the end of the runway. Expedite your taxi when ground roll is complete."

"Roger," replied John. We'd been in tight places before but this was a bit different. As we whistled over the top of the apartment building I noticed about 20 or 30 kids standing and waving in the middle of the grass strip just outside the barbed wire fence.

We were coming down like a rock so I pushed in a little power and we flared just in time to roll it on. "Wasn't bad for the first time in Berlin," said John with a smile in his voice.

At the end of the runway a standard follow-me jeep was waiting to escort us to the unloading area in front of the impressive terminal building. We were lined up behind a string of other C-54s in various stages of unloading. A few C-47s were scattered among the larger C-54s like chicks nestled with a mother hen. It was a beehive of activity.

The hanger overhang was three-quarters of a mile long, built by Hitler in the graceful shape of an eagle's wing, bent in a symmetrical arc as though the eagle were pulling out of a dive. The overhang was high enough that we could have taxied right under it if necessary, but that was not to be with this kind of operation where fast and unobstructed access was essential.

The jeep came to a stop. The driver was out in a flash and signaled us forward a few feet, then gave us the cut engines sign. He was off in a moment to pick up the next aircraft.

By the time our engines had quit turning over there was someone pounding on the back cargo door. Sgt. Elkins hurried to the back, opened the large cargo door. Immediately in front of the door was a huge semi-trailer truck loaded with men dressed in those characteristic black tattered jackets or blue foreign-looking mixtures of old uniforms or coveralls. They were glad to have whatever they could get to wear.

A wooden chute quickly bridged the gap from the cargo door threshold to the truck bed. Up it rushed five of these Berlin laborers as if they were going to a fire. The Berlin unloading crews had been pilots, highly skilled professional people, tank crewmen or ordinary

The C-47 "Goonie Bird" was the first to respond to the Berliners' need. They were phased out by the end of September, 1948.

laborers. It was my first close up, eyeball-to-eyeball meeting with Germans in their homeland.

Mixed emotions were going through me as I sized up this heterogeneous crew through my stereotyped eyes. As I looked from one to another to find the monster, the hardened stare, the "superior" eye, or the defiant look, it wasn't there.

I suddenly realized that the closest man to me had his hand extended to me for a handshake and the one behind him was raising his for the same purpose. Then I noticed the look in their eyes as they gazed at the flour bags, then back to us, as though we were angels from heaven delivering the news of the resurrection.

I tried to keep this picture in focus, still insisting there must be one of those hard, defiant, supermen, somewhere in this crowd. There was no hint of what I had expected, although I had discounted what to expect given the difference in circumstances now and during the war.

There was an expression of humble gratitude through body language, the tone of unintelligible greetings, the moist eye and the sincere thrusting forward of the hand of friendship. This exchange took but a brief moment before they were rapidly moving the heavy sacks of flour to their fellow workers in the truck bed.

There was so much communicated in that short moment it seemed more like ten minutes as I went back over the things that had gone through my mind as a young man and later during the war. The look in the eye was unmistakable. No matter what had gone on before or for whatever reasons, they were individuals, human beings. We were friends, working for a common goal: to be free.

A wave of emotion came over me. We were trying to bomb each other into oblivion just a few years before and now a tremendous feeling of working together, united for a common cause, replaced my search for stereotype reinforcement. It didn't come easily. I was being taught a great lesson about prejudging individuals because they belong to a certain nation, race or color. It would be helpful in the years to come.

We made this trip more than two weeks before General Tunner came on board. We wanted to see what Hitler's airport terminal looked like. Down the chute we went between sacks of flour and then into the terminal building. The snack bar had all the goodies we were used to: hamburgers, hot coffee, and hot chocolate. It was like a world apart

Flour for Freedom.
Former combatants working around the clock in harmony for the right to choose.

from what those laborers knew on the flight line only 100 yards away. Crazy contrast!

A friend took us out the back stairway to a tunnel that had been used during the war to assemble fighter planes. He had all kinds of stories to tell about this unique edifice, some a bit beyond belief. We talked to pilots who had been there before us. We talked about the Templehof approach, how Berlin looked, the manner of the Berliners unloading the planes, and all the strange sights and sounds that had saturated my senses these past two days. It was an exciting experience.

Time went too quickly and we hurried back to the airplane to find the truck gone and the people wondering where we were. How could they have finished the job so fast? When General Tunner came to town there would be no more visits to the terminal building. The snack bar would be put in several portable wagons and be brought to the airplanes and the weather man would come around in a jeep to update our weather. Before the last sack was removed from the aircraft, the pilots would have to be in their cockpit, ready to start the engines. General Tunner would make a lot of important changes.

The engines coughed to life with a few little puffs of white smoke, smoothed out, and in no time we had received clearance to taxi.

As we proceeded around the inside of the barbed-wire fence to the take-off end of the runway, we could again see the children in the open place between the barbed wire and the old apartment buildings. They were intently watching the landings and takeoffs,

Typical group of children on the East End of runway 27 at the beginning of the airlift.

with more interest than children around airfields at home. A few waved as we went by.

The totally impersonal mass of humanity had begun to break down into individual human elements with faces, fears, children, dogs, hunger, gratitude, but above all courage and a driving passion for freedom. They were temporarily free of the oppressive heel of a dictator. How long would it last, and what of the bleak future that stared covetously out of the eyes of the Russian bear just across the city border? How valiant would I be if the roles were reversed?

We were cleared for immediate takeoff. Without the ten tons of flour, the big bird leapt into the sky like a homesick angel. The instructions from Tempelhof Control were to establish our climb and at 900 feet turn left to 255 degrees and home in on the Wannsee beacon on a frequency of 308 kilocycles and an identification of WZ. We climbed to our assigned cruising altitude of 6000 feet and after Wannsee turned to a heading of 275 degrees toward Braunsweig. This route through the Center corridor is a shorter leg than the Southern corridor we used coming in. The British and the Americans used the Northern corridor and also came out the Center corridor. This allowed one-way traffic and some peace of mind.

We held 280 degrees until we intersected the 270-degree radial outbound from the Gatow beacon, frequency 259 kilocycles, call sign GW. At this point we corrected for wind drift to maintain a track of 270 degrees for the 115 miles it took to clear East Germany.

Over Braunsweig we turned to a heading of 217 degrees for the 95 miles to the Fritzlar beacon, frequency 315 kilocycles, call sign FZ. At Fritzlar a call was made to help position ourselves with other aircraft and to report to Frankfurt control. Our decent was to begin here if preceding traffic was favorable. We hoped to cross Staden beacon in 61 miles at 4000 feet. At Staden, frequency 305 kilocycles, call sign SD, we were about 28 miles from home. In spite of heavy traffic, we expected and got our clearance to Rhein-Main from over Staden.

The usual close-in procedure routed us by the Offenbach beacon, frequency 320 kilocycles, call sign OFN. From

Unloading coal in Berlin.

there we were cleared for a visual approach to the Rhein-Main airport and a contest with ten other aircraft to get it on the ground. John was flying it, for which I was grateful. This was a real cowboy operation. General Tunner would change all that.

Finally we were back in our hard stand after an elapsed time of five hours and thirty minutes. Three hours and fifty-five minutes of that time had been actual time in the air.

We were met immediately with a truck full of coal bags. The load master said he would have it loaded and tied down in 45 minutes. That was enough time for us to get a meal at the mess hall near the flight line. Within an hour we were fueled up and back in the air, repeating the procedure all over again. There would be one more round trip after that before we could retire to the barn at Zeppelinheim. It was 03:00 hours when we crawled up that ladder and fell on our bunks.

6

Aerodromes, Airplanes, People and Politics

The next few days and nights were all mixed together in a hodge podge of breakfasts at dinner time and visa versa. Sleep and fly, sleep and fly. New faces and aircraft were appearing daily from places like Alaska, Hawaii, Panama, Kelly Field, Guam, Japan, and Westover Air Force Base in Massachusetts. Troop Carrier C-54s from some of these places had preceded us, as had 35 Military Transport Service C-54s.[20]

James D. Braham, now from Richardson, Texas, was a personnel officer when the airlift started. He stayed right at Rhein-Main sorting out the unbelievable challenges the influx of airlift personnel caused. He also had the responsibility to plan the evacuation of permanent party personnel dependents in case the cold war developed into a hot one. In many people's minds that was a distinct possibility.

It was seldom, in those days, that his wife and daughter got to see him. For those assigned just to fly the airlift there were no families in Germany. James didn't get much sympathy from the airlifters on that score.

When General Tunner assumed command of the airlift, it wasn't long before his great administrative skills were evident throughout the operation. He came across as a man with a mission, in a hurry to be somewhere. On the surface he was tough as nails, but underneath he had great compassion for those who served. We knew immediately that he was primarily interested in the safety of the flight and ground crews.

From the directives that began to flow we knew that he knew how to run airlift. What had been a rat race to see who could get around the corridors the fastest became a highly organized and disciplined operation. We all drew a breath of relief, and more than one bull session gave grass roots support for the changes.

Airspeeds, altitudes, position reports, location in that string of pearls, all became a way of life that we were required to live day and night. These changes occurred within a very short time after General Tunner took command on 29 July 1948.[21]

The British, French, and American authorities worked hand-in-glove to accomplish what seemed, at the beginning, to be an almost impossible task. The British called their operation "Plainfare." The British RAF had begun operations in lock step with their American USAF counterparts. They had a larger variety of aircraft in their operation including Dakotas, Yorks, Lancasters, Hastings, Halifax, and flying boats well represented by the Sunderland. It may sound strange to list flying boats among aircraft supporting Berlin.[22]

The city was once one of the most beautiful capitals of any nation. There are 76.8 square kilometers of forest land and 31.2 square kilometers of lakes and rivers within just the West Berlin city limits. These natural assets present a beauty that allows nature lovers to become reasonably happy city dwellers.

The large amount of water surface provided ample space for the ten Short Sunderland flying boats from RAF Calshot. These aircraft operated out of a temporary base at Finkenwerder just west of Hamburg on the river Elbe. Their principle landing point in Berlin was the Havel See which was quite close to Gatow Airfield, the British main landing terminal in Berlin. These Sunderlands and two British civilian Short Hythe flying boats were the only aircraft that could handle a very special cargo. These aircraft had received anticorrosion treatment to withstand salt in their cargo bays. They flew great amounts of salt to the besieged city.[23]

The scheduling of these aircraft posed a sticky problem because of their different flight characteristics. During bad weather they had more difficulty in making their water landings due to inadequate ground [water] navigation and landing aids.

As one can imagine, the British had a much greater challenge in providing support, maintenance, spare parts, technical know how, and air corridor space necessary to accommodate the many different varieties of aircraft and their different flight and mechanical characteristics. They did their job well.

The principal RAF bases in the British Zone of West Germany were Schleswigland, Lubeck, Celle, Fassberg, and Wunstorf, plus the flying-boat base at Finkenwerder. These bases focused the principal British effort into Berlin Gatow through the Northern air corridor.[24]

At the very beginning, Gatow was the envy of American pilots because they had ground control approach [GCA] radar. I remember several very foggy days that they landed me at Gatow when Tempelhof was closed due to the Tempelhof's less precision radio range landing aid.

The British invention of radar has greatly blessed the lives of Allied pilots through the years and contributed in a major way to the winning of the Battle of Britain. Without our radar landing aids and long-range radar the airlift would have failed.

In contrast to the varied types of aircraft employed by the British, the Americans relied almost entirely on the Douglas C-54 Skymaster. At the height of the operation there were approximately 319 C-54s assigned in support of Operation Vittles. Of these, 19 were assigned at the Great Falls readiness training unit [RTU] where replacement lift pilots were subsequently trained. Another 75 of the aircraft were in the maintenance pipeline to, from, and within the United States. The remainder of the aircraft, including 24 in the Navy VR6 and the VR8 Squadrons, were directly engaged in flying the airlift. Many of these aircraft were in local Squadron maintenance and not being flown or loaded.

When the Navy aircraft arrived at Rhein-Main in November, 1948, there were a lot of inservice jokes told back and forth between the Navy crews and the USAF crews. The two Navy squadrons did an outstanding job in the competition between all the units. They more than held their own.

The other aircraft for the United States were the C-47s that began the airlift, operated by the 60th and 61st Troop Carrier Groups, a few C-82s of short duration in September 1948, and one C-74 from my old outfit in Brookley. The C-47s peaked at about 100 aircraft at the beginning and were gradually phased out by the end of September

The Douglas C-54 Skymaster replaced the C-47s and are shown here on the ramp at Tempelhof.

1948. On 5 August 1948 there were 80 C-47s and 80 C-54s assigned to the operation.

The principal USAF bases in West Germany were Rhein-Main near Frankfurt, and Wiesbaden [Y-80]. Rhein-Main was the best equipped base of any during the airlift but was located considerably further from Berlin than the bases in the British Zone.

Rhein-Main was the home base for many airships including the Graff Zeppelin and the ill-fated Hindenburg in the German fleet of lighter-than-air ships in that era of aviation. On the 3rd of May, 1937, the Hindenburg was launched from Rhein-Main, Zeppelinheim, on its way to a fiery death three days later in Lakehurst N.J. It was 803 feet long and 135 feet in diameter and had just concluded its 54th flight, 36 of them across the northern or southern Atlantic Oceans.

During the war Rhein-Main was a German Luftwaffe fighter base. Toward the end it was home for the advanced ME-262 jet fighters. Their presence brought heavy bombing pressure, culminating in a raid on Christmas day, 1944, that leveled 75 % of the buildings on the base. In March, 1945, the Germans destroyed everything that was left and abandoned the site. After the invasion, the U.S. Army Air Corps restored the facilities and used the base for their P-47 Thunderbolt fighters.[25]

From our bunks in the loft of the barn in Zeppelinheim, we were almost eyeball-to-eyeball with the aircraft coming in to land on runway 07 left at Rhein-Main.

Wiesbaden was a German fighter base during the war and had a good runway 5000 feet long. It was 456 feet above sea level, 87 feet higher than Rhein-Main.

Other bases not in the class of these two were Fritzlar and other support or maintenance air fields.

As the C-54 fleet increased dramatically, the British airfields of Fassberg and Celle were used very heavily by the United States Air Force. Nearly half of the C-54 fleet would eventually be hauling coal from those two bases. They were much nearer Berlin than the southern bases. Two aircraft could haul as much from the British Zone as three aircraft from Rhein-Main.

There was a very important contribution from civilian aviation, by both the British and Americans. As one might expect, there was a little friendly rivalry between these complementary efforts. One night

A British Airman directs the loading of coal in an Air Force C-54 at Fassberg in the British Zone.

we were approaching the number two position for takeoff when the tower called and asked us to pull off to one side and let another aircraft pass. As he passed in front of our lights we saw that it was an American Overseas commercial DC-4. They were doing a good job helping the effort with their limited fleet. The pilots of these commercial planes were highly professional and dedicated. As the aircraft passed and took the take off position in front of our number one aircraft, I recalled a conversation a few nights before in the club.

The commercial pilots were the envy of many military pilots. Whether it was true or not, some pilots thought the commercial jocks got preferential treatment such as we had just witnessed. Some military pilots defended that arrangement with the explanation that the commercials had a contract and to perform it they couldn't stay in line waiting for all the Big Easies to clear. Sounded reasonable.

The commercial pilots were nicknamed "The Golden Boys." "Why is that?" asked one of the Lieutenants. "Do you know how much money they make for every trip to Berlin? That's why," answered a self-appointed expert. "How much is that?" came back the query. Some thought they were paid on the number of trips they made, not by the

month like we were. It was obvious that no one really knew. Most
agreed it was a certainty that the salaries were nowhere in the same
ballpark with ours.

"They have more experience and more invested than we do,"
answered Lt. Guy B. Dunn, a C-47 and C-54 check pilot. "Even so,
they don't do any better job getting the goods to Berlin than we do,"
replied Pickering with some pride.

*Jack Bennett (right) the pilot with the most flights to Berlin. He has 40,000 hours in the air
and currently lives in Berlin. Photo in Berlin on the 40th anniversary of the end of the blockade,
12 May 1989.*

The envy came more from the feeling that the "Golden Boys" were
more experienced, getting a lot more money, appeared to
get some preferential treatment, and could go home if they really
wanted. Their operation was a small but important part of the tonnage
hauled. Their chief pilot, Jack Bennett, was a pilot's pilot, a real pro.
It is likely that he had more trips to Berlin than any other pilot on
the airlift.

One thing we did agree on was that these guys were good pilots
and we were glad they were on the team.

In spite of the talk, there was a real esprit-de-corps among the military pilots. An example was Lester R.D. Stillwell, a Captain out of San Antonio, Texas. He was proud of the qualified military pilots from world-wide MATS bases and also the C-54 Troop Carrier crews. Lester was a veteran of 180 missions over the Hump [Himalayas] into China during the war. General Tunner was also his commanding officer in that operation. Lester had come to the airlift from a passenger and cargo operation out of Kelly Field in San Antonio, Texas, one of the MATS outfits. He was to settle down years later in Carmichael, California.

We were quick to agree with his observation that "We've got the most proficient bunch of pilots in the United States Air Force flying the airlift. Their instrument and night experience is exceptional. They fly the precision routes as General Tunner has set them up and I wouldn't mind being a passenger in the back end during any instrument approach these guys make."

Lester went on to explain that the C-54 crews assembled on the airlift had more varied experience than the "Golden Boys" had, having flown tough air environments from Alaska to the Far East. Stillwell put some of the pride back in us.

The discussion had hit a resonant chord with Lieutenant Stan Mitchum. He had been stationed in Great Falls flying the run to Alaska with his home now in Houston, Texas. "This thing is a milk run compared to some of the weather and the bases we had to fly through and land at in Alaska. If you want to have some fun, try making an approach in a white out, without proper navigational aids, to a strip that is paved between two peaks. There is only one way out and the runway is so steep that you have to keep about 50% power on after landing to get up to operations. I think the route to Berlin is not too much of a challenge after logging a few hours around that Alaskan beat," Stan said with pride in his past experience. We had gained a better feeling for our civilian compatriots and our own self-image.

The Berlin bases for the USAF were Templehof at first and Tegel later, with some occasional traffic into Gatow. In the beginning the biggest problem with Templehof was the grass and pierced steel plank [PSP] runways and the approach over the five-story apartment buildings.

In October the first flights began to use the newly constructed hard-surfaced runway 270 at Tempelhof which was lined up with a graveyard on the approach. It was finished just in time before the PSP runway became unusable. Rain-slickened PSP caused a number of accidents and blown tires.

The new runway location did away with the approach over the buildings. Now we were below those same buildings in the latter part of the final approach. In instrument conditions it was interesting to suddenly see an aircraft emerge out of the stratus cloud in the groove below the red light on the corner of the apartment building.

Peter Hoffman, now a journalist in the United States, was a young boy during the airlift. He lived in those apartments. One very foggy night he was alarmed to hear the roar of four Twin Wasp engines right outside his room and witness the belly of a C-54 almost flat against his window. The pilot had drifted off the GCA center line and corrected almost too late for the crew and Peter. The spirit of these Berliners was the remarkable cement that held things together. It was the almost-fanatical drive of the people as a whole to choose their independence over capitulation that would make the airlift succeed.

It became obvious that such a complex and intertwined operation involving the aircraft of two nations in such a confined airspace should be combined and directed centrally.

General LeMay, Commander of the United States Air Forces in Europe, and General Tunner met with General LeMay's British counterpart, Air Marshal Sir Arthur P. M. Saunders, Commander-in-Chief of the British Air Forces of Occupation. A combined, centrally directed operation won out over any other concerns. The final agreement was reached on 14 October, 1948, just before General LeMay left Europe to be the legendary commander of the Strategic Air Command. He and Sir Arthur signed a lengthy directive setting up the Combined Airlift Task Force [CATF].[26]

General Tunner was designated Commander of the Combined Airlift Task Force, Air Commodore J. W. F. Merer of the RAF, a fine, dedicated officer, was named the Deputy Commander. Merer continued to command the RAF's Operation Plainfare. The Royal Air

Force effort also included elements from New Zealand, Australia, and South Africa. There was an equivalent of 10 RAF squadrons.

The United States Air Force had the equivalent of 20 squadrons, and the Navy had two squadrons. Both of these elements were assigned to the Military Air Transport Service.

The logistics of such an undertaking were beyond my comprehension as a simple pilot in such a complex operation. Even now, as I look back, it is remarkable what General Tunner and his staff were able to do for the American contribution. The British contribution was just as remarkable.

Politics were always present and employed in the contest for West Berlin. Not long after the blockade had begun the Russians offered West Berliners the opportunity to obtain fresh vegetables, coal, and other essential commodities if they would sign up for East Berlin ration cards. This offer was made to drive a chink in the West Berliner's armor. It must have sounded pretty good to people eating dehydrated food in insufficient amounts.

Areas around Berlin were good producers of vegetables, fruit, grains, and livestock. Delicious strawberries and asparagus were native to the surrounding areas. Now the Russians were offering to make those delicacies available. Just sign your name.

The number of West Berliners who signed up for these rations has been estimated to be between 20,000 and 90,000. Even the highest estimate represented only about four percent of the blockaded population. This overwhelming vote for personal freedom and the Berliners' support of the British, French, and Americans spoke more clearly than any words of the special spirit and mentality of those under siege.[27]

Edward A. Morrow reported on October 16, 1948 that during the blockade the East Germans were smuggling a considerable amount of produce and raw materials to their countrymen in West Berlin. Some of the success of this action was credited to the assistance of minor Soviet officials, probably anti-Stalinists. These sympathetic efforts were contributory to breaking the blockade.[28] The Washington Star on 16 October 1948 reported, "The Russians tightened their blockade to prevent any food from slipping into Berlin's Western Sectors from the surrounding Soviet zone. Passengers on all trains, inland waterways, and motor vehicles would be searched for foodstuffs or other rationed articles. These articles would be immediately confiscated, especially if the passengers carrying them were bound for Berlin."

The move of the Soviets to take over Berlin resulted in the practical division of the two Germanies and the bonding of West Berlin to the West. In addition, the blockade was responsible for an increased feeling of empathy from the East Germans for their relatives in the West and their countrymen generally. There would be a component of that feeling for the West behind the bloody East German revolt of 1953 against Stalin's henchmen, the exodus in 1961 which led to the erection of the wall, and the mass exodus to the West in 1989.

The aircraft were taking a real beating with the high number of heavy takeoffs and landings. Engine changes, mechanical repair, and electrical systems needed countless hours of attention. Coal and flour dust was raising havoc with everything from radio equipment to control systems. Maintenance was of growing critical importance. In a move characteristic of his fertile imagination, General Tunner contacted a former German Luftwaffe Major General, Hans Detlev von Rohden. The General had been in air transport and was familiar with the kinds of problems we faced.[29]

Within a very short time he was able to locate many Germans who had been aircraft mechanics, have maintenance handbooks rewritten in German, and work the men into our maintenance force. They were very good and very numerous. Their help was a real factor in keeping the aircraft in the air.

As the pressure grew on Tempelhof and Gatow, it became readily apparent that there must be another airport built if the airlift were to succeed. The French agreed to provide the real estate for such a field in their sector, on a site used by Herrman Goering for the training of anti-aircraft divisions during the war. It was an ideal location in the country, with no obstructions on either end of the proposed runway. It was to be called Tegel.

Colonel Swallwell, a veteran of the Hump who served on General Tunner's staff there, and Colonel Peterson of the Engineer Corps, developed the plans for the new Tegel airbase. When the plans were completed Colonel R. Whitaker, Chief Engineering officer for the Post of Berlin, was given the job to see that it was constructed. His men worked around the clock until it was finished.

The labor force came from volunteers among the citizens of Berlin. The pay was 1.20 marks per hour plus a hot meal. At the peak of the construction a total of 17,000 German citizens worked around-the-clock in three eight-hour shifts. Approximately 40% of the work force was women.

The material for the runway base was readily available in the remains of the once-proud buildings of Berlin. Forty thousand cubic meters of crushed rubble, taken from streets and alley ways, formed part of the foundation which was from 24 inches to 60 inches thick. Wheel barrows and hand carts were the most-used construction equipment in the final placement of 1,000,000 cubic feet of crushed brick, the equivalent of ten destroyed city blocks, which was put into place by the citizen volunteers subsisting on very lean rations.

When the work was begun on September the 5th, 1948, an optimistic finishing date was set for 1 January, 1949. The enthusiasm and dedication of the work force was underestimated and the target date was shortened to 15 December, 1948. The extraordinary effort and cooperation between this mixed work force provided for our first landing at Tegel on 5 November, 1948. Theirs was truly a remarkable achievement. This now provided the capability for a landing in Berlin every minute, with each airfield capable of a landing every three minutes.[30]

Bob Ramer, now of Lexington, Kentucky, was a young Sergeant operating the new tower at Tegel. He still marvels at the accomplishment of bringing an aircraft across the threshold of that runway every three minutes and the team work that existed between the French, British, Germans, and the Americans. It gave him a feeling of well-being to see this diverse group of citizens exchange a wave of the hand, a smile, or verbal greeting while crossing the compound or going about the job. The realization that the same thing was being repeated concurrently at Gatow and Templehof gave Bob a feeling of teamwork he had never had before.

Although the runway at Tegel was located in an ideal spot, with flat terrain and open approaches, there remained a major flight safety hazard. The obstacle was a 200-foot-high radio tower positioned near the runway. Removal of the tower would be an easy physical task but nothing in Berlin is easy, especially in those times. It happened that the radio tower, although it was located in the French Sector, was

owned by a communist-controlled radio station in East Berlin. The
Soviets had refused repeated requests for it's relocation. We had offered
to pay for all relocation costs and still it stood there.

The French had no aircraft resources to contribute to the airlift,
but they were full partners and cooperative in every way in which
they could participate. They were pleased for the opportunity to
provide the real estate for Tegel and were on the verge of making
another morale-boosting contribution.

On the 20th of November French General Ganeval formally
requested the Soviet Commander in East Berlin to remove the tower
by the 16th of December 1948. General Tunner's book,*Over the Hump*,
relates the situation as he observed it on the 16th of December, 1948:

> General Ganeval invited the Detachment that we had stationed
> there, composed of some 20 officers and men, to come up to his
> office for a mysterious meeting. When all had arrived, General
> Ganeval shut and locked the door. The procedure seemed
> somewhat strange at first but the General served such excellent
> refreshments, and exuded such Gallic charm, that all suspicions
> were allayed. Suddenly, in the midst of the merriment, a mighty
> blast rattled the window panes and shook the room. French and
> Americans alike dashed to the window just in time to see the
> huge radio tower slowly topple to the ground. "You'll have no
> more trouble with the tower," said the General softly. The Reds
> screamed to high heaven and attempted, as the French had
> anticipated, to lay all the blame on the Americans. Our
> Detachment had an iron bound alibi, however: they had been
> under lock and key.

Years later in Berlin, I met a French member of that demolition
crew who described his experience. "The broadcasting crew at the
tower had been busy sending out their propaganda and music to all
who would tune in. In the midst of this tranquil scene we trooped
in with our demolition experts. The leader of our team tapped the
station manager on the shoulder and said, 'You have about five minutes
to get out of here unless you want this tower around your ears.'

"A quick look at my French commander's face left no doubt in the
Soviet radio station manager's mind that what he had just heard was
really going to happen. He quickly sounded the alarm and led the
charge out of the office located under the tower. It was not much longer

than five minutes before the explosion was heard and the tower came tumbling down."

There were cheers in the living quarters and clubs of all the airlift bases when the announcement came over the radio. I heard the news over the aircraft radio on the way back to Rhein-Main. "Those Frenchmen are alright!" said John, slapping his side with an accompanying roar of approval.

7

Flight Experiences
in the Corridors

The flights were increasing almost daily. It was during one of our second round trips in a very busy period when we experienced some especially difficult flight conditions.

We were over East Germany and halfway through the corridor to Berlin. It was in the waning hours of daylight with storm clouds bringing darkness a half hour earlier than usual. The horizon was illuminated with lightning bolts of spectacular proportions. Just before total darkness we saw what seemed to be a miniature sand storm coming across the normally green and verdant countryside cross-stitched with fields and forest.

Directly below us was one of the Russian tank training grounds. The tanks were engaged in a major exercise, tearing at the soil as they maneuvered to and fro. The tank tracks were spewing the dirt into the air and the wind gave it no chance to return in the place from which it came.

Our normally stable flight platform was being tossed about. "Better go back and check the tie downs on the coal," Capt. John suggested to Sgt. Elkins. "This is getting rough." The ground disappeared as we slammed into the middle of a growing cumulo-nimbus.

The static on the radio was obliterating any recognizable signal. That tank training ground was in the middle of the corridor so we knew for the moment we were where we should be. Just before total darkness we crossed the river Elbe, right on course.

We suddenly were in alternate severe up- and down-drafts, and the rain was beating so hard on the fuselage that the sound of the engines could hardly be heard. "Better turn the cockpit lights up, John, we may see some lightning," I suggested. It was no sooner done than a brilliant bolt with ragged edges sawed its way across the windshield directly before us and disappeared off the right wing. The hair on the back of my neck stood up as the static electrical field swept by.

"Wow, that was close!" Elkins gasped. Even with the cockpit lights turned up it was a few moments before we got our normal vision back. The last weather we heard had Tempelhof in the clear and, sure enough, in five minutes we broke out into a beautiful star-studded sky with a very clean windshield.

"I've been in a few good drive-through car washes, but nothing to beat that," offered John as he shifted a bit to avoid a growing rain puddle in his seat from a leaky side window.

"Try and get Templehof range on the bird dog and give airways a call, John," I suggested. It had been futile up to then. Communications were suddenly crystal clear and we were cleared for our approach.

The stop at Templehof was routine and we were soon on our way home through the Center corridor. Things went pretty well until near Fritzlar where we ran into the remains of the front and a stack of C-54s trying to get into Rhein-Main and Wiesbaden. Frankfurt Control put us in a holding pattern.

We pulled back on the power to 26 inches of mercury and 1550 RPM. This gave us 400-brake horsepower per engine and cut our fuel flow from 334 pounds to 180 pounds per hour per engine.[31] "Stay out of the 1601 to 1699 RPM range," warned Elkins. "That area is restricted because of excessive vibration on the tail section. We are real light. This power setting will keep us in the air for a long time."

We had just enough fuel on board to get to Berlin and back and to an alternate in the area. "Hope it won't take too long," John observed. "I'm hungry."

In the one of the few times I remember, GCA went off the air and they were only getting one aircraft out of the stack on a radio range approach every 12 minutes. There was only 20 minutes gas left in the tanks when we finally touched down at Rhein-Main.

As we checked in at operations an old head who had been in Germany for two years broke into our commiserating with one another, "Look, you guys are lucky to have this kind of weather. Just wait until winter. There won't be any lightning but there will be more than enough fog, freezing rain, snow, and sleet. You'll be lucky to get into Templehof when that sets in."

"The airlift will be over by then," I said more confidently than I had any right.

One late afternoon flight, in the middle of East Germany, we were startled by a sound of strange origin right under our nose. Almost concurrently the blurred shape of a Yak-3 pulled straight up before us. He immediately went into a vertical roll. "Hope there is not one of our guys just above," shouted John, louder than he needed to be heard. "Wow! That was exciting," joined in Sgt. Elkins. Other reports were coming occasionally of like incidents. "Better than being shot at and it does break the monotony," I responded.

There had been no reports of a cargo aircraft being fired upon. Harassment seemed limited to head-on approaches with a last minute pull up, coming up from behind right under the aircraft, and formation flying just off our wing.

The thing that gave us reassurance in the face of such tactics was President Truman's action in ordering B-29 Superforts to airstrips in England.[32] He made it clear to the Russians that the bombers had the atomic bomb capability and to keep their guns out of the action. Needless to say, we each renewed our resolve to support President Truman. None of us were aware of how serious the international poker game had become.

We got back to Rhein-Main at 22:00 hours anticipating our second round trip back to Berlin. The weather had steadily deteriorated to the point that we knew it would not be a fun trip.

After debriefing we made our way over to the snack bar and wolfed down meat loaf that must have been left over from the evening meal, and then headed back to the aircraft.

The rain was coming down in sheets and the lights from the auxiliary power units were sparkling like fireflies in the night. Inside the aircraft we pulled off our wet coats, checked the tie downs on the crates of bottled fresh milk, and headed toward the cockpit. "Those kids in Berlin are going to be glad to see this," Sgt. Elkins said with a smile.

John Pickering was a big, easy-going, fun guy to fly with. He had a way of staying calm in the midst of chaos. Besides an oil leak on number 2, a low right main strut, a generator out on number 4, and an inoperative auto-pilot, we were in good shape. He shrugged it off with "I've seen worse."

With the forecast turbulence for the route, we would be hand-sticking the bird anyway so the auto-pilot was not a big deal. Some of the other items, maybe.

Taxiing to takeoff, we could see the barn right in front of us just across the autobahn. That lumpy mattress would feel pretty good about now.

With gusty conditions on the takeoff roll, we held her down to pick up an extra 10 miles per hour before lifting her into the soggy, rain-soaked night. The first 900 feet came slowly. Then we started hitting a few updrafts

The most appreciated cargo by the children of Berlin, fresh whole milk.

in the cumulus which put us back on our climb schedule. The static made it hard to pick up some of the departure fixes but we did manage to nail Fulda right on the money.

We had some difficulty in getting the time of the previous aircraft crossing Fulda. It wasn't a good night for communications. The radio compass needle was swinging all over the place, making tracking outbound a bit inaccurate. The proper identification of this useful direction finding device is the AN/ARN7 radio compass. It has four bands between 100 and 1750 kilocycles. The "bird dog" needle points in the direction of a tuned-in ground station, either automatically or manually, by rotating the loop to receive a null. At least that is the theory.

Forty minutes later we were desperately trying to get a bearing on Tempelhof. John was doing his best. "Wish they would hurry up getting that CPS-5 long-range radar installed," he moaned. "Between static bursts I'm getting two different readings on the same frequency."

We were now fairly free of static but hadn't seen the ground since we took off and it was so dark it wouldn't have done much good. We really didn't know our position. The identifiers for Tempelhof range seemed strange and the needle was going back and forth as if between two stations. One signal was suddenly stronger but the direction was 30 degrees off our nose. "We're not that far off," John observed.

"We've got that decoy station the Soviets have set up on the same frequency as Tempelhof. Those darn Russians shouldn't do that," he exclaimed as he took off his headset and hung it up in disgust. What a big, gentle bear of a man, whose nick name was the Silver Fox. No expletives, bad language, only a nod and a little disgust. "Nearest I've seen you to getting mad John," I observed with a smile.

Ten minutes later he was back at it. The weather wasn't improving and there was no direction-finding service functional. The reception was so bad we couldn't clearly distinguish the A or N quadrants of the Tempelhof range. It seemed a very long time before we were able to get a reliable signal, to find that we had already passed Berlin and were probably not far from Poland.

We started a quick 180-degree turn when a severe vibration shook the whole aircraft. "We've been hit!" shouted Elkins. "Number 2 is on fire." Immediately the three of us confirmed the fire visually and from cockpit instruments.

"Feather number 2 and place the mixture lever to idle cut off on that engine!" I ordered Sgt. Elkins as I pulled the number 2 fire extinguisher selector handle. "Pull your CO_2 cylinder discharge handle, John," I said with some urgency. Trail your number 2 cowl flap, Sgt. Elkins," I urged as I turned on the landing light and looked out my window at the offending engine. The propellor was dead still and the blade feathered perfectly, the leading edge pointed directly into the airstream. So far so good. It would be nicer if we really knew where we were. The very possible prospect of a forced landing in Poland or East Germany reared its ugly head. John mumbled something about flying without parachutes so we could haul more cargo. "You know we never use parachutes in our standard MATS operation," I reminded John.

"This isn't a standard operation," John reminded me.

"This old gal will get us to an airfield on three engines if we can find a field," I answered John. "At our weight we can almost hold our altitude on two engines and if we have to we can drop some fresh milk to the local farmers."

"Not likely the Russkies will turn on any of their landing-field lights for us, and they aren't flying in this kind of weather," countered John. He continued, "If we are going to crash-land at night in a storm, I'd rather take my chances with a parachute."

Attending to number 2 engine Sgt. Elkins had quickly placed the Vacuum Pump Selector Handle in the proper position; turned the ignition switch, booster pump, and generator switches off; closed the cowl flap; and had gone back to do a visual check on the engine.

The manner of Sgt. Elkin's return to the cockpit and the ashen look on his face told me immediately that we had more problems than a shutdown engine and not knowing where we were.

"There is still a fire out there and if it gets past the fire wall it will be into a main fuel tank. That would blow us to bits! Better hit it with the other bottle," urged Elkins.

In just a moment I discharged our last CO_2 bottle and we all said a little prayer. "Go back and keep an eye on it, Sgt. Elkins, and let us know." A night crash landing or being blown out of the air was begining to be a distinct possibility. Our best chance was to get to Tempelhof before the worst happened.

"Give Tempelhof another call on emergency frequency and double check the bird dog, John," I suggested.

John's voice went out calm and clear. "Tempelhof Airways, Tempelhof Airways, this is Big Easy 555. Mayday, Mayday, Mayday, come in please. We have a fire in number 2 engine. Do you read us?" John paused between several transmissions and then it came.

A faint response, "Big Easy 555 this is Tempelhof Airways. I read you three by three, give me your position."

Almost concurrently we were picking up a better reading on the bird dog. "We are east of your field about 30 miles. Request crash trucks stand by."

About 10 minutes later we saw the dim lights of East Berlin and shortly after the Tempelhof beacon. What a beautiful sight! Elkins came forward and gave us the second good news of the night. The flames were out and the smoke was decreasing. The aircraft seemed sluggish on the controls coming down the final approach on three engines and a smoke screen trailing the fourth. I knew that the added problem was due in part to the accumulation of coal and flour dust in the control cables and pulleys.

The landing weather wasn't bad and we were soon on the ground with an escort of fire trucks illuminated with flashing red lights. "Sure great to have a reception committee like that when you need it," sighed Elkins.

The engine was soon foamed down but a close inspection failed to disclose any sign of being hit by a projectile or other foreign object. We were as happy to get rid of that load of milk as the Berliners were to get it. That was no milk run! We left old 555 at Tempelhof and hitched a ride home on the next flight out.

On arrival in Rhein-Main John indicated a need for a drink at the club before climbing the ladder to the loft. By then it was about 04:00 hours and there were several seats available at the big round table in the club. A lively discussion was already underway on the wild time everyone had that night with the weather. There were others who had experienced the same radio problems.

One pilot said things weren't that bad and related the story of RAF Squadron Leader Denys Horner who was headed to the Havel See in a Sunderland. He found himself above a Soviet practice bombing range and suddenly surrounded by clusters of practice bombs dropping in front of his windscreen from the Ilyushins above him.[33]

Incidents of Soviet flares, ground-to-ground rockets, air-to-ground fire, too-close-for-comfort Yak buzz jobs, and blindings from searchlights were all brought into the discussion to make our evening seem a little less unique.[34]

It is just as well we hadn't seen the 16 October 1948 Washington Star which reported: "The Russians announced that they will practice anti-aircraft fire at towed targets in the allied airlift corridor. American authorities charged that it would be a dangerous violation of air safety rules. They [Russians] also announced they will conduct 'local flying' drills at various other points in the Allied corridors."

There was a steady change of participants around the table as new crews came in from their flights and those who had been there awhile went to the barracks. Soon it was our turn to bounce our way to the barn in the back of the weapons carrier shuttle.

The next day we received word that there had been a second fatal airlift crash of a C-47. The fully loaded Goonie Bird fell into the already bomb-scarred apartments in the Friedenau borough.[35] The Berliners mourned the loss and in a special ceremony named the adjoining streets for the crew members. Mercedes and her mother attended the honors. The crash was close enough to their apartment that they had heard the impact and had seen the flames.

The crash of a fully loaded C-47 into already devastated apartments in Berlin. All the crew were killed.

Even when things were going well, we naturally flew with mechanical conditions that under normal flight operations would have caused a delay or cancellation of the flight. One such case was a C-54 flying out of Fassberg. The pilot assigned for the night flight to Berlin was Captain Ray Kingsbury from Orlando, Florida. The big bird had just been loaded up with coal. Ray was doing the preflight inspection under a wing with his flashlight. Moisture was dripping down the back of his neck and onto his wrists. He knew it was raining but he thought the big friendly wing would give him better protection than that. But a quick sniff of his wrist told him immediately that the annoyance was not water but gasoline.

Ray stepped out from under the wing and called the nearby maintenance chief over. He said, "You know chief, we've got a regulation that says we can't fly an airplane when it is leaking over six drops a minute. There are four places that are leaking gasoline. My best guess is that there are at least three times the allowable six drops a minute coming out of holes in that wing."

The maintenance chief scratched his head while he did some arithmetic and then asked, "Captain, don't you know that means not more than six drops out of every hole?"

Captain Kingsbury got to Berlin and back with his crew but wrote up in the Form 1, "There is more than one hole leaking more than six drops a minute coming out of our right wing." The crew had measured it and denied making the situation worse by a bad landing at Tegel.

New crew members and aircraft were continuously coming in from the States. Stan Wilkinson, now of Homosassa, Florida, just finished his marriage ceremony in time to leave for Germany. He arrived in Wiesbaden late one evening, turned in his records to the operations people, and was on his way to Berlin in short order. His new squadron commander was flying in the left seat and Stan was co-pilot. Stan's second mission was in the left seat as aircraft commander the very next day.

He was later assigned to Celle as a coal hauler, using the shorter Northern air corridor to Berlin. This would be the beginning of 280 missions with only two missed approaches. Stan would later return home with a good feeling about helping people worse off than himself. He would stay in the Air Force and was proud to say that he learned to appreciate the great Berliners and to have worked with them in the preservation of freedom.

8

Cultural Shock

About the only place that crew members had a chance to interact with one another was in the mess halls and Airmans' and Officers' clubs. The living quarters didn't lend themselves to cozy gatherings and the people were in an out of the quarters like a revolving door. The mess hall at Zeppelinheim was a fairly social place where incoming crews could meet those who were just going out. That occured at any hour of the day or night. the clubs were more comfortable with easy chairs and even some music.

When a crew was off duty and enroute from a cockpit to bed they often would stop by a club for a few minutes of conversation and a drink. It was a short break at the end of a 12- to 15-hour day. With this kind of arrangement it was understandable that some of the chatter was about the most recent trip, the crazy condition of the world, and how long it would take the diplomats to get the Russians to the bargaining table so we could go home. These sessions were also filled with stories about problems at home, accounts of friendly frauleins near airlift bases, and noticeable cultural differences.

The disruption of families on such short notice to support the airlift fostered many build-in problems. The indefinite nature of the assignment was one of the most disruptive factors. General Tunner took care of that by specifying that pilots assigned full-time duty flying the airlift would be sent home after six months.

The subject would get around occasionally to the nonfraternization policy with the German Frauleins. There were many bachelors who made it sound like the policy just as well not have been written. It surely wasn't any hinderance to them.

The new pilots at these gatherings were privileged to buy the drinks. I usually got an appreciative glance when I ordered an orange juice instead of something more expensive. "What's your problem?" was a frequent query. "It's just my way of life. I respect your choices and I hope you will do the same," was the usual reply. After the first query it never seemed to be a problem. It was an aspect of military life that had worried me from the day I signed up for Aviation Cadet training. The people I associated with in the service were sharp, principled, and patriotic citizens. Almost without exception they were tolerant, broadminded, and willing to look at all sides of an issue. Their attitude toward my beliefs made me look at myself to see that I reciprocated their acceptance. There were many others who had a life style similar to my own. Some of them were of other religious faiths or of no religious belief at all but they lived a personal code that seemed to work for them. To find I could be me in the Armed Forces was a relief of major proportions.

The more I heard in these sessions about the independent nature of the Berliners, the more I realized that I had underestimated the value of freedom in my life. Every time I landed in Berlin it reinforced that feeling and appreciation. People in America took freedom too much for granted. There were a few friends of mine that I would like to have dropped off in Berlin for a couple of days.

The morning after a night flight John and I were headed across the compound to the shower room. On the way we noticed a small group of fellow pilots standing at the barbed wire fence talking to some women. Out of curiosity we detoured over that way and listened in.

The women were passing some packages wrapped in newspaper through the barbed wire fence to several fellows I recognized who lived in the tar-paper shacks.

"Hey, Lt. Hartnell, what have you got in the package?" John called out to our old buddy from Mobile.

"Nothing very exotic, just some clean shorts and stuff. These gals do a lot better job than they do in the base laundry and we get door-to-door delivery. May even get a phone number," came back Charlie's matter-of-fact reply.

"What does it cost for a week's wash?" pursued John.

"Two candy bars, or a candy bar and a package of gum," he replied.

I turned to John, "What do you think it would cost for the same wash in Berlin?"

"Based on other differences, I'd guess you could get it done for three sticks of gum," he said as if the mathematics were a problem. "It is ten times as tough there as it is here."

"With our week's candy ration we could really have a ball in Berlin," he mused. "Those folks haven't had any of that good stuff for their kids in three years. They are just staying alive."

That night, after our second round trip to Berlin, we got the good news that we didn't need to do a third. A few more pilots were gradually building the pool. It was appreciated. The time was 23:30 hours and a real dark night out. "Let's get something to eat at the flight-line mess hall," Elkins suggested. "It's better than that Zeppelinheim morgue."

We were hungry and the food was better than usual. Still there was some left on the trays. "Looks like our eyes were a little bigger than our stomachs again," quipped Elkins, who was the thinnest of the three but sported a clean tray. John and I ignored the gentle reprimand and headed out into the night to scrape our trays into the garbage barrels.

The barrels were located right on the edge of where the darkness mixed with the light shining out of the mess hall windows.

It had happened before but I was never prepared for it. No sooner had we scraped the last of the scraps from our trays and dropped our silverware in a can of sudsy water, there was a flurry of movement out of the shadows.

Three full-grown men in tattered pieces of clothing that didn't match rushed to the barrels and contested for whatever edibles were there, whether they were mixed with paper napkins or not.

The graphic demonstration of a fellow human being stripped of his dignity, relegated to animal instincts to survive, and totally oblivious to whoever might see, almost left me sick.

We had just been joined by a sergeant from the mess hall who had come to pick up the silverware.

"You look a little surprised," he observed. "The scraps are not for them but for their wives or kids who can't come on the base. The workers get enough to eat for themselves. We save all edible leftovers for people like that. Sometimes they beat us to it."

The experience took away the good feeling we had after the meal and replaced it with some sobering thoughts. How terribly lucky we were. How much more the scene must be played out in Berlin than here; unfortunately with people who were not acting but living the part on the cruel stage of life, erected by war and directed to that scene by a madman. The missions to Berlin seemed doubly important after that midnight meal.

My mind was far away as we made our way into the club for a bull session before bed. We lucked out— a couple of easy chairs were just waiting.

This time the discussion was about the things that were so different in the environment in which we, crew members, found ourselves. Cultural shock seemed to be the topic of the evening.

One of those subjects was the scene at the mess hall. Another experience most often noticed by new pilots occurred when a cigarette butt was flicked away. The men at the garbage cans were reserved compared to the rush put on to retrieve the smallest tobacco remains.

Tobacco could be traded for anything. It was the gold standard in most war-torn countries whose national resources were all but destroyed. The fragrant-smelling material was craved more than food, yet in it's traitor role, like a Trojan horse, destroyed the tissue of the host who took it in. It was a small pleasure in a time when even small pleasures were scarce. Could an outsider judge it as of no worth when others saw it so differently? Because it wasn't for me didn't mean it might not have some special significance for someone in these circumstances.

My first experience with the importance of tobacco had been shortly after my arrival. Several of us were in a jeep stopped in front of a railway crossing bar which blocked the road while a train lumbered past.

A number of pedestrians and bicyclists were also congregated at the barrier. Our sergeant driver, knowing that we were new arrivals said, "Watch this."

He flipped his half-smoked cigarette out the window away from the line-up at the barrier. The small movement that it took to flick the butt and the resultant trajectory of that neat white package could have been a red distress flare and not received more attention and response.

Suddenly there were people flashing in front and in back of our vehicle to claim the prize. That butt was prime barter material. More than half the time the cigarette butt was not for personal consumption, but to be used to trade for something else. Others told of similar experiences.

The topic of conversation shifted when a tall, gangly lieutenant with a drawl as long as his frame said, "One of the most interesting things I've noticed around here is that everyone is a navigator."

"What do you mean, a navigator?" I asked.

"You know, a navigator always has his brief case or flight case with him," he replied.

"Oh yes" everyone chimed in. "We know what you mean. We have seen that too—everyone has a brief case."

Brief cases of all descriptions were used to carry barter materials or personal possessions that needed watching.

The conversation drifted to the perennial subject of many bull sessions: women. After all, what is more important to a man? Some new arrivals made the observation that there didn't seem to be any married German women in the area. "How's that?" asked an old timer.

"Well, I haven't seen a woman yet who had a ring on her left hand," quickly replied the newcomer.

"I'll be," joined in the tall Texan. "Someone give this junior birdman the word." Several volunteered and several others were listening for the answer.

The Texan took it upon himself, "Over here married women mostly wear their wedding ring on their right hand. We ought have a class on culture for you greenies. Better watch your step."

"Time to leave," John said, "let's go to bed." We boarded the weapons carrier and bounced off down the road to the barn in Zeppelinheim.

9

Anticipating the End

As those first days went by, I began to wonder how long Stalin could take the pounding in the world press that he was getting for his inhuman act against a vanquished foe. In Stalin's priority list, world opinion was secondary to the need to remove the challenge presented by West Berlin.

The hottest subject of conversation around the bases, after the lack of social life, was how much longer can this airlift last?

A shiny silver RAF Dakota parked on the operations apron added fuel to the rumors that some high-level negotiators may be returning from Berlin. The distinguished Sir Anthony Eden had been seen in Base Operation. These indicators made the rumors sound pretty good. I didn't think it would be too long until that new Chevrolet and I would be back together. Rumors seem to receive the most nourishment from among those who would be the beneficiaries if the rumors became reality. There was a lot of nourishment being provided by air and ground personnel at Rhein-Main.

Among our group in the barn we discussed what the procedures would be for deployment back to the States if word came tomorrow that the airlift was all over.

"I can tell you what is not going to happen," Lt. Peyton said hopefully. "There will not be time for anyone to go to Berlin on a sightseeing tour, that's for sure. They will send everybody home just as fast as they sent us over here."

For a farm kid, and one who was very much interested in seeing historical sites, the thought of missing out on a close up look at Hitler's bunker, the Rheischtag, and the Brandenburg Gate after so many trips to Berlin didn't sound so good. I already had these exciting places plotted on a map and had seen them at long distance from the air. I wanted to see them close up and said so.

Peyton went on, "They can't send me home fast enough, I've seen enough of Berlin." I understood his reasoning. He had left his wife just as fast as I had left my car. They had no children yet and from the last letter their expectations that things had got started before he left proved to be false hope. He needed to get back on the scene.

Alta's letters were of about the same frequency with a little extra warmth in her surprise about my new location in Germany. The rendezvous with my red Chevy had a greater meaning behind it, an immediate departure to Utah whenever we did get back. Still there would be time for one quick trip to Berlin if I had the chance. Although I didn't think Lt. Peyton had a corner on the crystal ball, many of the other pilots thought what he said would likely happen. More importantly, I thought that is what would happen.

The steady fly, fly, fly, interspersed with six or seven hours sleep left no time off to look around on the ground in Berlin. Even when an aircraft broke down in Templehof the crew would be sent out on the next plane to pick up a loaded one in Rhein-Main. No reservation was needed. There were a lot of empty seats going west.

With all these factors and the rumors in my mind, I immediately began to plan how I could get a picture of me standing in the Tiergarten rubble to show my kids sometime in the future. Another record for posterity must be movies of planes popping over that darn apartment house on the end of the runway. The location was about two miles across the field from the terminal. A shot from inside the barbed wire, at ground level, would be more expressive than a thousand words. I must get to Berlin with some free time. It would have to come at the expense of sleep.

The ruthless Stalin and his policies toward Berlin were taking a beating in the World Press and I thought the Soviets should capitulate any day. His policies didn't represent the Russian people. If the world had known of the murders that Stalin was heaping on his own people at the time, his starvation techniques would have appeared less severe. There was no sympathy in the world for the Soviets starving a city of women and children who were already down and out.

A little serious thought on the inadequate tonnage we were delivering to Berlin at that time and the short time the blockade had been in effect would have quieted my anxious and almost compulsive behavior regarding a sightseeing trip.

It was just after the middle of July, 1948, and I had a plan to visit Berlin on the ground and get those pictures. My movie camera was a 1947, Revere eight-millimeter single lens roll-fed spring-actuated devise that had seen many miles and better times, but it did a good job.

The opportunity presented itself one early afternoon when I returned to the 17th MATS hard stand area at Rhein-Main from my last scheduled flight. Lt. Bill Christian, my roommate, was headed for his planeload of dried potatoes. "Got room for a passenger?" I asked seriously.

The ever-present children cheering us on. I would soon meet them face-to-face.

"You bet! We could use some company," he shot back. I turned to John and said, "I'm going to take a busman's holiday to Berlin. Don't wait up for me. I'll be back for our next flight. Get some sleep for both of us." John was at loss for words but nodded his understanding.

In 45 minutes we were in the air headed back to Berlin, the first time in my experience as a passenger. Lt. Christian was still a little surprised about how fast I had taken him up on his offer. He had been in on the discussion in the barn and commented that he knew I was interested in this trip but didn't think I was that serious.

Capt. Larry Caskey was one of my best buddies, in the air and on the ground. He had given me a contact at Tempelhof who, he said, would arrange a jeep and a driver to run me around Berlin. All I would have to do is give the sergeant an hour's notice. A quick check in my wallet confirmed that the telephone number was right where I put it.

"You'll need a jeep to get where you want to go," Larry had warned. "The side streets are still half full of rubble."

The plan was falling into place. Soon as we would land I'd call the sergeant and then head for the apartment building, two miles around the perimeter fence, for the movies. By the time I would get back to the terminal he would have me a jeep.

The weather was great and so were my spirits. I'd show Stalin. Those pictures would be in hand before he could lift the blockade.

10

Little Things Mean a Lot

Lt. Christian nosed the Big Easy down the taxiway toward takeoff position. We were soon in the air. Being a passenger seemed very strange but fun. The weather was beautiful as we took our place in that long string of airborne grocery stores. All seemed well with the world. The Berliners were going to receive a record number of tons that day but it would still be well below the amount needed for survival. Could we provide an even greater amount when the weather got really bad? Looking up ahead in the corridor we could see some airspace where a few more planes could be squeezed in, but could the two airfields in Berlin handle the required increase? At this time the pilots were not aware that the planners were way ahead of us in considering an additional airfield. Stalin's bet that we couldn't do it looked good to the odds makers. Most thought the airlift would certainly fail with the onset of the normal Fall and Winter weather. There were a few pilots in that group who were also believers. Tunner's Chief of Staff, Col. Milton, now a retired General, has said that General Tunner was the only one who knew the job could be done by air.

We soon took our place in the line up in the sky for a landing at Tempelhof. The aircraft swept over the tall apartment buildings on the end of the runway and in the next ten minutes we welcomed aboard the eager, friendly Berliners to extract the plump sacks of dried potatoes. I never got tired of the warm, genuine greeting extended by those grateful souls who burst through the cargo door to relieve the big bird of its precious cargo.

I rushed into Base Operations and called the number for the sergeant with the jeep. In two minutes it was all arranged for a pick up on the flight line in one hour. Just enough time to get pictures of the airplanes popping over the apartment buildings across the field and to get back.

I hurried along inside the barbed wire fence and in about 20 minutes I had covered the two miles and was looking through the barbed wire fence at the apartments. The grassy open place across the fence, just before the apartments, was a little wider than it looked from the air. The terminal building and the runway were at my back. The end of the pierced steel plank runway was very near and the terminal building was all the way across the airfield.

The first thing that caught my eye was about thirty kids in the middle of that grassy strip watching the planes swoop over the roof tops to a landing just behind where I was standing. Now the children were watching me, an American pilot in uniform.

The airlift became a game for the kids to pass the long siege hours. Their bricks are in the shape of the Tempelhof hanger.

By the time my Revere movie camera had recorded a few feet of film with aircraft seemingly popping out of the chimneys, half of the kids were right up against the fence across from me.

It didn't take long to exhaust my German vocabulary with, "Guten Tag, we gehts?"

I was immediately greeted with a torrent of responses that were geared to someone with a greater command of the language. We were soon joined by the rest of the children.

It was a mixed group. Most of them were between the ages of 8 and 14 and evenly split between boys and girls. They were not especially well dressed but their clothes had been kept in good repair. Some were patched. All were clean.

After a few giggles and animated discussion between themselves, they appointed two or three as spokespersons for the group. Children were taught English in the schools and several of the kids spoke it quite well.

The group was there because they had a tremendous investment in the outcome. Besides, it was interesting to see such a concentration of aircraft dedicated to their survival. Some children were timing aircraft arrivals and could tell of the weekly increases in the number of landings.

One of the first questions was, "How many sacks of flour does each of the aircraft carry?" There had been some discussion about how many equivalent loaves of bread came across the fence with each aircraft. Were we really flying in fresh milk for the younger children? What about the other cargo? How many tons? One question came one right behind the other.

Then I received a lesson about priorities. They were interested in freedom more than flour. They fully recognized that between the two there was a real relationship but they had already decided which was preeminent. I was astonished with the maturity and clarity that they exhibited in advising me of what their values were and what was of greatest importance to them in these circumstances.

In the months between the time the aircraft over Berlin changed their cargo from bombs to flour the children had witnessed an accelerated change in international relations. These young kids began giving me the most meaningful lesson in freedom I ever had. Here

I was, an American, almost bald-headed at the age of 27, yet I was learning about something I obviously took too much for granted.

One of the principal spokespersons was a little girl of about 12 years with wistful blue eyes. She wore a pair of trousers that looked as though they belonged to an older brother and a pair of shoes that had seen better days on someone half again her size.

"Almost every one of us here experienced the final battle for Berlin. After your bombers had killed some of our parents, brothers and sisters, we thought nothing could be worse. But that was before the final battle. From that time until the Americans, British, and French came into the city we saw first hand the communist system. We've learned much more since that time. We don't need lectures on freedom. We can walk on both sides of the border. What you see speaks more strongly than words you hear or read." Her sentences came out with difficulty and not just as quoted but with the same points of emphasis.

A boy, not much older and standing near continued, "We have aunts, uncles, and cousins who live in East Berlin and in East Germany and they tell us how things are going for them. When they are here they use our library to read what is really going on in the world. They can say what they think when they are over here among family or with known friends."

It was soon obvious that these young people had been schooled and tested in a laboratory far more rigorous than any classroom situation. The lessons they had learned were deeply implanted over the scars left by the trauma of war.

None had asked if I had been in one of those bombers in former times. I certainly wore the uniform they had been taught to hate; a symbol of death from the skies. Yet in none of their conversation or in their tone of voice was there a sign of resentment or hostility. It was freedom, not flour, that they were concerned with that warm July afternoon in 1948.

Those who had parents, or a single parent, or only brothers or sisters, all believed that someday there would be enough to eat, but if they lost their freedom they feared they would never get it back.

What they referred to as freedom was the idea that they could be what they wanted to be, to choose their course in life without being told what they would be, that they could really have open access to a free press, and speak freely their thoughts on a subject without fear.

Very high on their priority was to be able to travel if and when they had the means.

The wistful blue-eyed girl made the point that they could get by with very little for quite awhile if they knew they could depend on us to stick by them and do the best we could.

The conversation, labored as it had to be given the language barrier, coupled with its interest, had consumed much more time than I had allowed. My thoughts returned to the jeep and the driver and my worry was that he would not wait. More than an hour had already passed.

My thoughts were interrupted again by the little girl, "You must not believe that Berlin weather is always like today because if the blockade is not lifted by late fall it may be impossible to bring us enough, even the littlest amount to save us. The weather is very bad in early winter."

She said more but her words were washed away by four Twin Wasp R-2000 engines directly over our heads, responding to a pilot's demand for a little cushion to break his decent before impact with the runway. The added power was enough, but even then you could see the main landing gear struts almost bottom out.

I scarcely heard her words before the airplane. My thoughts were on the jeep. In a moment I whirled to go, then paused long enough to thank them, to reassure them that more planes and crew members were coming every day, and to marvel to myself about what I had heard and learned from those so young.

How much their aspirations matched the advertised goals of our great land. These were the enemy? Or was it just their leaders or the system? Were any of these Hitler's youth? Somebody was. What did they really think of the situation now? Were they being honest with me or telling me what I wanted to hear? Too much to ponder, I had to run.

My preconceived prejudice was melting like the proverbial January thaw. The children got to me more than the flour "unloaders" had.

"Sorry kids, I must go," I waved over my shoulder. My overriding thoughts were to get that jeep and make up for precious lost time. It would be nice to get back to Rhein-Main in time to have one or two hours sleep before our flight shifts started again. In that frame of mind it was unlikely that a totally different outside thought could get inside my head and affect my course of action, but it did.

At first it was hard to identify the intruder. It was ever so soft, so small a probe as to be indistinguishable. But there it was. By now I was 50 yards away, headed for the jeep, but my mind was still back at the fence.

What really makes those kids so different? The query was soon turned away and my mind was fixed hard ahead on the jeep. Again the probe got in with a little more persistence. It was quickly answered. They are mature beyond their years. They have been through experiences and come to conclusions that are not representative of children at this point in their developmental cycle. That complicated answer, good as it seemed, didn't take care of it.

But why are they really different, in what other way? persisted. The question demanded closer scrutiny. I stopped in my tracks.

They had forgiven a previous enemy in uniform, but that wasn't it. Then the answer came with a rush.

Not one of almost 30 kids, most of whom hadn't had any gum or candy for two or three years, was willing to become a beggar and ask, verbally or by body language, if they could have some chocolate or gum. They must have wondered and believed that I had at least a taste.

I was sure that the image and memory of candy and gum, the special prize of any child, must have been held tightly in their minds. For years it hadn't been for real, tightly held in their fists or secured in their pockets.

They were so grateful for freedom and our desire to help them with these meager food supplies that they refused to tarnish their feelings of gratitude for something so nonessential and so extravagant.

For all to refuse the beggar's role without exception or pre-agreement made it the more remarkable. I do not believe grown-ups would have shown the same restraint. The gentle probe now concerned getting to the jeep, but it didn't have the same quality as its predecessor.

The contrast that gave the moment meaning was my experience during the war and afterward. In South America, Africa, and other countries, an American in uniform was fair game on the street for kids with a sweet tooth. Thousands of American G.I.s filled the special craving of countless little ones and did so willingly, even by design. It became a conditioned response: a group of kids, their immediate, strong request, hand in the pocket for pre-placed goodies for such an encounter, and the pleasure of dispensing same. Here there had been no request.

Against the Berlin backdrop the difference was staggering. I had been there for over an hour. They had ample opportunity to ask. Not one had given the slightest indication of his or her thoughts.

Instinctively I reached in my pocket. There had been no preparation for such a moment. All there were was two sticks of Wrigley's Doublemint gum.

Thirty kids and two sticks, there will be a fight, I rationalized, making a last ditch attempt to resume my course to the jeep.

That was not a satisfactory answer. Such a little thing, two sticks of gum. Will you share it with the kids is the question? Scrooge could not answer that question in the negative, but that was not the issue. The issue was time.

I glanced over my shoulder. The children were there, even pressed against the barbed wire fence, still waving as is the European custom, until the departed guest disappears down the road.

Now was the moment of truth. To the jeep or back to the fence? I didn't know it but if I chose the fence my life would never be the same again. My father had taught me that good things would happen if you did something for someone without expecting anything in return.

I turned abruptly and headed for the fence.

11

The Commitment

Within the first three return steps the children stopped waving. They expectantly awaited my arrival at the fence. Then they saw my hand come out of my pocket and something, unmistakably, was in it!

Their interest and intensity of expression changed in a flash. There were some who jockeyed for a better position to discover what I had. My fears began to rise that the pushing would take an ugly turn but it was too late to turn back. I was commited.

In the last few steps to the fence I broke the two sticks of gum in half and headed for the children who had been the translators.

Their hands were now through the barbed wire. There was no need to await my verbal offer. My actions had already telegraphed my intent and they had accepted.

The four pieces were quickly placed. There was a short gasp as one boy engaged a fence barb in his forearm because of the excitement. In all my experience, including Christmases past, I had never witnessed such an expression of surprise, joy, and shear pleasure that I beheld in the eyes and faces of those four young people. Nor do I remember seeing such disappointment as was evident in the eyes of those who came so close. The disappointed looks were transitory and tempered by their much more difficult trials and disappointments over the past months. The pleased looks of the four were frozen in time.

There was no fighting or attempts to grab away the prize given to the four who were busy carefully removing the wrapper. No chance could be risked that the smallest piece might fall to the ground.

The quiet was broken with a rising babble from the rest. They were requesting a share in the tin foil or the outer wrapper. Strips were torn off and passed around. The recipients' eyes grew large as they smelled the bits of wrapper and recalled better times.

After a brief moment they placed the tiny wrapper in their shirt or trouser pocket as though it were a $50.00 bill. There was someone special in their lives who would believe their story if there were some evidence.

My eyes were sending me a message that my brain couldn't understand. What an impact from just a tiny piece of wrapper, let alone the expression of the four who had received the contents.

I must have been a sight, standing there in wide mouthed amazement. What I could do with 30 full sticks of gum! They could have the wrapper and all, quickly went through my mind.

Immediate thoughts of when I could come back to the fence were answered by: It will be a long time. You'll be flying without any sleep for twenty-four hours and that can't be repeated soon.

Just then another C-54 swooped over our heads, across the fence and landed. Two little plumes of white smoke came off the main tires as they touched down on the pierced steel planked runway and squealed up to speed. That plane gave me a sudden flash of inspiration.

Why not drop some gum and even chocolate to these kids out of our airplane the next daylight trip to Berlin? We will have such a flight the next day, this suggestion came to mind so fast it caught me unawares.

You will get in a heap of trouble if you are caught, came a quick and rational response.

This whole blockade is a violation of human rights. Compared to mass starvation this shouldn't get me any more than a minor court martial, I answered myself.

Why not get permission? You know how long that will take? The airlift will be over by then and it is just a one-time thing, besides, we'll only be about 90 feet in the air, answered my desire.

To my own astonishment and dismay I found myself in the next moment announcing the plan for all to hear.

At first their response was cautiously reserved for fear they had misunderstood. I took the opportunity to add, "I will do this thing only if the persons who catch the packets will share equally with everyone in the group."

By now, those most proficient in the language had confirmed this crazy, unbelievable proposition to the others and the noisy celebration had already begun. Added to the celebration were shouts of "Jawohl! Jawohl! Jawohl!" from everyone in answer to the requirement to share. Then it became very quiet.

The little girl with the wistful blue eyes was prodded to be the spokesperson. "They want to know which aircraft you will be flying. Such a small package would be too easily lost, especially if you come late and we have tired by watching all day in vain," she excitedly stammered out while gazing intently into my face.

My face had a frown. There was no way to know what specific plane I would be assigned on any flight, let alone that special one. It would be a four engine C-54 for sure. If I did know which airplane, there would be no way to identify it from all the rest of them coming over the apartment building. Then another flash of inspiration from my days flying over the farm in Garland, Utah.

Why not wiggle the wings? The thought passed through my mind like a lightning bolt. That was the answer!

"You kids watch the aircraft approaching Tempelhof, especially when they pass over the field. When I get overhead I will wiggle the wings of that big airplane back and forth several times. That is the signal," I said with noticeable enthusiasm.

Now the frown was on blue eye's face and several others standing nearby. Now what is wrong, I wondered. It seemed so good and so clear.

"Vhat is viggle?" she asked with a wrinkle on her nose. With both arms extended I gave a demonstration that could have won an Oscar. It did bring some laughs. The enthusiasm continued to build.

There just didn't seem to be anything more to discuss. Action was clearly the next step. A few suggested that I leave and get the project started. My thoughts quickly returned to the jeep.

Luckily, the driver was still waiting. I was very late.

The young driver was from Boulder, Colorado, smartly dressed in his well-tailored uniform and spit-and-polish boots. "Did you get your pictures, lieutenant?" he asked. "You bet! Sorry it took so long." I replied with no hint that something else more important had occurred and was about to burst my calm exterior.

The jeep motor caught immediately and we exited Tempelhof gate at a brisk pace into a scene of man's inhumanity to man. England, Japan, Russia, and countless other countries could give like evidence.

We wove our way in and out of the rubble-strewn streets. In between the streets, gutted buildings without roofs or windows stared up at the open sky in an unchanging trance, a web of twisted girders fell crazily across bomb craters that dotted the city's face like small pox scars. Down the Unter den Linden we arrived at the Brandenburg Gate.

Even in it's tattered war-torn cloak, the majesty of the 1791, eight-story edifice, mounted on it's twelve enormous Doric columns was splendid to behold. Gotthard Langhaus designed it after the Propylaea in Athens.[36] The chariot, quadriga, astride the top of the gate, proceeding toward the East, listed to one side with pieces of the chariot, wheels, charioteer, and four horses lost amid rubble, remaining and removed. It would be ten years later until the structure was fully restored, and 13 years before it would be blocked from the West with an ugly grey wall.

Our jeep was parked in front of the Brandenburg Gate in the middle of the Unter den Linden, the once-bustling great highway, the East-West Axis. It was the site of the last active airstrip that was to serve Hitler directly. Light planes had come and gone bringing special documents, passengers, or material, using the highway from there to the Victory Column as their runway.

In early April, 1945, the removal of Reichsminister Albert Speer's ornamental bronze lamp posts and the trees from beside the great highway had been the subject of furious debate between the Reichsminister and the Commandant of Berlin, General Reymann. The removal of these obstructions, both so symbolic of the sophisticated heart of Berlin, was necessary to make room for the wing span of larger aircraft to assuage the death throws of Berlin. By then it was far too late. The argument was academic.[37]

From there we drove the short distance to the Reichstag, the center of the City and prime target for the competing Soviet Generals Zhukov and Koniev. It was a stupendous ruin, originally dedicated to the German people, set fire first by Hitler's Nazi henchmen in 1933, a

Top photo is the Brandenburg Gate and the bottom photo is the Reichstag, through the gardens planted to aid the Berliners' survival. Pictures were taken on my visit with the jeep, just after speaking with the children at the fence. (July, 1948) Moments later we were pursued by the Russians.

flaming foot stool on his ascendancy to power. It was to become a more raging funeral pyre to the Third Reich, not far from Hitler's final resting place, the Bunker.

In a few minutes we were driving past the Brandenburg Gate again and were soon at Hitler's Bunker. There was not much to see.

We wouldn't be there long. The driver suddenly exclaimed, "Jump in the jeep quick, let's get going."

I didn't need a repeat of the message because of the urgency with which it was delivered. By the time I had thrown my leg over the seat on the passenger side he had the engine started and the wheels churning dirt and gravel. My curiosity was running a close second to my pulse rate. A look over my shoulder revealed a pursuing jeep with Soviet markings, driven by an apparent madman in a Russian uniform. He was being encouraged by a comrade of like demeanor and dress in the passenger seat.

"Why are they chasing us?" I demanded.

"It happens that the Bunker is on their side of the border and lately they don't take very kindly to Americans and airlift pilots in particular," he replied somewhat apologetically. "I was watching for them at the Brandenburg Gate. Didn't think they were out today."

The driver continued, "They have a couple of Americans in jail over there now. They had a British Officer, John Sims, in a stinking cell for three nights at the Russian Kommandatura. He just got out a few days ago."[38]

Although we were quickly back on our side of the border, we maintained our speed until the pursuers abruptly broke off the chase.

"It's getting late. Let's head back to Tempelhof," I suggested. I was relieved but still a little peeved that I hadn't been made aware of the sensitivity of the situation. There would have been some disappointed kids and a real angry Lt. Colonel Haun if my afternoon in Berlin had turned into an overnight.

Back on the ground at Rhein-Main I found that our crew was on the schedule for a 02:00 hours departure the next morning, back to Berlin. A little quick arithmetic indicated that we should have one trip at a reasonable hour in the daylight.

As I crawled into the loft John was sound asleep. How we could sleep up there, so near the Rhein-Main final approach, with an aircraft whizzing by every few minutes, was not really a mystery if one considered our flight schedule. If I hurried there might be two hours sleep available for me.

Tired as I was, sleep wouldn't come. It seemed like a whole week of unreal events had been crowded into the last 12 hours. How to keep the commitment I had made to the kids was the current prime stimulant. We could buy a very limited amount of gum and candy. The amount was strictly controlled by a ration card. There wasn't enough available on my card to do justice to the kids. I needed Pickering's and Elkin's rations as well. How would they react to my request, and more particularly to the reason for it? At least the Base Exchange was open for such purchases 24 hours a day.

If we put three rations in one package and they lost it, they would loose all. The one package wouldn't be very big, but going 115 miles an hour it could make a big impact if it hit one of the targets too directly. At that altitude they wouldn't have time to duck.

It made some sense to split the drop into three packages. It made even more sense to put a handkerchief parachute on each package to slow the fall and mark the treasure. There was an emergency flare chute right behind the pilot's seat that was within Elkin's reach. He could push it out just as we passed over the roof of the apartment house on the final approach.

That decided, I dozed off just in time to be awakened. "Glad you made it back, Hal," yawned John matter-of-factly. "Have a good trip?"

The sales job on my two buddies was effective because their hearts were as big as usual, but the goods weren't obtained without some words of prophecy.

"You are going to get us in one big mess of trouble," said John. Elkins cast a similar vote as they somewhat reluctantly forked over their neatly packaged and fragrant rations of chocolate bars and packages of gum. The sight and smell of it, and the thought of the kids, sent a thrill all through me. If they thought half a stick of gum was great wait until they got some chocolate and gum with wrapper!

A firm pact of utmost secrecy was mutually taken and we were on our way to Berlin. The first flight was in the dark, and being pre-Tunner days, we had some unusual traffic delays.

The second flight was just right. We were going to arrive over Tempelhof on prime time, just before noon.

We strained our eyes to catch sight of the kids as we approached Tempelhof at 1500 feet. Sure enough, there they were, all together in a little knot in the middle of the grassy strip in front of the apartment building. They appeared to be scanning the heavens.

"Looks like they haven't told another soul," I said with a grin. "Reckon there is about the same number as yesterday."

With that I rolled in left aileron and fed in a little left rudder. The wing went down and just as the nose started to turn I fed in right rudder and right aileron, almost crossing controls to keep the wings wiggling and the nose straight ahead.

The recognition was instant. That little band literally blew up, waving, jumping, circling, and sending, we were sure, a few silent prayers. In my minds eye I could see the little blue-eyed girl in those oversize shoes and trousers. My bone-tired weariness was completely gone.

Rhein-Main, preparing for the first drop to the Berlin children at the fence. The other two parachutes were already aboard. (July, 1948)

We swung around the pattern, briefed Elkins again on how he would do it on my signal, and quickly we were on the final approach. The three loaded handkerchiefs were attached to the goodies by strings about 14 inches long. The handkerchiefs were folded in a special way ready to drop. By now the kids were out of sight behind the apartment building.

Excitement and concern for what we were about to do was growing in the cockpit. What if we dropped the packages on top of the

An artist's conception of a recipient.

Some of the waiting children

apartment or beyond the barbed-wire fence, onto the runway?

"What if an aircraft waiting for takeoff would happen to see the parachutes and get our tail number?" asked John with a frown. "Give me full flaps and 2400 RPM," I replied. No time to change our minds. We were commited.

The apartment house came under the nose of the airplane in a blur. For an instant the group of kids were visible, still waving, all turned toward the building, faces skyward.

"Now, Elkins," I shouted. With a quick thrust he had the little packages out of the flare chute and almost as quickly we were on the runway.

The question on all of our minds was where did the parachutes land? We would have to wait for the answer.

Unloading seemed to go slower than usual. Little was being said. Everyone was deep in their own thoughts and concern for what the results of this impulsive act would bring.

12

Operation Little Vittles

The engines coughed to life and Tempelhof tower came through crystal clear, "Big Willy 495, you are cleared to taxi to takeoff position. Call when number one."

In moments we were proceeding down the taxi strip inside the barbed-wire fence, headed for the takeoff position opposite the apartment buildings. As we made the last right turn we could see down the barbed wire all the way to the buildings. There was the answer!

Protruding through the fence were three little parachutes extended by several animated arms attached to three vibrant bodies. The little parachutes were being waved without discrimination at every crew as each aircraft taxied by. Behind the three with the parachutes were the rest of the cheering section with both arms waving above their heads and every jaw working on a prize. The long trousers quickly identified blue eyes. She was radiant!

"Guess they got it O.K. and it looks shared," beamed John's deep voice. "Sure does, I must have hit them right on the head," said Elkins proudly.

"Wish they wouldn't wave like that," I added somewhat seriously as I slid back my side cockpit window to give the children a return wave.

Pickering, noticing my reserve added, "Don't worry, you didn't have a name tag on when you talked to them. You didn't give them your name, did you?"

"No I didn't, and I didn't take my hat off, so they don't know I'm almost bald-headed," I answered with a little more hope. "They don't know who we are."

The next daylight trip we noticed a few more in the group on the end of the runway, all waving at each aircraft, landing, taxiing, and about to take off. We figuratively held our breath each day, waiting for a summons that didn't come. We were grateful for that.

Several conversations were overheard in the mess hall and base operations between pilots wondering why the kids were making such a fuss on the end of the runway. We renewed our pledge of secrecy.

A few days later, after we had finished unloading our cargo of coal, we couldn't get number 2 engine to turn over. The starter motor was out. Very little maintenance was done in Berlin. If we weren't able to start the engine we could feather the prop and take off on three engines then start it in the air. That was strictly an emergency procedure to be used as a last resort.

We were about to ask for Operations approval when up drove a maintenance jeep. "Those engines take a Jack and Heintz 1015 starter motor and we sure don't have any. There isn't enough wind out there for Operations to give you a three-engine try. We've got something better in the person of Ebert Herman," said a grizzled, old master sergeant.

"What can he do?" I quizzed.

"He and a couple of sharp mechanics can start you with a bungee cord," he said matter-of-factly.

It turned out that Ebert had developed a way to attach a bungee, a heavy elastic cord, to the tip of a prop, stretch it to a given limit, and quickly release the prop. Warm as the day and the engine were, it should work.

I watched with great interest as Ebert and crew went about their job. With all switches ready in the cockpit they released the prop with a twang. The engine coughed twice and was soon running smoothly.

"I'll be darned," muttered Elkins, "I've seen everything now."

A week quickly went by. The crowd of kids was noticeably larger and still enthusiastic. When we were able to buy a new week's ration we knowingly looked at each other. On the spot we again pooled our resources, came over Tempelhof, wiggled our wings, caused a celebration, and delivered the goods on target.

Another week went by and the group on the end of the runway was now a good-sized crowd. We knew that a lot of kids in the group hadn't received any goodies and we set about to correct the inequity.

Every time we wiggled the wings of that airplane we were treated to a remarkable spontaneous demonstration of sheer joy. This third group, swelled by newcomers, gave us the biggest demonstration yet.

A few more days went by and the forerunner of things to come, a dense fog bank, swept up from the south and fell over our West German bases at Rhein-Main and Wiesbaden like a down comforter. We literally took off on the gauges from Rhein-Main to Berlin. By the time we got over Fulda, the weather broadcast said the stuff had blanketed most all of Western Europe.

"Wonder what will be open on our return flight?" asked John. "This stuff is practically zero zero."

The mobile snack bar established by General Tunner and the personal service of the weatherman, who provided plane-side briefings, were welcome additions to operating procedures. In turn, we were to stand right by the aircraft and depart the second the big semi-trucks cleared our tail.

The traveling snack bar and the weatherman's jeep at Tempelhof.

That flight the weatherman wasn't there. With limited fuel it was essential to know where we had the best chance of getting in upon returning to West Germany. After waiting a few more minutes, I told Pickering I was going to run into Base Operations and see if I could get a quick look at the weather map.

As I came into Base Operations there was a large planning table just inside that would accommodate extended maps, charts, and flight-planning materials. At the moment it was stacked high with what appeared to be mail. Strange use for the table, and a stranger way to treat mail, I thought as I sidled up for a better look at this unorthodox display.

It only took a glance to freeze me in my tracks. The letters were addressed to "Uncle Wackelflugel [Wiggly Wings]" and "The Schokoladen Flieger," Tempelhof Central Airport, Berlin.

I flew back out the door without the weather but with an even larger burden.

"Holy cow, guys," I blurted out. "There is a whole post office full of mail in there for us!" The three of us decided not only to lay low for a while but to quit. We had done more than was expected and this was the point to stop.

It was a few days later that our flight over Berlin on 12 August 1948 took place, the near mid-air collision in the cloud, holding over Wedding beacon at 10,000 feet.

Our resolve to not make any more drops held firm through two ration periods. The crowd was bigger than ever. That meant there were quite a number who hadn't received a sweet surprise.

Again we looked at each other knowingly and Elkins said, "What are you guys doing with your rations these days?" In a moment it was determined that we had all saved our rations for both periods. A short conversation resulted in, "Just one more drop and that is absolutely all."

It took about six overloaded handkerchiefs to handle all the goodies our pooled rations required. We had them on the flight deck ready to drop on the next day trip. The weather was good as we approached Tempelhof. The crowd was easily picked up at a pretty good distance. The reaction to the wiggling of the wings was reward enough for the last drop. Elkins, now an expert, called, "Bombs away!" We were soon on the ground and in the unloading process.

Taxiing out for takeoff, the testimony to our proficiency was displayed all along the barbed wire fence. As we nosed the aircraft down the runway and smoothly shoved the throttles to the wall we made a solemn pact that this really was the last of the drops.

The next day on arrival back at Rhein-Main from Berlin, an officer met our airplane. That was not a normal procedure.

Without much of an introduction the officer led off with, "Col. James R. Haun would like to speak with the pilot." If there had been any doubt in my mind whether I was the pilot, my crew buddies put that question to rest.

The military secretary announced my arrival to the Colonel. I felt my marginal blood pressure cross the border. I wasn't kept waiting.

"Halvorsen, what in the world have you been doing?" came what seemed to me a very stiff query from the good Colonel Haun.

"Flying like mad, Sir," came my best reply.

"I'm not stupid. What else have you been doing?" came a better question.

Then it was that I knew that he knew. For a moment it seemed like that long thin thread leading from the sugar beet field in Garland, Utah to Berlin was about to break. "Oh well," I thought, "there must be something in the world besides flying."

This fine commander who had accepted my transfer from the C-74 squadron in Mobile in order that I could join the airlift was now in a position to correct the error. He was much firmer than I had ever seen him before.

"Didn't they teach you in ROTC at Utah State to keep your boss informed?" came a burst that cast questions even on my earliest military training, let alone a great University. More seriously, it also indicated that he had been going over my file. How else would he know where I had those two quarters of college work? Things looked grim.

Then in one motion he reached under the desk, as though he was reaching for a whip, but came up with the *Frankfurter Zeitung*, a newspaper, and put it where I couldn't miss it.

"Look at this," he invited. "You almost hit a reporter in the head with a candy bar in Berlin yesterday. He's spread the story all over Europe. The General called me with congratulations and I didn't know anything about it. Why didn't you tell me?"

My reply was rather weak, "I didn't think you would approve it before the airlift was over, Sir."

"You mean to tell me that after we had dropped thousands of sticks of bombs on that city and the Russians are now trying to starve the rest of them to death, that you didn't think that I would approve dropping a few sticks of gum?" he ended incredulously with volume to spare.

"Guess I wasn't too smart, Sir," I admitted.

"General Tunner wants to see you and there is an International Press conference set up for you in Frankfurt. Fit them into your schedule. And Lieutenant, keep flying, keep dropping, and keep me informed." he smiled for the first time as he finished and shook my hand.

I left the office in much better condition than I had entered. "Wished I had the nerve to ask him exactly how he really knew it was me," I wondered. "The newspaper man must have got my tail number yesterday and thought he was doing me a favor."

The newspaper article had probably saved us and the operation. The press dubbed the project, "Operation Little Vittles" taken from the big operation, Vittles, and so it remained.

Pickering and Elkins were waiting for me. "Are we going to have a new pilot?" Elkins asked. It was a rhetorical question. They already guessed all was well from the look on my face.

The next trip to Berlin the three of us went into Tempelhof Base Operations with our arms full of bags to pick up the mail from the Berlin kids. We didn't have time to read it and even if we had we couldn't. Some letters were written in English but most were in the native tongue.

Colonel Walter S. Lee, the Base Commander at Rhein-Main, provided two German secretaries and a place to call home for the operation. There would be no change in our flight responsibilities so the extra help, plus many other volunteers, were essential and appreciated.

The secretaries began the work of sending out replies to the letters. There were about four form letters that took care of most. The rest were given special treatment. With the help of the secretaries those letters that needed special care were translated and given to me for action or reply. Gisela Hering, a native German secretary, was the main helper that kept things moving.

With the secret out, I would come back to the old barn and find my cot covered with cases of candy bars and chewing gum. They could have brought their owners several German cameras on the black market. Handkerchiefs for parachutes would often be stacked along side the goodies. Because of the great value of these materials on the black market I was especially concerned that these and other donations were put to their intended use. I stopped paying the ladies at the Zeppelinheim fence with candy and gum for laundry.

We soon ran out of handkerchiefs and used old shirt sleeves for candy bags and shirt tails for parachutes. That phase was short lived. Our supply officer, Capt. Donald H. Kline, was able to obtain twelve beautiful silk chutes about three feet in diameter. They would handle a very healthy load.

Looking them over and being short on parachutes, I naturally wanted them back to use again. Most everyone laughed at my idea. "Boys and girls will have those things made into shirts and unmentionables before you get out of town," several said almost in unison.

Displaying one of the larger silk chutes used.
May 1963.

I had Gisela write twelve notes in German that said, "Please return this parachute to any American Military Policeman that you see so it may be used again." Next to it I wrote in English, "Please return this parachute to Tempelhof Base Operations for Operation Little Vittles."

We had enough rations to make the most of these beautiful pieces of cloth. "You'll never see them again," said Lt. Bill Christian, a usually upbeat and optimistic friend. But that afternoon, we watched the crowd celebrating as the larger chutes billowed and serenely sailed on a gentle breeze to different parts of the group. I could even almost hear an "AH!" from below at such a sight.

That afternoon, on a subsequent flight, I ran into Operations to see if some might have been returned. My expectations were not very high so it was a double pleasure to find six of the twelve waiting for me. Eventually that group was reduced to one. It is in the Air Force museum at Wright-Patterson Air Force Base, Dayton, Ohio.

It didn't take the children in Berlin long to hear about our parachute shortage. The letters we received began to include parachutes the kids had caught that were returned for refills. Those who hadn't caught any made parachutes of their own. The parachute usually had a companion piece, most often a map.

The secretaries gave me a letter from Peter Zimmerman who was about nine years old. His letter included a crude piece of cloth of about the right size, with four stout strings attached to the four corners. He had seen a real one first hand, moments too late to claim it.

His map was a classic. The letter went on to say that he couldn't run very fast and wasn't doing too well. "Please note the map," he had written. "As you see, after takeoff fly along the big canal to the second highway bridge, turn right one block. I live in the bombed-out house on the corner. I'll be in the back yard every day at 2 PM, drop it there."

In good weather conditions the tower would allow me to fly special deliveries after departing Tempelhof and to join outbound traffic when they could fit me in. Most pilots like to fly low sometimes and I was no exception.

There was a polio hospital in West Berlin that was full of kids with severely limited mobility. It was visited on a regular basis by an American health officer, James J. Gibson, to make sure the children received what they needed from the airlift. On one of his rounds the Doctors handed him a packet of letters from the kids for delivery to me.

The letters were pretty much the same, not an expression of self-pity but an expression of thanks for the daily flights in good and bad weather to support the needs of their beloved city. They went on to mention, almost apologetically, that they were unable to run or walk in an attempt to catch a little parachute.

The main point they all wanted to make was for me to disregard the quiet sign on the streets outside the hospital. The doctors had promised it would O.K. to fly low over the hospital and drop the goodies in the yard. The doctors would bring the parachutes, with the attachments, to the children's beds.

"We have read about your drops and heard of it on the radio. Every time we hear an airplane close, we hope it could be Uncle Wiggly Wings. Could you try especially for us?" they pleaded.

Something would have to be done. The hospital was located in an awkward place for airlift traffic and an excursion in that location probably wouldn't be approved.

A little girl seven years old wrote to me. Her name was Mercedes Simon and she had a problem.

"We live near the airfield at Tempelhof and our chickens think your airplanes are chicken hawks and they become frightened when you fly over to land. They run in the shelter and some moult with no more eggs from them."

The final paragraph was the pay off.

"When you see the white chickens please drop it there, all will be O.K."

Your little friend,
Mercedes

A load of coal and a load of "Little Vittles" for Peter Zimmerman.

I couldn't find the white chickens and enlisted the help of squadron buddies. They couldn't find the white chickens. We made some extra drops around the Tempelhof approaches but didn't hit the chicken yard.

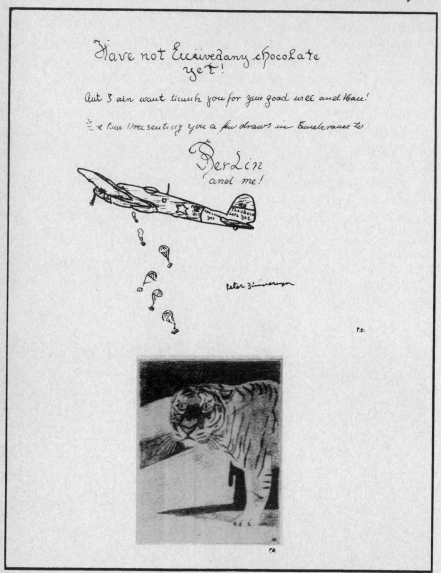

Peter Zimmerman's complaint, "No chocolate yet."

We carefully followed the map to Peter Zimmerman's house. Kids in the back yard. Bon Bons away! Next week a letter from Peter, "Didn't get any gum or candy, a bigger kid beat me to it." The next try was futile. His letters had always contained pencil sketches of animals or landscape scenes. One picture depicted an aircraft with little parachutes coming out of it. The words, "No chocolate yet," were written on the tail section and suggested his continuing plight. The last letter didn't have any of these works of art, only:

"You are a Pilot? I gave you a map. How did you guys win the war anyway?"

We gave up on dropping candy to Peter. I packaged a good assortment of candy and gum, took it with me to Tempelhof and mailed it to him through the West Berlin Post.

The thoughts of the 300 kids in the polio hospital were back on my mind. Supplies were coming in fast and furious. The newest contribution was a case of Paris brand bubble gum.

The first big carton of bubble gum. The hospital kids were supplied from this box.

I gathered up a good supply of Clark and Hershey bars, plenty of bubble gum, and hitchhiked back to Berlin for the second time.

James J. Gibson, Jr. met me at the aircraft and in 30 minutes we were at the hospital.

Thinning sugar beets in the dust with a twelve-inch hoe was not conducive to blowing bubble gum bubbles, and I never was a baseball pitcher. At least I could blame my ineptitude on those excuses. How was I going to show these kids that the gum had this special quality? Bubble gum was unknown to them.

Reluctantly Mr. Gibson disclosed that he had practically been a bubble-blowing champion. All he needed was a few minutes practice in the back room. His only handicap was a small wiry moustache!

The chocolate was really appreciated but the bubble gum was the hit of the day. It wasn't long until we could hear bubbles popping up and down the wards. The bright, excited chatter of the children was enough to diffuse some of the concern the nurses had for sticky pillowcases and sheets.

The TB and Polio hospital and Mr. Gibson doing his duty.

If my heart had been full before it was now overflowing with the reaction and spirit of these marvelous young people who couldn't chase a parachute.

One day I stopped at the mail room at Rhein-Main, hoping for a letter from Alta or the folks. It had been over two weeks without any mail from them. I was taken aback when the mail room clerk asked me a second time for my name and then my I.D. card. The reason was soon apparent.

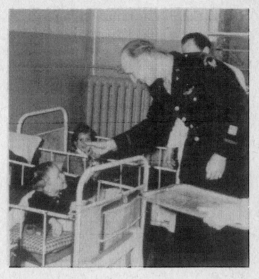

Visiting children at TB and Polio hospital.

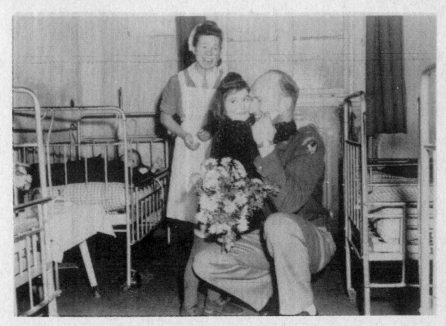

A little girl recovering at the TB and Polio hospital.

The clerk went to the back room and returned with a half bag of State side mail. "Bring the bag back when you get through, Lieutenant," he said with some wonderment. Others who hadn't received a letter that day gave me some hard stares. I didn't know any more about it than they did although it was likely related to Operation Little Vittles.

One of the many mailbags full of envelopes with handkerchiefs for parachutes.

We were on the way back to the barn and in a few minutes the mystery was solved. Most of the letters were from the East Coast. All of the envelopes were stuffed with handkerchiefs for parachutes. The wire services had carried my report of shortages and the radio stations up and down the East Coast and from out West were playing tunes if the requester would send handkerchiefs to Operation Little Vittles. *The Weekly Reader* fans responded most generously from across the Nation.

Many handkerchiefs had the donor's name and address written on them. The wire services also made mention that I was a bachelor, which explained the black-laced and perfumed contributions. We dropped them all.

Since receiving Mercede's letter we had not been able to find the white chickens. Remembering Peter's solution, I packaged a goodly supply of gum and candy, took it to Berlin and posted it to Mercedes at her home, 15 Hahnelstrasse.

By this time the crowds were so large on the end of the runway we feared someone may be injured in the mad dash to retrieve the packages. The method of operation was changed to eliminate drops next to the airfield and the focus was shifted to playgrounds, parks, school areas, and church yards all over free Berlin. The drops were made with no advance announcement.

Supplies were coming in from Armed Forces people in West Germany. Readers of *The Weekly Reader*, the elementary school publication, were sending more letters and increasing their contributions and requests for pen pal names and addresses.

Chicopee, Massachusetts had built a new fire station and converted the old one at Grape Street into a 24-hour assembly station for Operation Little Vittles. Miss Mary Connors, from Skeel St. Willimansett, an Elms college student and a chairwoman of the group, did a magnificent job. The leaders for the city were Mayor Edward O. Bourbeau, Will Thivierge, Claire Panzer, Delores Belcher, and Joanne Young. Some other officials of the ground force of Operation Little Vittles, Chicopee Chapter, were Mary Reardon, Laura Chapla, and Dorothy Lane. There were countless others.

The Chicopee operation was the Center for Little Vittles in the United States. There were 22 schools organized in full support of parachutes, candy, and packaging. Businesses furnished 2,000 custom-made shipping cartons, 11,000 yards of ribbon material, 2,000 sheets for parachutes, 3,000 individual handkerchiefs, and 18 tons of candy and chewing gum for this center alone. By January 21st, 1949, the committee's production was peaked at 800 pounds shipped every other day.[39]

Contributions arrived from Great Britain and as far away as Australia.

The Non-Commissioned Officers' wives club, the Officers' wives club, and the Service clubs at Rhein-Main set up assembly lines and handled much of my logistic problems.

The Rhein-Main Community Center and some of the first volunteers.

To accommodate the increased benevolence I posted a large map of Berlin in Operations under which was placed cardboard boxes filled and ready to go. Numbers on the map indicated the new drop areas that could be covered from our flight path into and out of the city. Departing crews from Wiesbaden and Rhein-Main could pick up a box and deploy the contents from altitude over the city. A crew member would go back and hold the cardboard box next to an open escape hatch window. The suction would take the little parachutes out into the slipstream like popcorn coming out of an air blown popcorn popper. It was quite a sight from the air, but even more impressive from a child's point of view on the ground.

We flew with our escape hatch doors removed to assist in the evacuation of coal and flour dust from the fuselage. The flight deck was protected from the draft by a bulkhead and crew door. Accumulation of coal and flour dust built up in the control cables and pulleys. Sluggish response to the aircraft flight controls was the undesirable result. In an extreme case coupled with other problems, the condition could be dangerous.

One clear day I spied a rugby match underway on a field not far from Tempelhof. Young people were playing with others watching.

A small load ready for delivery.

It took but a minor adjustment for my flight path to line up with the playing field. Elkins deployed a good load right over their heads. The ball was quickly abandoned and the spectators immediately joined

the contestants. A reporter from the publication "der Insulaner" may
have been in the crowd because their issue of 26 November 1948 carried
an artist's conception of what happened on the front cover.

Dropping from higher altitudes increased the surprise on behalf of
the recipients. One letter from Klaus Rickowski recorded such surprise:

> It was a perfectly normal school day in the blockade in the
> morning about 07:30. I was on my way to school with a few
> children from Pashener Alley, in Britz. We heard above us the
> humming of a Rosinen bomber and continued talking. We all
> recognized them, the big silver birds which found their way above
> us day and night. We collected pictures of the Dakotas and the
> Skymasters and built models of them. We were all technicians
> and we knew all about the airplanes.
>
> Suddenly there was great excitement on our street. Shouting,
> running and pointing up to the sky. A few little white specks were
> hovering there. That was something new. I had heard them
> talking a little bit about the parachutes with the candy and I
> wondered if that was something like this. I would certainly like
> to have one of those little things and the wild hunt began.
>
> The parachutes became larger and were coming down over
> the park in Britz driven by the wind over the area of the Fritz
> Carson school. The kids were already tearing around through
> the bushes looking for a parachute. I had two of them in sight
> and ran in the direction of a park where there was a little pond
> in the area.
>
> One parachute landed just in front of the pond and was
> immediately gobbled up by a whole bunch of kids. The other
> fell right in the middle of the water. My fear was very short.
> Throwing off my knapsack and my shoes, in I went. The fact
> that the water was very cold and dirty and that I was covered
> up to my armpits with algae and duck manure and mud was
> not noticed until much later. More important I had one of the
> parachutes.
>
> Then came some embarrassed faces. School had long since
> begun and we were coming late. In my class there were three
> crumpled up figures who asked the teacher for his pardon. When
> we had told our story the teacher, who usually was quite strict,
> was very understanding.

Because I was soaking wet I was permitted to go straight home. Even my mother who was very careful about clothes, that were so hard to get at this time, overlooked the mud and dirt and rejoiced with me.

Sincerely,
Klaus Rickowski

Another letter of surprise was from a father worried about what to give his son for a birthday gift. On the eve of the event there was absolutely nothing special that could be provided to eat or to play with. He had made an awkward attempt to shape a little horse out of a piece of wood but that had been a failure. The father said people who believed all Germans to be great wood carvers were another testimony against those who set up stereotypes.

The lights that were available sometimes between 2 and 4 AM were out and the dawn was approaching as he stared out of the broken and patched window of their top floor apartment, contemplating their plight. As his focus came back to the grey roof outside the window a light spot, not noticed before, caught his eye. What could that be? He came closer to the window. It was a piece of cloth and something was attached! With trembling hands he opened the window and with a stick he was able to retrieve the parachute and candy. Something very small had come to fill a very large need. It had come to a special place at a special time.

The kids in East Berlin wrote great letters explaining how they would come over to West Berlin and catch some of these wonderful surprises. They hoped I wouldn't take offense that someone from the Russian Sector was collecting bounty intended for the Free Berliners. They hastened to assure me that it wasn't their doing that they lived in East Berlin or even in some cases, East Germany. They didn't have anything to do with setting up the blockade nor the East-West boundaries. They had to live over there because that is where their parents lived. An admiration was often expressed for the Americans.

The bottom line in the letters from East Berlin always came down to, "Is there any chance that you could drop these packages to us in East Berlin when you make your approach to Tempelhof? You have to fly right over us before you turn to land."

"We see your wings wiggle and the packages come down. There are parks and school yards that would make good targets over here and there aren't nearly as many people," they pleaded.

A special load was assembled and the next trip over East Berlin the ample supply was showered down on the kids in the Communist Sector. Capricious winds distributed the parachute formation, drifting with eddying currents, over a large area. Little figures in hot pursuit of a wind-borne delight disappeared from sight as others could be seen gleaning the harvest.

The East Berlin kids will love this!

My recent experience in looking at my own stereotyped prejudices had made it easy for me to drop to the kids in the communist territory. Those kids were probably less communist than a lot of people in the United States. Anyway, it is the system, not the people, that causes miscommunication and misunderstanding between nations. The people on the eastern side of the border were no different than the people on the western side. The world doesn't have the problems person-to-person that we have nation-to-nation.

One of the most stirring events of the Blockade was fueled by one voice from almost 300,000 East and West Berliners gathered in the

Tiergarten, on the Platz der Republik, in front of the Reichstag. It was late afternoon, 9 September 1948. Overhead the great metal birds, cradling the sustance of life, set their wings for the hungry nest at Tempelhof while Westerner and Easterner joined ranks to cry out to the free world of the Stalinist's injustice to humanity on both sides of the border. The magnificent Mayor, Ernst Reuter, displayed the throb of the bruised Berliner's heart for all to hear:

> We cannot be bartered, we cannot be negotiated, we cannot be sold....Whoever would surrender the people of Berlin, would surrender a world....more, he would surrender himself." The Mayor finished his historic address with feeling and passion that touched every soul to the core:
> People of the world, look upon this city! You cannot, you must not, forsake us! There is only one possibility for all of us: to stand jointly together until this fight has been won.[40]

An instantaneous tumultuous roar of approval from East and West Berliners engulfed the speaker, the crumbling Reichstag's columns, and the ears of the Soviet officers standing in their staff cars behind the Brandenburg Gate. Within moments the Red flag would be torn from the chariot on top of the Brandenburger Tor and a 15-year-old youth would seal the moment with his life. The heart of Berlin had spoken and so it was to be.

After many requests from a fellow lieutenant in Mobile, Alabama, I agreed to sell him my almost new red Chevrolet parked under the pine trees on Brookley Air Force Base. It was not without some misgivings and heavy heart that I signed the title and put the acceptance message in the mail. With this act I was more firmly committed to the airlift than ever before. In a small way it seemed to me like the stories that are told of early settlers whose ship was burned on some far-from-home shore to take their thoughts from returning to the thoughts of doing where they were.

On return from Berlin one day there was an officer to meet my aircraft. He said "Halvorsen, what have you been doing over East Berlin?"

I replied, "I've been dropping some of the parachutes to the kids over there."

"You can't do that," he said with some authority.

The gentleman was a friend of mine and he didn't seem really shook up, which led to my flippant reply, "Why not? The law of gravity is the same on both sides of the border."

In my mind I visualized that it was the need that was the same on both sides of the border and had simply substituted the word gravity for need. He shrugged off my impertinence with, "The Soviets have complained to the State Department that your dropping to the kids on their side of the border is a capitalist trick to influence the minds of the young people against them. You will have to stop."

The Soviets had control over the airspace above that part of their territory so we had no choice or appeal. News media in the United States voiced the fear that the protest would apply to drops over West Berlin.

The *Holyoke Massachusetts Transcript* of 14 October 1948 carried the following head line: "Operation Little Vittles May Be Halted After Protest From Russia." The text said in part:

> One of this country's major goodwill missions, "Operation Little Vittles," may be snuffed out overnight because Russia has complained to the State Department that it "violates propaganda agreements." Born in the heart of 1st Lt. Gail S. Halvorsen, the "Little Vittles" project has brought joy to thousands of Berlin children who picked up candy-laden miniature parachutes dropped by American pilots flying the Berlin Airlift to break the Russian blockade. Word that the operation may be halted came today just as children of Chicopee were launching a plan for centralizing "Operation Little Vittles" in their city. News of the Russian protest was contained in an unconfirmed message from Frankfurt, Germany to a wire service in this country.

That article and others carried the news. The ban was limited to drops over Russian-controlled territory. The operation in Chicopee really bloomed after that.

On 2 November 1948 the *Springfield Massachusetts Union* reported:

> Operation Little Vittles is headed for the big time and the school children of this city [Chicopee] from grade 1 to the seniors in high school are mainly responsible. Latest developments in the amazing growth of the idea include the following: a donation

of 900 pounds of twine from Robert Nolen, a supervisor in the School Department of Education in Boston, a gift of 1100 yards of linen to make parachutes from Budd Textile Co. of Philadelphia, another large gift of cloth from the Chicopee Manufacuring Co. for the same purpose. The kids will stamp the following message on each parachute: "This candy is sent to you from the school children of America." The message will be in German.

The article went on to tell of a Lt. Grier who dropped into the Chicopee Walgreen drug store for a small purchase and to his amazement he was loaded down with 200 pounds of candy for Operation Little Vittles.

Years later, in 1969, I was greeted by a then-grown young lady with mock irritation in her voice when she found out who I was and exclaimed, "I lived in East Berlin. Why did you quit dropping those things over there?" I explained the situation and she went on to describe how she had caught 13 of the little parachutes over a period of two weeks. She had married just before the wall went up and they had escaped to West Berlin with just the clothes on their backs. They are now city planners in West Berlin.

I just finished my debriefing at the operations counter and had turned to leave when the Operations Officer said, almost as an after thought, "I've got a note for you, Halvorsen." The message simply said, "I want to see you as soon as possible," signed General Tunner. A cold September rain added to my nervous chill.

Our previous contacts had been brief and informal. I wondered if some of our contributions had found their way into the black market. I worried about that.

Inside the old hotel, in downtown Wiesbaden, I picked my way through the modest set of offices covered with charts describing every aspect of the airlift operation. General Tunner was outside his door reviewing the tonnage figures for the past 24 hours. He seemed pleased with what he saw on the charts and greeted me with a smile, "Good to see you, Halvorsen. Have a seat." His handshake was firm and friendly.

"I haven't got time to visit long. The Air Force has requested that you proceed to New York for interviews on the 'We the People' television program plus some other T.V., radio, and newspaper coverage. They want to hear about what we are doing and the details of your operation. Do you want to go?"

Captains Larry Caskey, John Pickering, Lt. Bill Christian, and Sgt. Elkins could keep things going as well as I could.

"When do I leave?" was my quick response.

"Tomorrow morning on the C-54 courier flight," he replied. As I turned to go he called after me, "By the way, Halvorsen, don't get the big head about this thing. Have a good time and hurry back."

Arrangements were quickly made and I was on my way back across the Atlantic. This time in the back of the big bird, in a fuselage that was spotless. What a difference from the coal and flour-dusted interiors I had become accustomed to.

It was a very interesting few days in New York and quite a change of pace. Fresh from the bombed and desolate landscape of a ravished city to the sidewalks of New York was like coming out of the darkness into the light. The streets were free of rubble, roofs were firmly in place, windows shone without a crack, a cascade of color pleased the eye, undamaged steel girders that guided neatly finished symmetrical walls into the heavens were in their places behind their smooth coverings, cars with single occupants clogged the side streets and thoroughfare.

The contrast with Berlin made my heart go out the more to those gallant souls who were giving their all for the first step in this ladder of progress, freedom. The crowds of well-dressed, over-fed people rushed by me, already that first step forgotten or taken for granted, intent on some invisible objective that drove them past me without a friendly glance.

What could be so important? No matter, it couldn't compare to that basic force which drove former enemies to work together around the clock in harmony and to even smile and to wave.

After the television, radio, and newspaper interviews were completed, an invitation came to have lunch with a Mr. John S. Swersey, a member of the American Confectioners Association. His association sounded right in my area of interest.

I arrived at the Manhattan Hotel on time and was greeted by the maitre d'. He ushered me to a beautiful table decorated with a bouquet of fresh flowers and linen napkins. A large, well-proportioned man arose and warmly greeted me. "I'm Mr. Swersey," he announced without any airs or reservation. "Have a seat."

The next thing I noticed was the plates—they were surrounded by four forks! I'd never been to a four-fork lunch. We had one fork at the table on the farm and used it for whatever came next. Mr. Swersey already knew about as much of Operation Little Vittles as I did. He wanted to know more. "How much of this stuff can you use, Lieutenant?" he asked sincerely.

There were just the two of us plus a waiter who didn't seem to have any other responsibilities. Mr. Swersey waved his hand and said, "Forget that question. Let's eat then talk about the serious stuff."

After the last fork was used he got serious. "I represent the confectioners of the United States and you have already received quite a few supplies. We are really excited about what is going on over there and want to do more. What can we do?"

If I had ever heard of a blank check this was it. I thought of how big each drop should be, how many guys were in our squadron, how many trips they would make to Berlin in 24 hours, multiplied that by 30 days, to put it on a monthly basis, and gave him a number that I thought would give him indigestion. I honestly don't remember what that number was. It must have been ridiculous. He didn't bat an eye.

There was still a glow from the television show and the radio interviews. Not long after we were off the air, the studios received calls from people and organizations pledging support in quantity. But Mr. Swersey's proposition was staggering. Who said these New Yorkers weren't interested in anyone else?

I gave him my heartfelt thanks for the meal and more especially the pledge of support. John Swersey, a Jew, was vice president of Huylers Candy Company. Just before we parted, he took just a few minutes to explain that kids were the hope of the future and whatever had gone on before was now in the past.

In a few hours I was on a military flight headed back across the Atlantic, still puzzling the dynamics of Operation Little Vittles.

After a brief written report to General Tunner I went back to work. There was mail to be answered and flour to haul.[41]

The November weather was the acid test. It was the first time that we hadn't increased tonnage week to week. If it hadn't been for the long range radar and the ground controlled approach [GCA] radar

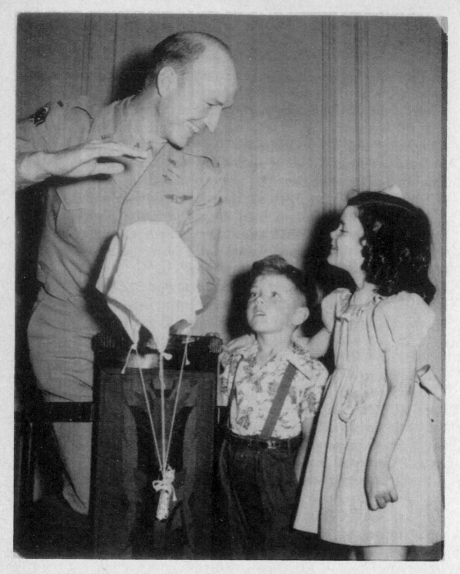

Some New York children receiving instructions on how it is done. Trip to New York, Sept., 1948.

of the 1946th Communications Squadron and their exceptional people, we could have lost the battle right there. Those men and women were great.

On the next flight the weather forecast for Tempelhof was for worse-than-usual conditions. "Don't be surprised if you have to bring the load back this trip," the weatherman warned. "It doesn't look good."

John picked up a big box of Little Vittles. "From the sound of things we'll probably have to drop these in a location identified by radar this trip," he said with a chuckle. "A blind drop makes for a big surprise."

The closer we got to Tempelhof the more accurate the forecast looked. We were getting bounced around and were picking up some ice. I said, "Sgt. Elkins, get ready to flip the windshield anti-icing switch on, and follow up with John to see he opens the control knob just off his right knee. If we're lucky enough to break out in time, I want the ice off the windshield." Elkins really didn't need the reminder. He wanted us to see through that windshield as much as we did. The ice on the leading edge of the wings was thick enough to activate the de-icer boots. Elkins had the Aldis lamp checking every few minutes. The prop de-icers were working. The rat-tat-tat of ice coming off the props against the fuselage was keeping us awake.

"Give radar a call and ask for a fix over the Britz area. Let's unload these little parachutes before we hit the Wedding beacon. They don't need anti-icing," I said with anticipation. We didn't have long to wait.

Elkins was dispatched to the escape hatches in the cargo compartment and returned a short time later to report that he had not only deployed the chutes but had been over generous by contributing his wrist watch. The expansion wrist band on the watch was very loose and the slip stream had caught it just right to include the watch with the candy and gum. "Hope that darn thing works better for them than it did for me," he said without a great sense of loss.

We all had a much-needed good laugh before the seriousness of the immediate approach and landing again demanded all we had. The sleet was coming down in torrents and the turbulence tested our abilities to stay on course.

"Hope the GCA doesn't blow a fuse tonight," John said with some concern. Into the approach pattern we picked up GCA right on cue. After turning final and responding to the Final Controller's request for a communications check he took over with:

> This is your final controller. You need not acknowledge any further transmissions. You are approaching the center line from right to left. Your landing gear should be down and locked. You are five miles to touch down. Approaching the glide path, approaching the center line. Turn right five degrees, heading 269,

prepare to begin rate of decent at 550 feet per minute in about 30 seconds. Heading is good, on the center line, approaching the glide path. Begin your rate of decent now. You are drifting left of center line; turn right two degrees to 271. Your glide path is good, coming back on center line. Turn left one degree to 270. You are 100 feet above the glide path. Adjust your rate of decent. You are on the center line very good adjustment, coming down on the glide path. One mile to touch down. Weather reports 400 foot ceiling and one mile visibility in freezing rain, braking action poor. Turn on your windshield wipers at pilot's discretion. You are on the glide path, on the center line, very good rate of decent. You are one half mile from touch down looking very good. Over the approach lights. Over the end of the runway. Take over visually and land.

John had called to me a moment before that he had the approach lights, the wipers were on and the windshield was clear. The runway lights were on bright but we could only see about half of them as we broke clear of the ragged edge of the overcast. They were a little

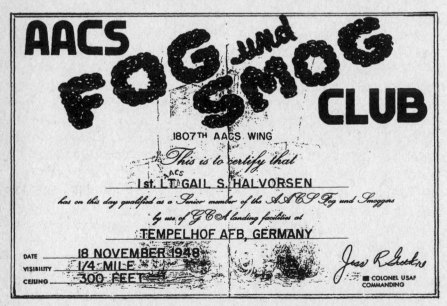

Made a member of the "Fog and Smog" club as a result of below-minimums landings at Tempelhof.

generous in their ceiling and visibility readings. "They get more planes in that way. The minimums for Tempelhof are 400 foot ceiling and one mile visibility so that is what you get," quipped John.

"We are lucky if we had 300 and a half," I replied. We got her stopped in spite of some ice patches on the runway.

The calm, soothing, deliberate voice of that final controller was the best high-blood-pressure antidote ever devised for such an occasion. "Did you see the red clearance light on the roof of the apartment building on the right?" asked Elkins.

"I had my head in the cockpit," I replied. "That red light and the building is always above us when we're just off the end of the runway.

What a feeling—on a stormy night when you're worn to a frazzle—to have a crew like that put you at ease and guide you to the end of the runway. We prayed for those guys. Many a pilot took time to visit the GCA shack with some heart-felt thanks for a job well done.

Jake Shuffert is one of the greatest cartoonists I have ever followed. He kept us loosened up and laughing at ourselves with his airlift humor. We all looked forward to his next creation. One of them was the depiction of a GCA shack. The weather was terrible. The GCA operators had just guided a plane in for a night landing at Tempelhof. Knocking on the door of the shack was a flight crew looking like they had just come out of an explosion. Soot, smoke, and coal dust all over them. They were holding the aircraft control column in their hands. The controller opens the shack door. Light from the inside illuminates the three smoldering crew members standing on the step. The pilot takes a step forward and says, "Would you please repeat that last transmission?"

We returned from Berlin to Rhein-Main early in December with a light snow falling and were met by an officer in a jeep. "Wonder what little surprise he has for us today," quipped John as he swung his big frame out of the seat into the aisle.

"Yesterday's drop was one of the biggest yet. Wonder if there was a problem," Elkins added.

I was greeted with, "Halvorsen, jump in the jeep—I want to show you something." In a few minutes we were at the railway spur on the base. On the railway track was a box car with a couple of armed guards around it.

"Who have you got in the box car?" I asked in surprise.

"It isn't who, it is what. There are 3,500 pounds of chocolate candy bars and gum in that car for your operation. There is almost enough stuff to buy King Ludwig's castle on the black market," replied the officer.

"Wow!" I whistled, "Where did it come from?"

"Some guy named Mr. Swersey in New York," he replied. "It came by ship to Bremerhaven and by rail from there to here."

The next week was a repeat of the same scene. This time there were 3,000 pounds. I quickly gathered a trusty crew and transported it to the secure place in squadron supply with the previous shipment. That Mr. Swersey really meant what he said! Fantastic! But what would we do with it all? We already were dropping a great amount, much of it from the Little Vittles Center in Chicopee, Massachusetts. It wouldn't be too efficient to drop this 6,500 pounds.

We moved finally from the barn to some barracks on Rhein-Main. Although the barracks were of frame construction, the change was most welcome. Showers in the same building! We were practically next door to the Officers' club. The secretaries were doing a great job, not only with letters but with organizational matters as well. The new location in the barracks made coordination easier. We had barracks bags full of German kids' addresses who wanted American pen pals and American kids who wanted German pen pals. The secretaries shuffled the letters and sent them out. Peter Zimmerman drew a family in Palm, Pennsylvania. He would get at least a new pair of boots out of that relationship.

I became increasingly concerned about the big cache of goods from Mr. Swersey. Something had to be done quick. John triggered the answer, "It's almost Christmas—let's give them a Christmas party."

I found a jailhouse in Berlin not far from the flight line. It had several empty cells. With a little persuasion we arranged for those cells to accommodate the candy. There was enough separation between the cells to prevent the inmates from snitching the goods. My buddies would take about 100 pounds of candy on their flights to Berlin. We would call Tempelhof tower with the code, "This is a Little Vittles flight. We have cargo." An officer would meet the airplane and take the 100 pounds to the jail and lock it up. Five to ten buddies would get to Berlin each 24 hours. It was a foot race, but we got it all to Berlin before the 23rd of December, 1948. A super captain in Berlin

I heard some children would be on the ramp at Tempelhof so we didn't drop these until we landed.

arranged with the Air Force and the German Youth Association for Christmas parties and the distribution of the goods in Free Berlin.

With no evening electricity the parties were held Christmas Eve afternoon. It was a very special Christmas for me knowing so many kids had such an unusual party during a siege just as real as when the castles of old were cut off and starvation was used as a conquering tactic.

Unfortunately, I was not able to attend any of those parties. But the fireworks were very much in evidence, late on Christmas Eve, as we flew near Frankfurt on our way to Berlin with a load of dried potatoes.

That 1948 Christmas had none of the normal gifts, food, family, tinsel, and decorations others have had. But my heart had never been so full of the Christmas spirit, all for two sticks of gum! I gave a silent prayer that special Eve for all those who made it possible, but more particularly for the Prince of Peace, the fountain of hope and man's free agency.

There was no let up in the pace of the airlift. At Fassberg, Irvin Martin, a captain with a lot of flying experience, now living in Orlando, Florida, was contributing to that pace. The pilots at Fassberg and Celle flew mostly coal and had a shorter run into Berlin through the Northern Corridor than we had through the Southern Corridor. Their tonnage figures were very impressive. Irvin was adding to that total on Christmas eve with three round trips into Tegel.

When Irvin filled out the aircraft Form 1, he noted with a wry smile that they had flown more hours on instruments and in the night on those three trips than they flew in daytime and clear of cloud. He didn't know what was going on back in the United States while he made those trips to Tegel. It was not until days later that he found on Christmas Eve, his wedding anniversary, that his wife had presented him with a brand new son.

One day there was a note in the mail box that several of us were being transferred to Wiesbaden. It was a fighter base during the war and often called by it's wartime designation, Y-80.

The first thing we noticed was that the barracks were much better, being of masonry construction. Congestion on the flight line and loading ramps was not nearly so bad and the surroundings were considerably more pleasant at that time than at Rhein-Main. One personal benefit was the ease of access to town. The city of Wiesbaden was snuggled up against the Taunus mountains and had the air of a resort. It had escaped the heavy bombing heaped on Frankfurt.

One of the first pilots I met in Wiesbaden was Captain Eugene T. Williams, a good natured and enthusiastic leader. He had already been

Capt. Williams succeeded me and Caskey. He kept the project going. He took care of 2,500 different needy children placed on Berlin's Peacock Island every two weeks. Willy dropped more than Caskey and I put together.

one of the outstanding supporters of Operation Little Vittles at Wiesbaden. It wouldn't be long before my rotation date would come up and I was looking for someone to carry on the operation the way we had it going. Larry Caskey would be responsible during the month or so before he had to leave. Willy sure looked to be the ideal person. From that time on we worked closely toward that objective.

It was January, 1949. My rotation time had come and had then been extended for one month to accommodate some of the Little Vittles responsibilities. It was time to hitchhike another trip to Berlin, wiggle the wings and say goodbye to some good friends on the east end of the greatest air show on earth. With goodbyes said it wouldn't be a long wait for a ride in an empty airplane back to Wiesbaden.

The last hour on the flight ramp at Tempelhof in Berlin brought back many memories of the things that had occurred at this historic terminal—things that would affect me for the rest of my life.

Just as I was preparing to leave an often repeated scene unfolded. Two little girls dressed in heavy winter coats, bearing a bouquet of fresh flowers and accompanied by a grandmother, were crossing the wind-swept ramp towards some airlift pilots. I stopped to watch. With a smile on their faces and a deep curtsey they handed the flowers to the pilots as an offering of friendship and appreciation.

Fresh flowers in the dead of winter in a city that had been under military siege for seven months! Without the necessities of life they were offering a delicate symbol of something beyond their physical

needs. A token of hope, of peace, of beauty, of things to come. How
necessary, how important these symbols to the hunger of the spirit.

Larry Caskey, (right) my successor just before Eugene Williams.

The prim little forms, clutching their heavy winter coats about them,
gracefully accepted the American pilot's thanks and radiated back,
in countenance and gesture, appreciation beyond their capabilities to
verbally express. They turned and skipped back to their escort. How
many times that scene had been reenacted here.

I remembered the first flowers I had received and how the Berlin
coal unloaders smiled as I walked through the coal- and flour-dusted
cabin with those flowers to the cockpit.

One day Manfred and Klaus Meisner had waited hours with their
father for me to arrive. From the rubble around the Reichstag they
had collected some broken pieces of marble. For hours they had shaped
them. Two pieces had been set in metal bases to form a beautiful set
of book ends. Their eyes shone with pride as they pointed to the metal
plaques which read: "Lt. Halvorsen U.S.A. AIRPORT Thankful and
as a Remember from a Berlin boy." Their names were inscribed below.

Several weeks before on this same ramp had stood a father and a
son who spent months building a miniature Royal carriage with little

Children at the Tempelhof fence we dropped to the day before. Captain Pickering in foreground.

handles on the doors that opened and all the other details of the real thing. It was pulled by six magnificent wooden stallions.

The hours of painstaking care that such projects required was evidence of the genuine appreciation of the donors of such gifts. In every case the meaning beyond intrinsic value was the look from the depths of the soul reflected and amplified through that great expressor, the human eye. In every case the experience left me a more humble and grateful pilot.

The givers of these kinds of gifts and the flowers had one thing in common. They were all genuine in their desire to share something of themselves, something that had some special value or meaning to them personally.

None was more genuine than a ten-year-old girl whose name I never learned but who brought with her the greatest gift that she could give, her most cherished and perhaps last remaining personal possession, her little fuzzy teddy bear. It had been her constant companion in the cellar during the British and American bombing raids. She had explained in her school English that it had been a comfort to her during the last battle for Berlin. It was this fuzzy reassurance that she cuddled

A little Berlin girl, Irene Oppermann, who with her mother, baked me a gingerbread Santa Claus complete with parachute and mock candy bar.

as the Russian rockets tore away the last of the city's defenses. It was a small, brown, Berlin bear with the fuzz worn off the elbows.

"Please take my teddy bear," she said in halting English, looking up at me with big brown, expressive eyes rapidly filling with tears. Like a mother handing her child to a rescuer for safe keeping until they could be reunited in peace and freedom, she extended her offering with "Good care take of him for me."

Seeing immediately the measure of her treasure I attempted to return it to her but that occasioned a negative response. Although my offer was desired, it could not be accepted. It was important that the gift be given.

"Good luck he will bring you and your friends on your flights to Berlin," she stammered, fighting to control her emotions.

The gift meant the more to me not only for the obvious love with which it was given but that it was given without knowing that I was the Schokoladen Flieger, the Candy Bomber, Uncle Wiggly Wings.

She had come to present it to any airlift pilot representing all air crews and ground crews that filled that long umbilical cord over East Germany to Berlin. I just happened to be with my aircraft near the terminal when she, with her mother, had come to do what she had to do. I would never forget my feelings as the little girl curtseyed, turned, and waved goodbye only 50 yards from where I now stood, thinking of what had happened to me these past months in Berlin.

Hundreds of aircrew members had lived similar experiences and had been touched as I had been touched.

How it is that the little things in life can provide the most joy and the greatest blessings? Service to others, as the Savior taught, provides those magical moments. The exhortation to serve, to love, is so simple but its blessing is so complex.

"Halvorsen, if you don't get in here we're going to take off without you," awoke me from my gathering memories before the long trip to Mobile, Alabama.

Taxiing out to take off, along the barbed wire fence, brought back the moment of two sticks of gum. Several children waved. There were others by the apartment building who never seemed to tire of watching those big birds swooping in to leave their "catch" in the open, hungry mouth of Berlin. None of them were expecting parachutes from arriving aircraft. They were aware of the shift of our drops to the whole city.

The children's tattered coats were drawn tight about them against the bitter January cold. Snowdrifts hugged the fence posts that in turn supported the barbed wire.

The fog had come, plus sleet, snow, winds and darkness, but the tonnage flown in these conditions to Berlin from the start of the airlift to the end of January 1949 was 674,232.3 tons by the Americans and 229,368.9 tons by the British. On 19 January, 1949, the average ration for a Berliner was raised from 1600 calories a day to 1880 calories a day.

The airlift also had allowed the continued employment of 935,238 Berliners. A total of 81,730.6 tons of manufactured goods were flown out of Berlin by the Americans and the British during the blockade.[42]

In just a few moments we were off. Immediately we could see two C-54s, some distance apart, approaching Tempelhof. Ahead we could see British aircraft positioning themselves for Gatow. Off to the right we could see a string of C-54s proceeding to Tegel. From at least one

Wiesbaden winter conditions.

of those planes it was certain that some little vittles were wafting their way earthward. Some children would turn their attention from the grey of the winter and the tightness of the Red stanglehold on their city to remember better days and hope for a better future.

In a few moments the western border of Berlin slipped below the wing and was gone.

Would I ever see Berlin again?

13

Post Airlift Happenings

The short time I had in Wiesbaden to gather my belongings and to huddle with Captains Larry Caskey and Eugene Williams about the future of Operation Little Vittles became a blur of time, events, people, and emotion. In what seemed the next moment I was at Rhein-Main, a passenger in the back end of a plush C-54 getting ready to depart for Westover Air Force Base at Chicopee, Massachusetts, enroute to Moblile, Alabama.

As we began our taxi I could see the old barn across the Autobahn. What memories of comrades and a worthwhile mission that old structure held. Our aircraft turned down the taxiway, revealing the familiar scene of aircraft scattered about the airfield with mechanics huddled about them. The men were occasionally whipping their arms against their bodies to call up added blood cells for duty at the extremities. There was a sharp, chill wind driving a cold January snow shower.

Lines of heavily loaded semi-trailer trucks wove in and out of the silver birds like slalom racers, expertly avoiding the flags, homing in on an open cargo door like a magnet latching onto a nail.

My mind went back to the aircraft mechanics. The men were doing what had to be done to breathe life back into the grounded birds. I grimaced as I thought of the job they had to do to replace freezing metal, adjust it, fasten it in place securely, and try at the same time to preserve the skin on their sensitive fingers. It seemed to me that the aircrews were the ones that got most of the credit in the press and

A "Little Vittles" flyer Capt. Williams put together. (1949)

in the German communities. To me the real heros were the aircraft mechanics.

Too often the ground personnel are taken for granted or overlooked in major air events that are outcome centered. Great ones among these are the truck drivers, security policemen, the GCA operators, maintenance personnel, weather people, the communications experts, the traffic controllers, food service and billeting people, the base engineers, the runway repair and construction people, the fire department crews, the medics, the supply workers, personnel people, administrators, operations people, and a host of others. General Tunner, although a pilot, was an administrator.

If I were asked to pick one hero of the airlift it would easily be the General. He was tough as nails but fair, a genius at planning airlift operations, and truly concerned for the well being and safety of those called to serve with him. He was a foe of bureaucracy, and he was the source for Berlin.

The overriding heros and heroines of the airlift had to be the Berliners—men, women, and children. Without their knowledge of what freedom meant and their indomitable spirit and principled response, the airlift would have surely failed.

They were the ones that went home at night to bomb-damaged rooms without lights, heat, or enough to eat. People of other nations had been through the same, even at the hand of some Berliners. Forgiveness comes hard to the proud and insecure. But hope of change springs eternal and if there is to be progress some things have to give. Pleasantries had departed Berlin deep into the war. At the beginning of the blockade the Berliners consciously postponed the return to an easier life for something better later. They were the heros, the cheer leaders, and the examples. They gave meaning to our efforts.

We pulled onto the runway behind a C-54 departing for Tempelhof and in a few minutes we were on our way to Westover Air Force Base in Massachusetts.

I was bone weary, and before we reached cruising altitude I was sound asleep. My dreams were filled with things long missed. Alta being among them. When I awoke plans seemed to have been worked out in my mind for leave out West, friends, family, and a new life. We had already covered half of the Atlantic. The rest of the way seemed short.

We entered the traffic pattern at Westover Air Force Base and were soon on the ground. There was quite a military and civilian crowd on the ramp that had the appearance of a welcoming committee. The brown, fuzzy, Berlin Teddy bear with the worn elbows was under my arm.[43] I was on my way into base operations before Mary

Connors stopped me. Then the realization hit that the reception was for me. Other than from the kids in Berlin, I hadn't had a welcome like that before, ever.

The Mayor of Chicopee, Edward O. Bourbeau, was the official greeter. He and Will Thivierge soon saw that I had the key to the city, was made Mayor for the day, and hosted to a dinner fitting for the occasion. What a thrill it was to meet first hand some of those wonderful people who supplied and were still supplying Operation Little Vittles with the goods for the Berlin kids. Special among the welcoming committee was Mary Connors. People from all walks of life worked side by side under her leadership in that great community to accomplish the unbelievable. Will Thivierge was the real power behind the scenes, giving round-the-clock support to the operation. He made it all happen.

After some pretty fancy speeches we toured the countryside around Chicopee. Our first stop was the Savage Arms Company. After a good look at the assembly line I was asked the improbable question, "What one of these guns would you like to own?" I allowed, "That light-weight 12-gauge automatic shot gun looks pretty neat. My old Remington is just about finished." Vice President G. Noble Davidson said, "It's yours."

The next stop was the Spalding Sporting Goods Company. "I understand that you are a pretty lousy golfer," mused the president, Mr. Brown. My reply didn't do anything to change his mind. Farm kids of my acquaintance didn't play golf. The Vice President, Mr. Gerould said, "You'll need one of the better sets to do you any good. Take a look around the room and pick out the set you like. Collect a bag in which to put them." After I looked around and selected what I thought was a pretty good set Mr. Brown said, "I can see you really do need help. Put those things down and try these."[44]

He had noticed my ignorance in handling the different equipment and had already collected a full set of Robert Jones signature clubs and a double handfull of new golf balls. He handed them to me in a beautiful leather bag. By now my mouth was about as far open as the kids at the fence with the two sticks of gum. I had some of their same feelings. It was because of them that I was standing there getting these surprises. I was doubly in debt.

There was hardly time to catch my breath before they had me out the door and into another factory. "Didn't know that Chicopee had so many factories, Mayor," I said with some pleasure.

The next factory was definitely different. It manufactured baby clothes. As I came through the front door I came face to face with a lovely young woman who welcomed me like a saleswoman would welcome the representative of a baby store about to order their first supply.

"Just a minute. There is something I have to tell you," I broke in, "I'm not married yet."

"Nobody asked you if you were married. We don't want to hurry you along too fast but it is never too early to be prepared," she replied with a warm smile, "Besides, we hear there are prospects." By now I began to wonder where they were getting all their information. I looked at the USAF Information Officer who was clearing my activities. "Had to be him," I thought to myself.

"Just so we understand each other," I replied as my gaze took in stacks of undershirts, pants, blankets, booties, and diapers. By the time I got out of there I had all I could carry of each. What a dowry! This and a genuine proposal ought to convince her. The baby clothes eventually wore out, but as of January, 1990, the gun and golf clubs were still going strong.

We ended up at the Grape Street fire station to witness the famous Little Vittles assembly line. Here is where they had already processed over 15 tons of candy and the thousands of parachutes to make the drops. Mary Connors explained that at the time of the visit they were processing 800 pounds every other day. Fantastic![45]

What a great time I had in Chicopee. What wonderful people there are on the East Coast. My early impression of "Easterners" was as wrong as what my farm day thoughts about other people and situations had been.

There was one more essential stop to be made before heading to Mobile and then west. Another one of the greatest individual supporters was Dorothy Groeger from 59 Hillside Avenue, Hillside, New Jersey. Dorothy was different. She had to overcome great difficulty to achieve the fantastic level of support that she gave the kids in Berlin.

The Chicopee headquarters for "Little Vittles," the Grove Street fire station.

At 22, Dorothy had been an invalid for three years. In spite of that she employed the telephone, family, friends, and manufacturers to process 250 parachutes with goodies every day. Her packages were special. Each packet contained a toy from the Dillon-Beck Manufacturing Company in addition to the candy! The time I spent with Dorothy renewed all the warm feelings for the inherent goodness in people that had brightened my life these past eight months. My thoughts on arriving at her home were on how I might cheer her up. When I left it was I who was the beneficiary of an uplift from a brighter light.[46]

Arrangements had been made for me to pick up a car in New York. From there I drove to Mobile where there was another wonderful welcome home. What support that base provided and continued to provide the Berlin kids. My next destination was Garland, Utah.

No town can take the place of Garland with it's 1500 souls. They had a two-day celebration, which included permission to fly down Main Street and drop candy out of a Goonie Bird to the kids. The only casualty was a little girl when in hot pursuit of a parachute the lollypop came loose and gave her a scratch on the head. Dr. Wardliegh had her fixed up in no time. This town had been a great supplier of the operation. I was able to thank the Ladies Self-Culture Club, the American Legion, and the Lions Club for the hundreds of "Garland, Utah, USA" parachutes and candy payloads that they provided the Berlin children.

Homecoming drop over Garland, Utah. (Feb. 1949)

A short time after that it was a thrill to fly low over Salt Lake City and Ogden, Utah, to repeat the process. Governor J. Bracken Lee picked me up at the Salt Lake City airport and drove me to Uncle Leland's house on 9th East and 6th South. Dad and Mom, who had come up from Stockton, were pretty proud of their sugar beet thinner. I was still in shock.

Dad and Mom in Salt Lake City, Feb., 1949.

Time was too short to come to an understanding with Alta. Others we had both known had more of a part to play in our lives than was apparent at long range. Time ran out and I was back to Mobile flying the C-74 again.

Word came that the Air Force was in the final competition for an Oscar at the Academy Awards as the result of a documentary they had put together on the airlift. Colonel George Cassady, our Commander, asked me to drop by.

"How would you like to represent the Air Force at the Academy Awards in Hollywood and accept the Oscar if we win it?" he asked. He went on to say, "There are two tickets available. Know anyone who might want to go with you?"

I quickly thought to myself that if two tickets would be as efficacious as two sticks of gum I sure wouldn't turn it down. It would give Alta and me a little time to sit down and do some serious talking about where this slow-paced, long-distance paper romance was going. I had been carrying an unset diamond wrapped in a piece of wax paper in my wallet since I was stationed in Brazil five years before. At our speed she would be beyond child-bearing age or married to one of her two other boyfriends. I needed to cool my love affair with the big aluminum bird long enough to start something with an eternal warm spirit that had promise of future increase.

"You seem to be giving this thing some awful serious thought. Shouldn't be that hard to make up your mind." Colonel Cassady added.

"Sorry, Sir, I was mentally already on my way. I'd love to go, and there is someone for the other ticket, I hope."

The phone rang and rang, but no one was there. Finally, two hours later I was able to make contact with Alta. She was as excited as I was and it didn't take long to make plans for a meeting on the corner of Hollywood and Vine.

We met right on time and we were able to get in the theatre early enough to gawk at all the celebrities. Elizabeth Taylor was sitting right across the aisle with Lt. Glen Davis, the great Army football player. Barbara Stanwyck and Robert Taylor sat on the opposite side. Others that we had only seen on the screen were all around us. The fineness

Proposing to Alta, Boulder City, Nevada, Feb., 1949. The ring is attached to the parachute.

of the dress and richness of the scene made me noticeably uncomfortable, given the circumstance of my past eight months. The dress of the three men who came from the shadows to scrape the garbage barrels flashed before me and I struggled to reconcile my participating in this operation so soon after being in another so totally different.

Jane Wyman received the best actress award for her performance as the deaf mute in Johnny Belinda. Lawrence Olivier was the best actor for his role in Hamlet.

By the time the night was over there was some good news and some bad news. The Air Force placed second to the Army in the documentary. A general officer was there to accept the Oscar for the Army. I was proud that the Air Force had sent a lieutenant. The good news was that after the night across from Elizabeth Taylor, Alta came across mighty good and things were looking up.

Marriage 16 April, 1949, and for eternity in St. George, Utah on 16 September, 1950.

I don't totally credit those two Academy Award tickets, or the two sticks of gum and the kids at the fence, or the dowry of baby clothes for what followed, but I'm sure they all contributed.

Our wedding was on the 16th of April 1949, less than one month before the Soviets would capitulate in the siege of Berlin. It was a great honeymoon on the South Rim of the Grand Canyon. That Easter Sunday and the bride were the most beautiful that I had ever seen.

At the time I didn't realize it, nor did I consciously think of the airlift, but things were really happening in Germany. General Tunner orchestrated an Easter parade with the equivalent of 600 railway cars full of supplies flown to Berlin in a 24-hour period. There were 12,940 tons delivered on 1,398 landings in Berlin.

Presentation of the Cheney Award for 1948 by General Hoyt S. Vandenberg to Lt. Gail S. Halvorsen in Washington, D.C., May 1949. From left to right: General Kuter, Commander of Military Air Transport Service, Senator Watkins (Utah), General Vandenberg, Chief of the United States Air Force, Mrs. Halvorsen, Lt. Halvorsen, Mr. Symington, Secretary of the Air Force, Congressman Granger, and Congresswoman Basone.

* * * * *

Mercedes called to her mother as she came bounding up the stairs to her flat in the old apartment building near Tempelhof. "They have just increased our food ration to 2000 calories and there may be some fresh fruit!"

Frau Simon looked up with a half smile at her daughter's radiance. "That's good news Mercedes. I think we're certainly going to make it now." But her smile disappeared as she went back to the official envelope clasped in her trembling hand. "We regret to inform you that your husband was not listed on the last search by the Russian Department for German Prisoners."

Mercedes at nine years old.

"Have they found Daddy?" Mercedes asked, knowing immediately the nature of the communication.

All her mother could do was shake her head. "Go down and feed the chickens, Mercedes, and don't forget the water," Frau Simon requested in a voice drained of expression or warmth.

* * * * *

I was stationed at Brookley Air Force Base in Mobile, with Alta by my side. What a pleasure it was to have someone to come home to. We even invited Peter Sowa and family over for Sunday dinner.

Our stay at Brookley Air Force Base was brief before I received orders to report to the University of Florida at Gainesville to get the university degree. In my optimism I had told the Air Force I could get an Aeronautical Engineering degree in two years. Two years was all the time they would allow. Those two quarters at Utah State were helpful but wouldn't go very far in filling many requirements.

We loved Gainesville. Brad, our first son, was born there on the same day they made me a captain. We finished our bachelors degree

The first passenger trucks leave Berlin for Hannover, 12 May, 1949.

The official end of the blockade, 12 May, 1949. The airlift continued to 30 September, 1949, to ensure adequate supplies.

The end of the blockade, 12 May, 1949. A Navy plane, one from the two squadrons assigned to the airlift.

in Aeronautical Engineering in the two years and were invited to stay a third year for a Masters degree.

From Gainesville we were assigned to the Wright Air Development Center at Dayton, Ohio. My job involved research and the development of cargo aircraft. They hoped I would design a large cargo carrying capability and control systems that would take ample doses of flour and coal dust. We lived in an old converted schoolhouse in Byron, Ohio. It was out in the country and we loved the neighbors and the half-acre garden. It was much better than the Zeppelinheim barn! Denise, our first lovely red-headed daughter, was born there.

After seven years of assignments out of the country or in the eastern part of it, the fantastic happened. We were sent to Hill Air Force Base, Ogden, Utah, only 45 miles from the sugar beet field.

They always say you should never go back. I found to my distaste that I had been in the farming business much too early. The Germans had perfected a sugar beet seed that sprouted almost every time so they didn't have to plant an excess. The individual plants were far enough apart that you could use a long-handled hoe and didn't have to bend over to separate the double plants. Even that was not enough enticement for me to pick up where I left off. Young men's backs would never be as strong again. With my flying, engineering job, and fishing there was no time for the farm, even if I had the desire.

I stopped by the Brigham City airport to express my gratitude to my old instructor. Johnny Weir was long since back from the wars and chipper as ever. The runway that launched me on that first flight in 1941 was much improved.

Johnny Weir (left) my first instructor. Brigham City, Utah, August, 1989.

It was at Hill Air Force Base that I briefed my good buddy, Major Don Bowry, on how to drop parachutes. This time I was going to play the part, along with several of my fishing buddies, of the kids expecting a parachute from the sky. It was his task to find our group somewhere in the Uinta Wilderness area, half-way through our 100-mile horse-back trek through the tops of that great mountain range. He was to drop us some fresh beef steaks and roasts. We would be tired of fish by that time. We also wanted a note from our wives on how things were going at home.

A place at the 10,000 foot level in an open basin was decided upon as the drop zone. We both had a copy of the same map. It was not quite as well done as Peter Zimmerman's in Berlin, but it was adequate. Don was to come by on the fifth day, verify it was us from the description of our horses and my bald head, and drop it there. I was hoping for better success than we had with Peter or Mercedes because there was no way Don could mail the goods to us if he couldn't find us. The weather was really bad the fifth day and got us off our schedule. Lightning bolts followed by thunder bounced back and forth between the granite peaks, humbled our souls and kept us from tempting fate as lightning rods on top of our horses.

One day led to another. No airplane and no drop. I knew how some of the kids in Berlin felt.

My first day back in the office Don came in with a big smile, "Well how did you like it?"

"Like what?" I scowled. "Did you eat them yourself?"

His smile was quickly replaced with a real look of disappointment and especially concern. "You mean you didn't get 'em?" he stammered.

"That is exactly what I mean," I said with emphasis.

"Holy cow!" he exclaimed. "I borrowed a survival chute to drop that stuff. I'm signed out for it. It's worth $75.00." Then I realized the genuine basis of his concern.

"It's going to cost you more than $75.00. Those steaks and roasts were the best we had," I responded. "Where did you drop them?"

Don had gone to where he thought we would be the day after the storm. He found a group of fishermen. Their horses were the same color as our horses, one guy was baldheaded, and they were waving very friendly so he dropped it there. Peter Zimmerman would have understood my frustration. "Don, I don't know if you would have been much help in Berlin," I chided.

The nicest thing that happened to us at Hill Air Force Base was the arrival, on Alta's birthday, of our second lovely red-headed daughter, Marilyn.

Our next station was Maxwell Air Force Base, Montgomery, Alabama, for Air Command and Staff College. The school was for only a few months but that was long enough to a add a good Southern name, Robert E., to the red-headed list. He arrived on Sputnik day, 4 October, 1957.

* * * * *

Mercedes was now a beautiful young lady increasingly fascinated with being a pilot herself. She had never forgotten the airlift pilots and their silver birds winging overhead with their precious cargo. Mercedes had kept the gum and candy wrappers that contained the goodies mailed to her in November, 1948. Those souvenirs brought back memories of hard times that made her stop and give appreciation for how much better things had become.

The good feelings were interrupted by occasional feelings of foreboding conveyed by visitors from East Berlin. Each visit seemed to project an increased tension — a sense of helplessness to affect important events in the East Berliners' private lives. The tension in the visitors seemed to increase in direct proportion to improvements in West Berlin. The disabling seeds, the denial of free agency, had long before been sown and would reap the wall and a whirlwind of more dramatic events to follow.

Mercedes' sparkling, up-beat approach to life was also occasionally interrupted as she wondered what could have happened to her father. These thoughts were left on earth as she took to the sky. Mercedes discovered a natural ability in the air that would have made any airlift pilot proud. She was coordinated!

* * * * *

The United States Air Force space program was brand new and starting to grow. We were thrilled to find that would be our next challenge. The assignment was at the Space Systems Division of the Air Force Systems Command, Inglewood, California. The ballistic missile program had started not long before in the old schoolhouse and the Space Division branched off from that. I was lucky enough to have a great commander in Colonel (later General) Dave Lowe.

The excitement of the next four years represented some of the best in my Air Force career. By now I was a major.

The already high priority placed on the research of space boosters and space craft was given some impetus by the apparent lead of the Soviets. My main job was the development of space launch vehicles, principally the Titan III, for the lifting body Dyna-Soar space glider. I had previously worked on Titan I for the Gemini program and the Atlas for the Mercury program. Although the Dyna-Soar shuttle-type glider was cancelled, the Titan III went on to be a communication satellite workhorse. I don't believe we would have ever flown coal in that bird! They decided I should be a lieutenant colonel.

After four years in California an opportunity came to return to Germany. This time it was as an engineering coordinator of research technology available in Europe that would be of some interest to our space efforts in the United States. No sooner had we arrived in Wiesbaden than the stork landed right behind us with our Germany edition, Mike. He wasn't a redhead, but he was the last and a great addition.

One of our priorities was to get the family to Berlin and show them Tempelhof. It was a little while before Mike was ready to travel. When we did make it I was amazed at the changes that had occurred over the years. Things were all cleaned up and the place looked great. The flight line seemed to be changed the least. There were a few commercial airliners where the Skymasters had covered the apron. The apartment buildings across the way looked to be in much better shape. For a moment I closed my eyes and could almost see the kids at the fence.

There were many startling changes to our city of 1949 but none could compare in shock power to the feeling of separation and apprehension instilled by the monstrous wall.

This stark, grey concrete-and-wire barrier to human contact coiled its way like a giant snake around Free Berlin. Its only promise was death to those on the other side who would attempt a crossing from East to West. It would become an infamous monument to a flawed plan for the utopian destiny of the human race. As I stood on the elevated viewing platform at Bernauer Strasse and my eyes swept the death strip, a feeling of darkness swept over me like the accounts of the plague descending on the Egyptians at the time of Moses. How could this be the 20th century?

After Germany we were assigned to the Pentagon. I had always tried to avoid that assignment. It didn't seem the kind of a place for an outdoor country boy, and rumor had it that it wasn't easy to get a letter signed out. We had never been to a place we didn't like before so we held a family council meeting to get an attitude check. We resolved that this shouldn't be any different. We found a place to live in the Mount Vernon area among the trees and beautiful countryside. In addition, we bought a 17-foot aluminum canoe and began exploring the local waterways. The Shennandoah river was fun. We camped with the cows on the river bank during a two-day trip downstream. The cultural activities and museums were great. We liked it there too.

My job was with the Deputy Chief of Staff for Research and Development in the space area, with emphasis on manned maneuverable, reusable spacecraft.

On unexpected occasions there would be a reunion with someone who had flown the airlift and subsequent discussion about the world and values in life and the effect the Berlin experience had on us.

It was the middle of the week and I had just arrived home when the phone rang. The lady on the other end said, "You don't know me, but my name is Mae Jantzen. My husband, Ernie, and I have been trying to locate you for 17 years. We live in Jamaica, New York and have just found that you live in Washington. We want to take you and your wife out to dinner next week. Will you accept the invitation?" she asked in a burst.

Rather than answering her directly, I wanted to know what it was all about. She assured me they were not selling anything and would tell us all about it after the dinner. From the tone of her voice it sounded like a genuine request that was important to them. That, plus a free meal convinced me.

Arrangements were made and immediately on meeting it was evident that they were wonderful people. After a lovely four-fork meal Ernie and Mae took us to a small meeting room.

"Remember in 1948 when you ran out of parachutes?" Mae began. Then I knew the subject. "We heard the announcement over station WOR that they would play tune requests for those who would pledge to send you handkerchiefs for Operations Little Vittles. We sent you three with our names and address on them. In a couple of weeks we received replies from two of the kids who caught them. We have never been able to have children of our own. We informally adopted those kids long distance." By now her voice was full of emotion and her eyes were moist with feeling.

Mae continued, "We sent those kids 77 care packages. When the little girl grew up and got married we sent the wedding dress and when her baby came we sent the Similac. We saved our money through the years, and just two years ago we finally made it to Berlin to meet "our kids." She was unable to continue for a moment.

"Those kids have blessed our lives. They were an answer to a prayer, and all for such a little thing as three handkerchiefs! I think it was one of the littlest decisions we've made in our lives, writing our names on three handkerchiefs, but the results have exceeded all the good things that have ever happened to us." She paused again to struggle with her composure.

"I know, Mae, for two sticks of gum our lives haven't been the same" I said, taking hold of her hand.

We would spend some good times with this warm New York couple before we left the Pentagon. Little did we know that in a few years we would be in Berlin with the Jantzens meeting their adopted families.

* * * * *

Mercedes was happy with the knowledge that she could fly as well as anyone, but two competing interests entered her life. As thrilling as flying had become, she felt a need for a greater mental challenge. Medicine had always held a special fascination. The fascination turned into a strong desire that had to be dealt with. She wanted to become a physician and help alleviate pain, especially as experienced in children. The long road to that objective began. Along the way the second competing force, in the form of a young man, would intercept that trip. He would eventually become the central force in her life and replace, with their wonderful four children, the several other career opportunities that Mercedes was capabale of fulfilling. She would also contribute leadership to the school system, community, and politics that surrounded their family in the Berlin setting.

* * * * *

One day while I was in the middle of a design problem in the Pentagon, the phone rang and a familiar voice said, "How would you like to get out of the Pentagon a year early and head up a satellite-tracking facility at Vandenberg?" he asked. I struggled to come up with the identification. Then it came. It was my old commander from the space program in Los Angeles, Colonel Dave Lowe. He went on to explain it would entail changing the operation to military from civilian and I would be "frozen" there for four years. After a hasty family conference we accepted and again headed west.

With four years guaranteed in one place we decided to have a house built and settle in. The job was a good challenge, and that made life interesting. The kids always wanted horses and we hadn't had any. We added two horses to the family.

The lovely little town of Santa Maria was laced with horse trails, which made for good times with the boys and girls. Some of the rides were in the moonlight up and down the rolling hills.

July, 1969, came around, and those two sticks of gum were about to change my daily routine once more.

"Colonel, are you one of the guys that flew the airlift to Berlin?" came a voice from the Pentagon. A reply in the affirmative and he was off again with, "Are you Uncle Wiggly Wings?" I acknowledged his question in the affirmative. It sounded like a strange conversation from a full grown man. He continued:

Those kids that caught your parachutes in 1948 and 1949 have gone to the Air Force Colonel commanding Tempelhof, Clark Tate, and told him their little kids want to see what it is like to catch those parachutes. The United States Air Force still runs Tempelhof just like we did during the airlift. Once a year we open up the airfield to the Berliners for two days to show them the cargo planes we have to support the city, if needed, and make a little celebration out of it. We set up a bunch of stands and sell them American ice cream and hamburgers. They love it. Now they want you to come and drop goodies to their kids during that celebration. Will you do it?

It wasn't long until I was on my way. I had sent ahead a list of names from old letters. By the time I got there the Police had located a lot of the '48 and '49 kids with their children. We had a big lunch together, exchanged stories and laughed at the pictures they had sent me in their letters way back then. The children of the old timers got a bigger laugh out of the pictures than the parents did.

It was great to get back on the flight line, but even more nostalgic to fly over their heads and push out the little parachutes just like before. The kids ran just as fast as ever.

Colonel Clark Tate was a great man. It was obvious that the people that worked for him loved him and that he cared about everyone, especially the younger airmen who were struggling to make ends meet. It wasn't an easy life, even in the new Berlin.

That July, 1969, trip to Berlin was topped off with a lovely dinner at Clark's and Betty's house the night before I returned to California. Clark picked me up at the airfield for the ride to his residence in Dahlem for that special meal. His vehicle was a Mercedes complete with a professional German driver and communications equipment.

Clark went on to explain that the Germans provided the support required to run the airfield. Some of the finest German employees labored with pride to keep that airfield in top condition.

"The Berliners are still glad to have us here, although that can't be said for some, but not all, of the young people who didn't experience those former times," he said. A guaranteed functional airport anchoring the lifeline to the West was of ultimate importance to those who valued freedom of choice next to life itself. The investment by the Americans, British, and French was not inconsequential.

Although Clark and I were of the same rank, I marveled at the special kinds of responsibilities that fell on his shoulders and the unusual conditions in which he had to work. Berlin was a very different place from any other Air Force assignment I had seen.

As we pulled to a stop in front of his house, the driver was almost instantly at the side, opening the doors. I looked up at the stately building before us with some awe. There was still enough of the farm boy in me to cause a little gasp.

"Is this your house, Clark?" I asked.

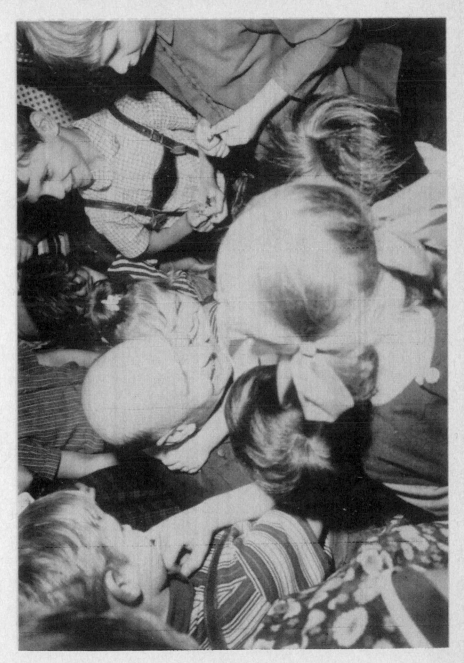

Return to Berlin 1969. Children of the children from 1948 and 1949.

Commemorative drop over Tempelhof, July, 1969.

Children of the 1948 and 1949ers catching the goodies like their parents. Tempelhof, July, 1969.

He nodded."You look a little surprised."

"I am a bit. How many children do you have?" I asked.

"We have one little boy." he replied.

"How many bathrooms do you have?" I asked.

With a surprised look on his face he replied, "There are five or six, I'm not sure. Why do you ask?"

"When I was a kid in Garland and had to go to the bathroom in the winter, I'd have to put my overshoes on first. Since then I've rated houses by the number of those facilities that are inside. Yours gets my top rating for a residence," I replied.

"If you think the outside is impressive, wait till you get inside," he answered matter-of-factly.

Just inside the heavy metal-strip-reinforced front door was a beautiful wooden shrank with an elegant scene of the Last Supper, hand carved in 1625. As we looked around the house, Betty went on to explain that the Germans had provided the place for the Commander of Tempelhof since the Americans took over the base from the Russians in 1945. It was furnished beautifully and Betty took care of it as though it were a German national treasure. "The place costs us our housing allowance but we've never had anything close to like this," Clark said, shaking his head. He went on to explain:

> My job isn't limited to running the airfield and the other interests the Air Force has in Berlin. My second hat consists of being the United States Air Force Representative to the city of West Berlin. In that role we are required to host the International community in this house and at the Air Base. We do what we can to further understanding between our Allies and the six American Sector Borough Mayors, their town councils, and the German residents of the American Sector of West Berlin. It may look like a posh job, but don't you ever believe it. Don't misunderstand me—I like it—but it sure does put some mileage on you. There is some official party or function every night somewhere in the city and we're expected to be there. In between there are shootings or incidents at the wall. I'm on 24-hour call. I've been in a lot of demanding jobs, but none that takes as many hours as this one does. When we're invited, protocol requires that we invite each host back to our place. A lot of our activity is with

the British and French officers and men of the airfields at Gatow and Tegel.

His long explanation was interesting to me and gave me a measure of the dedication of this man. My head was swimming with the unusual nature of his assignment and the thought that this was exactly the social-interaction kind of job that Alta and I had always believed we couldn't handle. What great representatives Clark and Betty were as down-to-earth human beings and Americans.

Betty went into the kitchen and Clark said, "Come on in the Winter Garden a minute and I'll pour you something to drink." We made our way through the attractive dining room into a large light room in the back of the house. It was all glassed in and was filled with green plants. The room was designed as a refuge from the long, dark Berlin winters. Clark pulled back a curtain and exhibited an exceptional assortment of bottles in various conditions of readiness.

"What would you like to drink, Gail? I've got whatever you want. If it is not here it will be in the basement," Clark invited. He went on to explain that the extensive bar was part of what he had to have to fulfill his entertainment responsibilities.

"You know that it's simply part of European custom to socialize with the help of alcohol. It's part of their culture and it isn't so different in the United States. I have a bar just as complete in my office on the flight line for guests who visit out there," he stated.

The explanations gave me a chance to read some of the labels. I had been in many officers' clubs in diverse locations and heard talk of products such as these. At least to a non-expert the selection was impressive.

"Thanks Clark, but could I have a 7-Up or an orange juice?" I asked as tough as I could.

"What's the matter, Gail, do you have ulcers?" asked Clark in a disappointed tone of voice.

"No ulcer. I'm a Mormon. I belong to The Church of Jesus Christ of Latter-day Saints, and the church teaches its members not to drink alcohol. You go ahead and have whatever you'd like," I replied and began to explain further.

But he stopped me with, "I already know quite a bit about your church. I go there occasionally, as I do to the Protestant and Catholic services. That is part of being the commander, at least that's the way

I see my job. I have several Mormon officers and airmen who work for me at Tempelhof. I'll have an orange with you."

Clark impressed me the more as a wonderful, concerned human being without prejudice or class consciousness, but exhibiting qualities that everyone admired. He was very attentive to Betty and their fine young son. On the ride to the house from the airport he had mentioned his deep concern that the job kept him away from his son too much and he had begun to resent it.

"How long is the commander's tour of duty here, Clark?" I asked.

"The longest since 1945 has been two years and eleven months. Don't know if I'll make it that long or not," he answered.

Betty had prepared a wonderful dinner that complemented the warm spirit I felt in the home. The time went all too quickly before it was time to leave.

The big Mercedes and driver were waiting for me at the curb. I gave my appreciation for the wonderful evening to Betty. Clark wrapped that big bear paw of a grip around my hand and said, "Give my best wishes to Alta and have a good trip."

"Sure glad I haven't got your job!" I said with sincerity as I headed for the car. "Thank you again."

My body fit the comfortable cushions of the big Mercedes in just the right places. I dozed off on the way to Tempelhof Airport.

East Berliners flowing into West Berlin, and West Berliners visiting East Berlin, over the Glienicker Bridge shortly after the Berlin Wall was opened, November 1989.

14

Back to Berlin

It was a smooth trip from Berlin to Santa Maria. I was flooded with questions from all of the children about what Berlin was like. "Did you meet any of the children who are now grown up" seemed to be the one of most interest. They all gathered around to hear for the third time how the children of the '48 and '49 kids ran all over the field gathering in the harvest. Some of the little ones were Americans from service families.

Our children particularly liked the story I was told by a Pan American pilot, Captain Bell, about the dainty little American girl who wasn't fast enough or assertive enough to catch any parachutes. She was sobbing quietly when a young German boy came over, put his arm around her and gave her one of his two parachutes with candy.

Alta seemed very interested in the house and what it was like. "How in the world could Betty keep a place that big clean?" Her question showed her empathy for another woman with a tough job. I explained that they were given some help for the house and the yard. Otherwise it would have been impossible.

The work at the tracking station was waiting for me. We had a few power outages which were devastating, but by working all night on two occasions they were able to get back on line without too much damage.

December, 1969, was too soon upon us. Our plans for Christmas were about a month behind schedule. In the middle of breakfast on the second Thursday into the month the telephone rang, "This is

Colonel Ryan calling from Washington. Colonel Halvorsen, have you put in for retirement yet?"

"No, I plan to retire when this tour is finished. Why?" I responded.

"I think you realize that if you have already put in your retirement papers I cannot reassign you. From what you have said, this is notification that you will be assigned overseas in July, 1970," replied Colonel Ryan.

"Wait a minute," I immediately responded with feeling. "I'm on a four-year 'frozen' tour and I've only been here 18 months."

"I am aware of that, Colonel Halvorsen. I am in charge of assignments in your field. There is a priority request for you personally and the Air Force has decided to honor it," he responded with some authority.

"Can you give me some idea why I am being reassigned" I asked as though his answer wasn't heard.

"There are at least two reasons. You have the Tracking Station ahead of schedule on the change-over to a blue suit capability, and the Berliners and General Holzapple want you to replace Clark Tate when he rotates next July" was his matter-of-fact-reply.

"I really care for Berlin and the Berliners but I don't want that assignment, Colonel Ryan. Get someone else who could do a much better job," I quickly suggested.

"I will be glad to relay your feelings, but I'm not sure that it will make any difference. There are a number of Colonels who would give their right arm for the job, and maybe some one else will fill the bill. I'll try," came back his more conciliatory reply.

"Thank you," I breathed as I wiped some beads of sweat from my bald head.

I turned to Alta and said, "Wow! that was close. They wanted us to replace Clark and Betty Tate, but he said he will try to get someone else."

The call was almost forgotten until a few days later when Colonel Ryan was on the phone again with the news that whether I wanted to go or not I would be assigned as the new commander of Tempelhof in July. General Holzapple thought it would be a good idea to have me return to the scene of my airlift days. My trip to Berlin to drop the goodies to the kids of the '48 and '49ers in July 1969 got the Berliners all fired up.

"Well honey, how are we going to handle this one? We've got two full-sized bars to consider," I sighed.

"We are not going to change or try to change anyone's life style, but we should have some say about what we do in our house there," Alta came back. She had always been the real level-headed one of this marriage and had been able to take the rough edges off many a thorny situation.

"There are still the clubs on the Base for those that want something stronger than they will find in the house," she reminded me.

"Well, you can't say this isn't going to be interesting. You are going to like the house," I said with a little more positive tone to my voice.

Alta was doing some hard thinking. She said, "It's one thing to choose what you will drink at someone else's party, but it's quite another to tell your guests what they will drink at your party. That part of it is going to be especially hard for me."

I nodded my agreement, then reminded her of her statement about the clubs on the Base. "It would be a lot simpler if we were just dealing with Americans, but the whole gamut of representatives from the friendly nations plus the Berliners we'll be entertaining is a separate issue," I acknowledged.

We started to think about selling the house we had so recently built and already learned to love. The landscaping wasn't all in yet and that needed to be finished to make it more saleable. At least the kids would be out of school by July and that would give us time to prepare them for the major relocation. That was going to be tough. They had just settled in with friends and were doing very well in their schools.

"Honey, we've got six months to figure it out. Let's not try to do it all at once," my pride and joy reminded me.

It proved to be one of the few times Alta was wrong. It was only a few days before the phone rang again, with Colonel Ryan on the other end.

"There has been a change in your orders, Colonel Halvorsen," he said.

"Great!" I shot back immediately before he was through talking.

Colonel Ryan continued, "You won't think so. You will have to report immediately." I was stunned and the look on my face caused Alta to put down the bowl of bread she was kneading and to join me at the phone.

"Why now?" I asked in a stupor of unbelief.

Colonel Ryan's voice suddenly became softer and more serious. "Clark Tate became very ill a couple of days ago. They took him into the military hospital in Berlin. Exploratory surgery was undertaken to find the cause. They found he is completely riddled with lung cancer and it has spread all through his body. He is at Wilford Hall Hospital in San Antonio right now. They can't really do much for him. They are trying the regular treatments but they don't expect him to live very long. You've got to report as fast as you can get there," came the reply.

That was a greater shock than the news of my early departure. My news was nothing compared to what Clark and Betty had received. I had learned to respect and admire this great man and his family.

It seemed a very long time until I was able to gather my thoughts and then to express my feelings about the tragedy. Then I said, "There is something that you need to know before we report. I am going to call Berlin and have the bar removed from the house."

"I don't know if you can do that, it's part of the job," came back Colonel Ryan's quick response, "I'll have to call you back."

A few days went by and I told Alta, "Honey, I think we are off the hook." The statement was a little premature.

The phone rang. It was Colonel Ryan. "General Holzapple says he doesn't care what you do with the bar. Get to Berlin."

"We'll be there, Colonel Ryan," I said as I hung up the receiver. I turned to Alta and said, "It looks like we are going back to Berlin for an extended stay for two sticks of gum!" I had already been to Berlin and back as a guest three times for those two sticks and would do the same at least eight more times between then and the end of 1989.

With what Berliners meant to me, I knew we would have some wonderful experiences. The worry was, would they like us when they got to know us? "It's going to be interesting to see how we do without the bar in the house and the office," I observed.

The next challenge was to convince our kids it would be great to learn more of other cultures first hand. The family council was set up for Friday night and it was soon apparent that this was not going to be a pushover. Leading the revolt were, surprisingly, the two youngest, Bob—12 years old, and Mike—7 years old. "We don't want to go because of our friends next door and other reasons," they announced in unison.

Denise, 17, and Marilyn, 14, were sorting out their feelings about friends and school. They were non-committal but struggling. Denise was a Senior at Righetti High School with only a few months to go. There was a wonderful family that wanted her to stay with them for that short time and the suggestion seemed possible.

Brad, 19, had a call to go on a mission for the Church and would be flying out the same day I would be leaving for Germany. He would be gone for two years. Marilyn capitulated but the two young boys weren't budging.

I could see it was time to play the ace. "There's something I haven't told you about that house in Berlin," I began. It was necessary to repeat it again to get Bob's and Mike's attention. After a short silence Bob asked, "What's that?"

With an "I thought you would never ask" look and voice I said, "In the back yard is a big old bomb shelter. It has a tunnel from the basement of the house into the shelter. The tunnel is blocked with a brick wall that is getting to be in pretty bad shape. They told me in Berlin that some of the plots on Hitler's life took place in there. I don't know what is inside, but I'll bet you could get those bricks down without much trouble and find out."

"Let's go," was the immediate response.

That taken care of, Alta said, "It would be better if we could all go together. What would that take?" Our new house was the main problem. If we could do something with it we could manage. With a family prayer and a helpful real estate agent the house was rented the next day for three years, starting from whenever we moved out.

We landed in Berlin in a heavy snow storm. "Just like old times," I quipped as the little guys were getting their backpacks on.

"The weather will never replace what we had in California," Marilyn observed as she pulled a scarf tightly around her neck.

Again, just like old times, there was an officer to meet the airplane. This time it was with a smile on his face. His name was Captain Niles Greenlaugh. "The bar is out of the house and the refrigerator is full of milk," he announced almost before anything else.

Niles was one of those Mormons Clark had told me about and was my Information Officer. Niles started right off, "Tomorrow you have

Arrival to take command in Berlin 12 February, 1970.

a special stag function at the French Officer's Club in Tegel Airport. They will probably honor the President of France. You will represent the United States Air Force."

I was anxious for the family to see their new home. I wasn't disappointed when we walked through the front door and heard the pleasant gasps of surprise. It wasn't long before Marilyn, Bob, and Mike were checking the condition of the mortar between the bricks that blocked the tunnel into the bomb shelter. They would be equal to the task.

The next day at the French Officers' Club I was a little apprehensive as I was ushered to the head table and seated between the Commander of the French airfield for Tegel and the Commander of the British airfield at Gatow. There was only time for a brief introduction and to answer a few questions on what I knew of Clark Tate's health. All of us were very concerned for him. I had flown down to San Antonio before leaving California and visited with Clark and Betty. He didn't

General Holzapple (left) and Colonel Smith, acting commander (right) handing me the reins.

look like the same man. Two months was the most anyone could expect that Clark would last.

The program started almost immediately and although he wasn't there it was obvious the next item on the agenda was to toast the President of France. All I could see to drink was the abundance of champagne in glasses placed on silver trays supported by a French legion of waiters in white jackets.

Breaking off in the middle of a sentence, I turned to my French counterpart and whispered, "I am sorry, I will explain later, but if there is to be a toast to your President I need to have orange juice, 7-UP, water or equivalent."

Although his English was quite good my unnatural low whisper was hard to understand, to say nothing of my request, which he finally understood on my third try. He said, "We have everything but Equivalent." I was certainly the dumbest one at the table. All the rest could speak two or more languages.

By this time our intense discussion had attracted the attention of some of the crowd, which had filled the ballroom elbow to elbow. The crowd had run out of small talk and were looking for a diversion. We were providing a good one. The look on the French Commander's face suddenly improved. He said, "That's not German champagne, it's French champagne!"

I wouldn't know until much later in discussions with a wonderful friend and subsequent French Commander, Colonel Marius Nari, that the French personnel in the city disdained German champagne and imported their own from France.

Time was really getting short and it didn't go well that the French Commander's happily diagnosed reason for my reluctance was not the problem. In desperation the French Commander asked, "How about some orange juice?"

"Great!" I replied with relief.

He stood abruptly and waved to an orderly. By now the crowd, without a major preoccupation, was all eyes even before he stood up. The orderly was dispatched posthaste through the crowd toward the kitchen swinging doors. Whispers followed him. I heard a nearby RAF officer query another, "You don't say, a bomb threat?" There wasn't room under the table or I would have given it a try.

All eyes stayed glued to those swinging doors. Open they came and through them the orderly, with a glass of orange juice, moved through the crowd like Walter Peyton behind the "Refrigerator" Perry. There was an almost audible sigh of relief from those assembled when the scene disclosed the purpose of the orderly's trip.

Now they wanted to see where the orange juice was going. "It's the new American Commander," some English speaker said loud enough to burn my ears.

The toast itself was anti-climatic, but not without a few murmurs.

When I arrived home that night I was pretty humble. "How did it go dear?" came the innocent query.

"Better do some sight-seeing, honey," I replied. "We won't be in Berlin very long."

In just a few days I was invited to a very formal affair at the Royal Air Force Officer's Club at Gatow. This time it was just a British and American celebration. There is absolutely no country in the world that can challenge the British when it comes to putting on a formal

Commanders of the three airfields of Free Berlin: Group Captain Wilson, RAF, Commander of Gatow; Myself, Commander of Tempelhof; Colonel Marius Nari, French Air Force, Commander of Tegel; and Alta, my commander.

silver, candlelight-and-lace happening. The British are simply unmatched. Again I was at an elegant head table and a toast to the Queen was quickly proposed. The wine had already been around for the toast but I had my wine glass upside down. I did have a full glass of water.

There had been a few comments among the RAF officers who had been to the event at Tegel, which accounted for much of the attention I was getting. As a result, my toast to the queen in water did not escape very many of those present. There was a fairly high buzz as we put down our glasses. Questions began to be asked about who this new guy was anyway. They were well aware of my Berlin airlift experience. That account had been in all the papers on our arrival but it didn't explain where this kind of behavior was coming from.

The next official obligation was to introduce ourselves to the International Berlin community through the traditional cocktail party in our home. This would be the moment of truth. The protocol officer said there would be about 100 guests from the Berlin protocol list. They were people we would be seeing at social events and interacting with during official duties as the Tempelhof Commander and the USAF Representative to the city. I began to wonder why a beet thinner and later an engineer got his wife into this kind of a predicament.

The waiter service for official receptions in our home was furnished by the waiters and waitresses from the Tempelhof Officers' Club. All of them were highly professional and prided themselves on being able to provide a guest his or her favorite drink without asking for a preference.

Alta and I didn't feel at all good about our game plan for that night. We had three large, beautiful, crystal punch bowls filled with non-alcoholic punch. The punch was of different colors and textures. One had a goodly supply of dry ice with the attendant cloud of vapor upon which was focused a red and green rotating spot light. It looked absolutely wicked.

The palms of our hands were clammy when the doorman welcomed the first arrival. As the people came through the door they greeted us warmly and headed for their favorite waiter. From the corner of my eye I could see the waiters and waitresses slowly shake their heads and point to the punch bowls.

There were some whose preference was well served and some who drank of it anyway. There were a number who left early.

We didn't feel very good about ourselves and reflected on some of the thoughts we had in Santa Maria before we came. We went to bed a thoroughly discouraged team that night.

The one thing that we completely misjudged was the tolerance and understanding of this principled, wonderful international community. In short order the word was around the entire circuit about why we were like we were. The people were absolutely fantastic. How we learned to love them and to anticipate an invitation to their homes. It was an exceptional opportunity to learn more about their backgrounds and special interests and tell them more about ourselves.

It wasn't long before we were greeted at their receptions by waiters with a tray of assorted soft drinks. I think some of them would have fought if we had tried to switch. How welcome they made us feel. Coming as we had with our apprehension, the acceptance was even more sweet.

It wasn't many days before Marilyn, Bob, and Mike came upstairs with mud and dirt smudges all over them. Success! They had dug their way into the bunker to find a partial cave in, water, old rusted cots, a few emergency supplies, and an empty petrol can.

"There must be some old guns or secret papers somewhere under that cave in," Mike said while he stripped off his soiled clothes. I could see that this would be a long-term project.

The reaction of the Berliners who had been kids during the airlift was terrific. Almost every one who had caught a parachute wanted us to come to dinner. The problem of selecting which invitations to accept was unsolvable. Our official duties had us out every night except for our family home evening night. On Fridays and weekends we attended two or more functions each night. If we accepted one private invitation how would we turn down another one just as worthy? We tried to get the word out to the public through the Information Officer. The effort and resultant understanding

My desk at Tempelhof, with a reminder of why I'm there.

were partially successful.

Alta worked out some very good things to serve at the frequent receptions that we hosted. She more than made up for whatever else we didn't provide.

We had some good times in that fabulous big house. Bob, Mike, and Marilyn were exploring areas I didn't know existed. I wasn't home enough to keep track of all that was going on, and there was plenty. I thought back to what Clark had said about the lack of time to spend with his son and I felt that pressure strongly.

It was but a few months before Denise joined us and quite a while longer when Brad finished his mission and arrived bright-eyed and bushy tailed.

As weeks went into months there were valuable contacts with Berliners who wanted to talk about the time of the blockade. They

From left to right: Brad, Marilyn, Mike, Alta, Me, Bob, and Denise.

would approach me in the street and at Tempelhof Open House events to recount with glowing enthusiasm the experience they had in catching a parachute from one of my buddies or myself.

On the Tempelhof flight ramp at one Open House, a mature young man came up to me and said he had been flown out of Berlin by the RAF with other children during the blockade. He had returned afterward and eventually married a lovely Berlin girl. He knew that his wife knew of me and wanted our family to come to their house for dinner. I reluctantly gave him the same reply as I had so many others. His name was Peter Wild.

During these Open House celebrations some would touch my arm in the middle of a hamburger or ice cream and with tears in their eyes tell me how much the flour, coal, and medicine meant to them during the airlift times. The expressed gratitude was of the same magnitude that the flour "unloaders" had expressed on my first airlift flight. Their feelings were for all the aircrews and the ground personnel and the 31 Americans, 39 British, and five Germans who gave their lives for the freedom of Berlin.[47]

During the two days of each year's Open House activity, several hundred thousand would visit the exhibits. Many lined up, rain or shine, to go through the old C-54 Rosinen Bomber.

In 1971 I had arranged to have the C-54 airlift veteran diverted to Tempelhof from a flight to the bone yard. The people of Berlin named it the "Rosinen Bomber." It became a memorial to all the aircrews, ground personnel, and other aircraft that flew the airlift. The aircraft is at Tempelhof today as a memorial.[48]

The C-54 I brought in for a memorial. The Berliners named it "The Rosinen Bomber." (1971)

In 1971 we were able to get the C-5 Galaxy for an Open House. It was the first time in Berlin and a real sensation. I was able to fly in with it and try the controls coming through the corridor. We extended our pattern to include more of East Berlin than usual: the Pope's revenge [the bulb on the television tower reflecting a cross], and the Brandenburg Gate. It was a reminder to the Soviets that if we could supply the city with 225 C-54s it would be a real snap with 17 of the C-5s.

That night we held the Open House reception in that C-5, orchestra and all. The city dignitaries were impressed with the capability of what certainly General Tunner had envisioned as an aircraft of the future.

At this same Open House I was approached by an East German who had escaped before the wall was erected. He told of several little Russian kids who had caught some parachutes when I was dropping them over East Berlin. These children were as thrilled as any others who were surprised by a small parachute descending above their heads. It was the first I had heard that a Russian child had been a recipient.

In 1972, a Four Power accord was reached that liberalized travel for West Berliners and West Germans to visit their relatives in the East. It was an exciting time as I had the opportunity to provide space at Tempelhof for the Ambassadors to hold some of their discussions.

Not long after the accord a West Berliner visited with me just after returning from his first stay with his East German cousin. His last visit was before the wall went up on 13 August, 1961. The West Berliner was about 39 years old and remembered the blockade as a young man. Now it was winter time, 1973. Even though there was a lack of sun he had a deep tan.

His East German cousin had asked, "Where did you get that tan?" The West Berliner answered, "Remember years ago how our families traveled to that ski chalet in Saanen Moser, Switzerland in the middle of the winter?" His cousin had a moist, far-away look in his eye as he simply nodded his head. "It was great skiing this year. Wish you could have been there," the West Berliner concluded. Too soon it was time to go. The cousin accompanied the West Berliner to the Wall at Check Point Charlie.

There the armed guards separated the Easterner from the Westerner. One had his freedom to travel and the other would loose his life if he attempted to make the same journey.

The West Berliner said to me, "Many have left all their worldly belongings and have given their lives in an unsuccessful attempt to enjoy the freedom we take for granted. We West Berliners are still very grateful for the airlift. That visit to my cousin really reminded me what would have happened to us without it."

He shook my hand and hailed down a taxi in the Luftbrucke Platz for his home in Dahlem. It would be 16 years before an escape attempt would not require bartering one's life for freedom in the West. The pain in the mind of the East German cousin would remain until it would be released in an explosion of feeling on top of the Wall with his countrymen and West Berliners, on 9 November, 1989.

We ended up being in Berlin four years. The myriad of contacts and experiences that came to our family would take too long to relate. Let me conclude with but two examples of contacts with the incredible Berliners.

Completing the four years as commander of Tempelhof, 12 February, 1974, General David Jones officiating.

The first involved Al Wehr. Al was a young man at the end of the war. He and his family huddled in their war-torn apartment waiting for the advancing Russians to knock on the door. Stories had preceded the advancing waves of troops. Reports were that the Soviet behavior with the conquered differed according to the particular Army Unit, the personal nature of the soldier, and the sex and age of the conquered. The first troops to sweep through the city were, for the most part, professional soldiers. Their behavior was much better than the conduct of those who were to follow. Many Berliners were warned by the Russians about the Soviet soldiers in the second wave.

What would the troops be like that would soon be storming through the door that held the Wehr family's gaze? The heavy thump of the big guns and the scream of the rockets had died away and now only occasional bursts of automatic weapons fire could be heard.

Then it came—the crash of a rifle butt against the door and right behind it a young Russian in a uniform decorated with the grime of battle. The soldier was alone. There was almost a friendly air about him as he began to collect wrist watches when a greeting by Al in Russian stopped the young man short. A brief, friendlier exchange followed, the watches returned, and the captor wished them well. He disappeared out the door followed by sighs of relief. Soon his heavy boots could be heard back and forth in the apartment above and then the unmistakable sound of a toilet flushing. That noise acted as though it were a starter's pistol for a race to begin. Immediately the heavy pair of boots came thumping down the stairs and again presented their owner at the Wehr's front door. This time the mood was not as friendly.

"Where are the cherries?" the Russian demanded in his native tongue.

"What cherries?" innocently asked Herr Wehr.

"The ones that came straight down from above," answered the Russian, brandishing his weapon.

The people in the apartment upstairs had somehow obtained the rare cherries and were saving them for a special occasion. They were covered with dust. A bowl with water was evident and the Russian had decided to wash them. While in the process he had inadvertently pulled the chain and the cherries disappeared toward the Wehr's apartment. The demand was to return them forthwith. A labored explanation and a demonstration on the Wehr's fixture finally sent the soldier on down the street to continue the occupation.

Al and his wonderful wife, Troude, have been two of the greatest ambassadors for understanding that we met in Berlin. For over 43 years they have dedicated their time and their home to guests of many nationalities, cultures, and from every station in life. Their exceptional children added a family dimension which extended the warmth of the welcome to more than just adults. They have hosted hundreds in an effort to understand others and to be understood.

The second case came to our attention in the Fall of 1972. One invitation kept coming: "Please come to our house. Bring your two youngest sons and join us for dinner. We have two boys of the same age."

For a year and a half there didn't seem to be a good time to accept this frequent invitation for a private, personal dinner. The friendly persistence and genuine nature of the request finally overcame our "mind set in concrete" mentality. We cancelled an official function with apologies, dressed the boys in their Sunday clothes and proceeded to the residence listed as 15 Hahnelstrasse.

We found ourselves on the doorstep of an old apartment building with overhanging balconies draped in flowers enhanced by a simple but elegant entryway. There were roses and green plants growing in the space on either side of the entry sidewalk. The building was not far from Tempelhof Airport. We were graciously greeted by a lovely young couple and their two sons.

Even before introductions they ushered us in and up some winding stairs to their refinished apartment. Without delay the young mother took us to the front room which held an old-fashioned china cabinet filled with artifacts of years gone by.

Among the little china figures nestled a letter, the object of her attention. She reached in, retrieved the old envelope as though it were very precious and very fragile, and with shaking hand held it out to me with a smile mixed with a look of keen anticipation.

"Please read this," she said in a voice that betrayed her emotions.

I quickly slipped the letter from its envelope. The first thing I noticed was the date, 4 November 1948, 24 years ago, and immediately thereafter the salutation,

> "Meine liebe Mercedes,
>
> Thank you for your small letter. Not every day I fly over your house but surely often.
>
> I didn't know that in Hahnelstrasse there lived such a nice little girl. If I could fly a few rounds over Friedenau I surely would find the garden with the white chickens but for this there is not enough time.
>
> I hope that through what is with this letter I give you a little joy.
>
> Dein Shokoladenonkel
>
> Gail Halvorsen

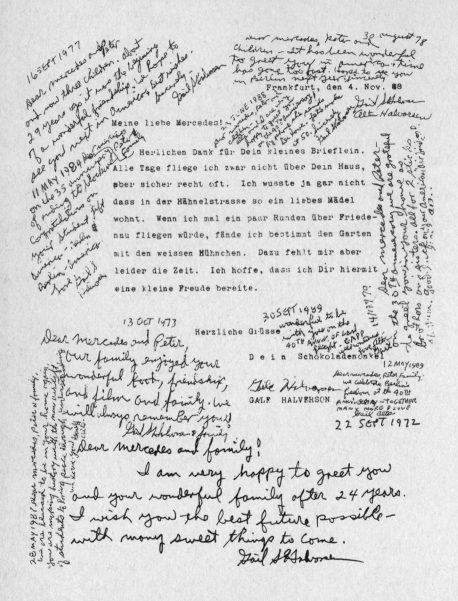

Frankfurt, den 4. Nov. 88

Meine liebe Mercedes!

Herzlichen Dank für Dein kleines Brieflein.
Alle Tage fliege ich zwar nicht über Dein Haus,
aber sicher recht oft. Ich wusste ja gar nicht
dass in der Hähnelstrasse so ein liebes Mädel
wohnt. Wenn ich mal ein paar Runden über Friedenau fliegen würde, fände ich bestimmt den Garten
mit den weissen Hühnchen. Dazu fehlt mir aber
leider die Zeit. Ich hoffe, dass ich Dir hiermit
eine kleine Freude bereite.

Herzliche Grüsse

D e i n   Schokoladenonkel

The letter I sent Mercedes on 4 November, 1948.

"You silly pilot, I am Mercedes. If you will take five steps over to
the window you will see for yourself where the white chickens were,"

she said with a twinkle in her eye. "I carefully rationed the candy and gum, and ate it little by little, but I will keep the letter forever," she added with meaning.

In a moment we were at the window. Down below in the horseshoe-shaped backyard was the place that held the white chickens and a shade tree like the one used for fuel during the blockade. Limbs from the old tree had warmed the broth made from the chickens that were not laying eggs.

Mercedes and me, 1972.

"This is the same window from which I watched the airplanes come in to land and hoped that a little package would come into my own backyard. In bad weather and at night the sound of the engines would tell us if there was trouble in landing or in finding the airport. The least difference in the comforting sounds caused us some alarm. In the beginning we couldn't sleep well because of the steady noise. Later we couldn't sleep well if the noise wasn't steady," Mercedes concluded.

She then introduced her children and husband Peter Wild, an outstanding science teacher in the Berlin school system. I had met Peter many months before during an Open House at Tempelhof.

In February, 1974, we had been in Berlin four years, one year and a month longer than any of the Tempelhof Commanders since 1945. Our length of stay greatly exceeded anyone's expectations, most of all, ours. The assignment, rather than being one to dread, was one of the most moving human experiences that we could have imagined.

Peter Wild is a great organizer and father as well as an exceptional teacher. He and Mercedes make a special team with a strong family of four wonderful children. They have provided a place for many visitors to stay. Alta and I, and at different times our children, have slept in the bedroom from which Mercedes wrote that 1948 letter. Now, it was our turn to host them.

Berlin Governing Mayor, Klaus Schutz, presents the German Service Cross to the Order of Merit and a Brandenburg Gate painting for service provided as Tempelhof commander from 1970 to 1974. Mrs. Halvorsen on the left.

After our return to Utah we invited Peter, Mercedes and children to visit us in Provo. During that visit we met Brent Chambers, a German teacher at Provo High School. When two great teachers of their calibre get together something good is going to happen. In this case, it was the birth of a new airlift, an airbridge of understanding from West Berlin to Provo, Utah.

A fully developed high school student exchange resulted with Peter being the outstanding organizer and manager in Berlin and Brent, later assisted by Barry Olson, of Timpview High School, doing the same on the Provo end.

Since 1980, hundreds of West Berlin students have visited Western America and have experienced the local culture by staying with host

The Berlin exchange students visit Brigham Young University.

The principal organizers of the Airlift of Understanding, Berlin-Provo, Brent Chambers, Provo High School and Peter Wild, Berlin. (Provo, September, 1989)

families. A similar number of Utah students have had a like experience with families in Berlin.

This new Berlin Airlift is alive and well and has been identified by the German Government as one of the best German-American exchanges. This operation, organized by Peter Wild and Brent Chambers, is an important extension of: one of the greatest air relief efforts in history, an interested little girl, some white chickens, and two sticks of gum. Much of the life blood now comes from the concerned German-American Partnership Program, Ministry of Foreign Affairs in Bonn.

Two of my Berlin trips occurred in May and September 1989, the 40th-year commemoration of breaking the blockade. The September trip included about 200 airlift veterans and their partners which made it a special memory.

One of the events was an air drop of little parachutes over Tempelhof from a Military Airlift Command C-130 to some Berlin children of 1989. Two of my sons were with me in the Candy Bomber. Four of the waiting children belonged to Mercedes and Peter. Three belonged to Alta and me plus seven of our grandchildren. It was the 30th of September 1989, 40 years exactly from the date of the last airlift C-54 flight to Berlin.

After the candy bombing we parked the C-130 on the ramp where in 1948-49 the C-54s had been lined up nose to tail in front of Hitler's familiar terminal building. On that spot there was a warm gathering with Alta, our five children and their spouses, our grandchildren, Mercedes, Peter, and their children all mixed together with the 1989

A Dick Kramer 8' x 16' oil painting of the airlift's many tasks. Presented to President Reagan in Berlin on the City's 750 anniversary, June 1987. It now hangs in the Tegel airfield reception hall.

Signing autographs in the Rosinen Bomber, May 1987.

These were some of the memories that were recreated on the Tempelhof flight ramp on 30 September 1989.

Our family in East Berlin, 30 September, 1989, just before the great exodus.

The 30 September, 1989 Candy Bomber after the drop to the children. The Halvorsen family with Peter Wild on the far right.

Berlin kids and 200 airlift veterans. I had stood on this place as a bachelor in 1948-49.

Suddenly a memory as clear as yesterday crowded out the present. The soft-but-distinct features of a little girl's face with big brown eyes, moist with emotion, came before me. Her hands outstretched, fingers lovingly wrapped about a gift that must be given, were presenting a fuzzy, brown teddy bear with worn elbows. All too soon she curtseyed, waved goodby and was gone. Was that her standing just over there, her several children's children receiving chocolate, now not so rare, from the airlift veterans? Each veteran had similar memories of this historic place.

The wiggle in my arms brought me completely back to a little girl of the present. My granddaughter, Heidi, was struggling to remove a candy bar wrapper. Her big expressive eyes glistened with anticipation.

That evening our family gathered in Peter and Mercede's apartment for a reunion none of us will ever forget. Later that night, beds and floors were covered with members of our family. The old 1948 letter looked down from its perch in the china cabinet with apparent approval at what it had been able to accomplish. It was 30 September, 1989.

While we slept, tens of thousands of East Germans were desperately preparing their young families to flee their familiar surroundings, homes, belongings, jobs, friends, and extended family for what the West Berliners had put their lives on the line to obtain in 1948-49, freedom to choose.

Within a matter of weeks over 150,000 East Germans would, like a tidal wave, sweep in a torrent around the obstructive Wall and its armed guards to freedom in the West. On the 4th of November, 1989, nearly a million East Germans would converge on East Berlin demanding the resignation of the 44-man East German Cabinet which would occur a few days later. The East German Politburo would be the next to fall. The constitution would be amended to exclude the right of the Communist Party to run the government.

The wild fires in Poland and Hungary, ignited by the spark of perestroika, encouraged by Mikhail Gorbochev, and borne of economic necessity, had leaped the borders and were out of control in hard-line East Germany, Czechoslovakia and Romania. The uniform cry was, "FREEDOM! FREEDOM! FREEDOM!"

In the early going it was reminiscent of a similar crowd in West Berlin at the Reichstag on 9 September, 1948. The call was the same and their deafening cheer answered Mayor Rueter's passionate plea, "People of the world, look upon this city! You cannot, you must not forsake us!"

Now, 41 years later, East German voices had reached a crescendo on behalf of East Germany and East Berlin, "Freiheit! Freiheit! Freiheit!" Truly a historic time and a stunning chapter in the "tale of two cities." But one of the great moments was yet to come.

It was 9 November, 1989. The masses of humanity crowding the streets of East Berlin had not diminished much from the demonstration a few days before. The East German cousin stood looking out his window into the street now filled with excitement. His 20-year-old son had already joined the milling crowd. The previous night the cousin had told his son about their family's pre-war traditions. One was an annual family winter trek to Switzerland for a ski vacation. The cousin hadn't forgotten the deep winter tan exhibited by his Western relative when he visited that January in 1973. Insignificant as the tan was, it provided the object for resentment of the "system" that had become almost unbearably oppressive.

The cousin joined his countrymen in the streets. Soon he found himself near Checkpoint Charlie, pushed by the crowd and inexplicably being drawn to the Wall like a mongoose to a coiled cobra. The partially retracted fangs were evident in the guard tower guns.

Then, almost as in a slow-motion nightmare, he found himself in the death strip with men and women all about him. He couldn't believe what his eyes were telling him. Every nerve was strung taut and each muscle braced against any eventuality.

He was almost to the Wall when a brute force followed by a searing pain between his shoulder blades flung him head-long into the dirt. His fingers clutched the loose soil that soon changed to mud. Some years before, not far from this place, Peter Fechter had fallen in a hail of bullets, the soil wet with his blood. Peter had slowly escaped through death.

The cousin stirred; others were getting up. Then it came again, water cannon at close range. An uncomparable feeling of relief swept over him; his whole frame shook. The guns were silent!

In moments all were at the Wall. Some stood on other's shoulders. Hundreds followed. The twain met, East and West in an explosion borne of 40 years in Stalinist bondage. It was over. Joy was rampant. A new era had dawned. Wave after wave of humanity from both sides swept over the Wall, celebrating its death, burying it with bodies thirsting to be free.

Now its former prisoners beheld what seemed to be the promised land. In a massive outpouring the East Germans and West Berliners were atop the Wall in each other's arms. Eyes were filled with tears, faces filled with expressions of joyful unbelief, and a spontaneous demonstration of enthusiasm borne of hope for things to come was everywhere. Most East Germans would look and return to their homes. Many would be disappointed with what they found.

At the end of the war East Germany came under a repressive regime. The airlift intervened for West Berlin; the East Germans paid with their blood for the 1953 revolt. The thread of freedom was just below the surface. They left in droves in 1961. The regime countered with the Wall. Almost 200 East Germans sacrificed their lives at that unholy altar for the desire to be free. Now the East Germans share what the West Berliners gained from refusing the Soviet 1948 food rations.

If controlled change can continue, the world could enter a new era where a Berlin-type airlift may not again be needed and a similar wall not again be built. However, starvation will not disappear and barriers to human understanding, physical or invisible, will continue to be erected to challenge our very existence and progress; person to person, nation to nation. May we be up to the task as the Berliners were. We haven't seen the solution to world problems but we have seen some progress.

On a visit to Rhein-Main, before boarding a flight to Berlin it was wonderful to see the majestic Airlift Memorial, its graceful arc a mirror image of its older [1951] sister at Tempelhof, standing as a sentinel over the gateway to the air corridors aimed at Berlin. It is a modern recommitment to man's freedom to choose.

Dedication of the Gail S. Halvorsen Elementary School at Rhein-Main, June 1985. From left to right: Chaplain (Col.) Mundinger; Mr. Leonard, Principal; Dr. Blackstead, Director of Department of Defense Dependant Schools, Germany; Col. (Ret.) Gail S. Halvorsen; Mrs. Ann Tunner, General Tunner's widow; Col. Peoples, 435th Tactical Airlift Wing Commander; and Mr. Brun, William H. Tunner Junior High School Principal.

Before my flight departed an event of special interest held me entranced. It was a visit to a school not far from the indestructible old barn where I slept those years ago. In 1989 our eldest son, Brad, his wife, Gaylene, and five children were stationed with the Air Force at Rhein-Main. Three of the five grandchildren had attended the school which bears their last name. The name of the school came from that chance meeting with some Berlin children of like ages at a barbed-wire fence 41 years ago.

As I strapped myself in the seat of that shiny, modern jet aircraft at Rhein-Main for the trip to Berlin, the flight attendant asked with a friendly smile:

"Will this be your first flight to Berlin?"

"No, I have been to Berlin and back before," I replied and under my breath said to myself, "for two sticks of gum."

I closed my eyes and my mind went back over 41 years. I could hear the roar of hundreds of Twin Wasp R-2000 engines driving three-bladed propellers. I could see them being maintained by valiant aircraft mechanics and being flown by hundreds of dedicated aircrews, determined to help the Berliners save themselves.

The freshness of the memory and the grand scale of the operation drowned out the sound of the jet engines of our modern craft as we lifted from the ground at Rhein-Main for the corridor to Berlin.

Mercedes and Peter would be there, and also like Jericho, a wall that came tumbling down.

15

Little Decisions
Continue To Be Important

This chapter is a mixture of several events that have occurred since the book was first printed in 1990. Many of them happened as a continuing, direct result of meeting those Berlin children at the Tempelhof fence in July of 1948.

Berlin, Dec. 1993. Farewell to the Allies in Berlin. There was a candy drop and these kids were some of the recipients.

The euphoria attending the first few months after the fall of the Berlin wall gave way to the hard and difficult work to find solutions to new challenges.

In the previous chapter I expressed the hope that the world would not require another Berlin-type airlift, but I recognized that starvation will not disappear and that barriers to human understanding, physical or invisible, will continue to be erected to challenge our very existence and progress person-to-person, or nation-to-nation.

Since that was written, the world has experienced events where lives have been saved and freedom championed by the employment of humanitarian airlift. One of the many trouble spots was and is the former Yugoslavia-Hercegovina-Bosnia area. This remains a deeply divided, devastated land filled with cries of human anguish. There are cries for dead or missing loved ones, homes destroyed or uninhabitable, and loss of personal peace with little hope for the future.

Not long ago a new-generation aircraft, a USAF C-17 cargo aircraft, arrived in Bosnia just in time to off-load its cargo of armed tanks. Crewmen were in the tank turrets and at the controls ready to fire, if necessary, as they rolled out of the C-17. Those they faced were about to violate their pledge to keep the peace. By this exceptional force projection, peace was preserved and lives were spared by the timely intervention of another airlift. This is the business of airlift—to support a Berlin or to prevent a war. Much of our airlift is done at the request of the United Nations.

Desired airlift capability is a collection of airlift resources. When properly managed, they will give the user the required throughput (materials), when and where the area commander needs it. The Air Force and Army team cooperation, as demonstrated in the episode, is not an isolated case.

Some years earlier, on 16 March 1994, the phone rang in my room in the Gateway Hotel on Rhein-Main AFB Germany, which was only 200 yards from the barracks I lived in while flying the Berlin Airlift in 1948-1949.

"General Loranger has approved your request to fly an 'Operation Provide Promise' night-support mission to refugees in Bosnia. You leave tonight at 18:00 hours. You will be provided necessary flight gear and a flack jacket. Any questions?" said the precise but friendly voice of the General's secretary. "Great! I'll be there," I responded.

Gail S. Halvorsen Col. USAF Ret. In flight gear ready for Bosnia. The flight suit below the jacket is his 1948 Berlin Aircraft suit. Rhein-Main Airlift Memorial in background. 1994.

My thoughts went back to those two sticks of gum and the 30 kids at the barbed wire fence in July 1948. I mused, "If it wasn't for those kids I wouldn't be here now. It is the little decisions that have determined the big things that have happened in my life."

I was excited to compare this airlift with the airlift to Berlin. The prospect of getting back in the air aboard a military airlifter with a blue-suit crew was like a transfusion. To help someone who is desperately in need gives the provider and the receiver a warm fuzzy. That feeling scratches an itch inside that, in my case, doesn't happen often enough.

The next few hectic hours were spent at various supply points getting outfitted with the cold-weather flight gear. Concurrently I was concerned about getting parachutes made so that the Bosnian kids could have the same experience as the kids in Berlin. The Rhein-Main AFB parachute section came to our rescue with parachute cloth cut to just the right size. A quick trip to the Base Exchange provided the chocolate payload and some suspicious looks.

The crew briefing brought back old memories. The briefing officer droned, "Some ground fire possible, little chance of opposition aircraft, and the weather is a bit spotty." With our fighters in the area, things looked good.

The veteran crew from Pope AFB, North Carolina, under the command of Cpt. Bryan White, now with C-130s in Alaska, made me feel right at home and I tried to stay out of the way.

Pope AFB crew. Aircraft Commander Capt. Bryan White is on the back row, third from left. The navigator is on his left.

Our target was approximately 70,000 refugees in the mountains about 20 miles out of Sarajevo, near the little town of Bradina. Our bombs were six pallets of food rations, blankets, medicine and other necessities. Each pallet weighed about 3500 pounds. The cardboard box with parachutes and candy bars was fastened to the last pallet to leave the cargo bay. A lanyard attached to the box would pull it open as the pallet departed. The tiny parachutes would then be free to scatter over a wide area.

En Route to Bosnia. Adding a few more parachutes. The same 1948 flight suit. Capt. Ray Cornelius, right.

Some of the aircraft dropping this night would use a similar procedure to drop tons of Humanitarian Daily Rations (HDRs) and Meals Ready to Eat (MREs), except they would have no parachutes! Their cardboard container, a Tri-Wall Aerial Distribution System (TRIADS), would be pulled apart by its lanyard as the box left the aircraft. The airstream would scatter the individually wrapped meals over a very large area. The meal's package provided some drag to slow the decent and the meals, for the most part, survived to do the same for the recipients. Advantages are a much higher drop payload and the meals are less expensive.

For those of us dropping supplies on pallets, it was a different story. Each pallet was supported by a large sheet of plywood that would be used by enterprising recipients with other sheets to provide shelters. Hopefully the large parachute on each 3500-pound pallet would slow it down enough to allow the refugees to dodge the impact. There had been previous reports of close calls, but no complaints against these welcome intruders hurtling out of the night sky. An organized distribution system on the ground kept some from seeing how close they could get to the gift without being smashed.

There were six C-130s assigned to our target. Our aircraft was first in the six-ship trail formation. We came down the east coast of Italy and then across the Adriatic Sea to cross the coast of Croatia at 16,000 feet mean sea level. One after another, all lights on and in the aircraft were turned out except interior red lighting which was necessary for the operation of the aircraft. The tinted light from the navigator's scope revealed the five blips in trail behind us, all at a proper and safe distance.

The navigator now had the formidable responsibility of using his ground-mapping radar to find the mountain valley that sheltered the refugees. He would need to call for the release of the pallets at just the right moment. There were no transmissions from our aircraft, but we could receive information on the wind at altitude levels below us. The wind direction and velocity were provided by orbiting fighter aircraft whose transmission to a central control aircraft (AWAC) was relayed to us. These winds would be entered in the plane's computer. The drop trajectory would then be determined and thereby the best estimated release point. We were well dressed with flack jackets and under cabin pressurization until we neared the drop zone. At 16,000 feet we were about 12,800 feet above the mountains.

In 1948 and 1949 we didn't have flack jackets or parachutes on the Berlin Airlift. We did have plenty of Russian Yak-3 fighters buzzing us and looking us over. We didn't worry too much because President Truman had the B-29s on alert in England. Stalin knew the Super Forts had the bomb capability and Truman wasn't afraid to protect those unarmed transports.

To my knowledge, except for a case with the British, the Russian ground fire in the Berlin corridors didn't get up to our flight level. There was no such guarantee over Bosnia.

I admit to scanning for ground fire or any unusual lights in the sky. We did have decoy flares we could deploy in case a surface-to-air missile came looking for our particular aircraft. The 1500 pounds of armor plate around the cockpit was also a pretty good security blanket.

Nearing the target, Captain White gave an adequate warning of depressurization and notice to don our oxygen masks. Soon the large cargo doors swung open wide with a roar. The aircraft nose pitched up as the rollers under the pallets delivered over 20,000 pounds of life support out the back into the pitch-black night. Hopefully it would land safely, and close to those in greatest need. Tail-end Charlie was the box of "Little Vittles," candy for kids.

In my mind's eye I placed myself on the ground with the 70,000 refugees, faces skyward, awaiting our aircraft. Ears would be strained for the first sound of those propjet engines! Where would the pallets land?

Flack jackets on. Going on oxygen ready to depressurize.
Halvorsen left, Maj. Rory Gardner right.

Where could I wait where it would be safe? If I could only see the pallets coming before they arrived. Listen for the rigging cords cutting the air and the air spilling out of the big parachute. The louder the noise, the closer the danger. If I were extra lucky, a few moments later I could get hit in the head with a "stealth" parachute and a candy bar.

But more important, imagine the anticipation for the blankets as a protection from the snow and the prospect of food for the stomach. The distinctive click of the metal cargo doors coming closed and locked brought me back on board.

That night 12 USAF, 1 French Air Force, and 2 German Luftwaffe aircraft delivered 104.6 tons of life-giving materials to people in three locations—people the crews most likely would never see.

During the Berlin Airlift, coal was dropped into the Olympic Stadium, but it was a very short experiment. Without proper equipment for air drop, the ground unloading capabilities at Tempelhof, Gatow, and Tegel made landing first the best method under the circumstances. I did like the few seconds it took to unload the C-130 at 16,000 feet but I missed seeing, meeting, and hearing from the people with the upturned faces like we did in Berlin. Words of receipt and gratitude came out of Bosnia, but it was a very slow process, for reasons readily apparent.

I like that C-130. A few years before I was in a C-130 with my son Bob as his crew delivered food, fuel, and newspapers to very remote bases in Alaska. The C-130, C-54, and the C-17 are my favorite cargo aircraft. I was a willing passenger in a C-17 during the Air Force 50th anniversary celebration at Scott AFB in June 1997. Just before that I had flown by in a C-47 and made a simulated "Little Vittles" drop. What a contrast!

The C-17 has exceeded all nominally projected in-commission and performance estimates. If we are going to continue to be an active player in the relief of suffering and champion peace with deterrence, we need more C-17s than we have to replace the aged and weary C-141s and the C-130s.

One of my soul's friendly glows is fed by the memory of military members and their families generously giving of time and resources to those in need, even former enemies. The Berlin Airlift is a precise example.

Another example occurred at Rhein-Main AFB just before Christmas in 1993. Chaplain Steven A. Schaick, Linda Young, and Gail Loranger were a few who organized and supported "Operation Provide Santa" for the surviving kids in Bosnia.

In his letter asking for volunteers, Chaplain Schaick wrote:

Since July 1992, Operation Provide Promise, a multi-national humanitarian airland/airdrop mission, has been providing food and medical supplies to the former Yugoslavia from Rhein-Main Air Force Base, Germany. Despite the relief offered by this operation, many will face starvation and death brought on by the deprivations of both war and winter. The most innocent of these victims are the children. Operation

Provide Santa is a non-political, non-profit volunteer program patterned after the historic Berlin Airlift and designed to enhance Operation Provide Promise by offering shoes, clothing, toys and candy to children.

Tons of warm clothes, candy and toys were donated by caring military and civilian individuals and families. These donations were dropped to the refugee children in the regular food pallets.

Gail Loranger at Rhein-Main AFB asked me to write a letter of appreciation to those volunteers who made "Operation Provide Santa" possible. Dated 15 November 1993, I wrote in part:

Forty five years ago right now, whatever moment you read this message, the air around Rhein-Main reverberated with the sound of reciprocating engines propelling aircraft on wings of mercy, filled with tons of dried food or coal for innocent victims in Berlin who were caught in a struggle to keep their free agency.

If you pause a moment you may hear the different sound of jet engines intent on a very similar, even a more dangerous mission. Added to the threat of starvation for the innocent victims is the possibility of violent and sudden death. Your personal efforts on behalf of the peoples of the former Yugoslavia have not gone unnoticed in the world.

Unfortunately it is most often the case that when power is unrighteously exercised by selfish adults, it is the innocent victims, the children, who disproportionately suffer. This seems true whether it occurs in our homes or in the world.

You have identified yourself as a caring person who stepped forward to do whatever you could to provide some measure of brief and momentary happiness to a young spirit whose world has run amuck and whose tomorrow may never come. You have helped provide a light in the middle of a nightmare. You have provided that which cannot be bought: Hope.

At the time I wrote that letter I had no idea that a few months later I would be in one of the Operation Provide Promise aircraft with candy on parachutes, headed for Bosnia and the children.

After my flight I was able to visit with the United Nations Inspection team at Rhein-Main AFB where the great airdrop bundles were being assembled. The team was headed by majors from the Netherlands and Portugal. The members of the team were: Halilovic Mufid (Bosnia, Sarajevo), Klacar Neboisa (Serbian), Mitrovic Slobodan (Serbian), and Turtkovic Vlatko (Croatian). Their task was to insure that the pallets we dropped did indeed contain humanitarian aid and not war materials.

The atmosphere was tense as I walked into the room among the representatives of the warring factions. Not long ago they all could have been called Yugoslavians. The youngest was the Bosnian from Sarajevo. He had been seriously wounded in Sarajevo by a Serb two years before. I was the only American in the room. The conversation was polite but not friendly.

I explained my interest and asked permission to take a video of our discussion. Permission was slowly granted. Talk of their job was not loosening up the dialogue. Then inspiration intervened, similar to the flash at the barbed-wire fence in July 1948. This time the content was different, but just as helpful. I found myself saying, " I'll bet I know someone that each of you know." That stirred some interest and a lot of disbelief.

Who doesn't know Kresmir Cosic?" I asked with confidence. Instantly each face was pleasantly transformed. Their immediate and simultaneous response was full of interest. Smiles broke through the cloud and the tension was gone. Each wanted to tell me how they knew him.

Kresmir was a Yugoslavian from Croatia. He was a national hero as a member of the Yugoslavian Olympic basketball team, winning one gold and two silver medals, and became the coach of their Olympic team in 1984 and 1988. But he turned down NBA offers to return to Yugoslavia and helped build a team for his country. In the hearts of every member of that United Nations Inspection Team he was a world-class human being. We had a common denominator. It was the spirit of a good brother.

Turtkovic (from Croatia) was particularly proud. He said, "Kresmir went to Provo University in America. He was their best player and even became a Mormon. He is a wonderful man." All agreed.

Then eyes turned to me. "Where did you know him?" "Well," I said, "That university is Brigham Young University in Provo, Utah. He was the best player, but I didn't get to see him play [1969 to 1973]. I was back to Berlin as the United States' Air Force Commander of Tempelhof, because of some gum. Much later I met Kresmir, in July 1993, when we were two of five people who were honored by receiving the Freedom Award given by the City of Provo. It was part of their 4th of July celebration. I rode in the parade with Kresmir. I am also a Mormon and from Provo, Utah."

We were almost as one in that room.

At that point I asked each of them about their families. All were married but Halilovic. All the others had children and spoke with tears in their eyes as they recounted a common theme of death or separation.

In February, 1992, Croatia voted to secede from Serb-led Yugoslavia, and the struggle is not yet satisfactorily closed. At that time, Kresmir was assigned as Deputy Ambassador to the United States. He later represented his country at the highest level in other assignments. He passed away in about 1995.

In those few minutes with the United Nations Inspection team, I witnessed the principle reaffirmed that had become my personal belief from years of experience: we are all kindred souls, regardless of frontiers. We have the potential for familial love and respect, one with another. Problems arise when greedy, selfish men or women take power upon themselves and tell others what they should be and what they should think. There are some systems that facilitate the rise to power of such personalities and these systems bring grief to mankind. It is not the common people in those countries who are the enemies.

* * * * *

In 1995 my experience with airlift took an unexpected turn. This time it was because of a parachute from my C-54 caught by a Berlin, Steinstucken boy, Gert Knecht in 1948.

Years later, in a visit to Steinstucken, Gert mentioned to me that he had the parachute but didn't know where it was.

Much later it was found, and Gert and friends made contact with NASA. US Army Astronaut Colonel William (Bill) S. McArthur Jr. took the parachute aboard the United States Space Shuttle, Atlantis. Bill and the parachute were launched from Kennedy Space Center, Florida on 9 November 1995, the sixth anniversary of the fall of the Berlin wall. On 12 November, Atlantis docked with the Russian Space Station, Mir. Once on board, Bill took out the parachute and explained its significance to Russian Astronaut Air Force Major, Yuri Gidzenko.

Mir Space Station Commander, Major Yuri Gidzenko, left; NASA Astronaut Col. William McArthur, right. The parachute is in the middle. Two Russian stamps are on the lower left of the parachute. A picture of Yuri Gagarin is between Icons above the flags.

It is conjecture but Yuri may have said, "The Blockade of Berlin was Stalin's doing, not the Soviet people."

Yuri did require all items brought on board Mir to be logged in. With a framed photo of Yuri Gagarin (the first man in space) and Russian and Ukraine Icons looking on, the parachute was duly stamped twice and made an official part of the Space Station's gear.

On 20 November 1995 Atlantis separated from Mir and landed on runway 33 at Kennedy Space Center, Florida. It had completed 129 orbits of the earth and traveled 3.4 million miles!

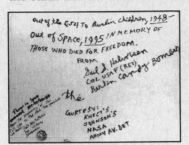

Bill McArthur wrote on the parachute, lower left, "From the beginning of the Cold War to the End— This parachute was there."

The parachute, none the worse for wear, was displayed in the Johnson Space Flight Center. It now resides in the small museum back "home" in Steinstucken, Berlin. In our visit there, April 17, 1997, they presented us with a framed pictorial treasure of the well-traveled parachute. Before its launch, I had written on it, "Out of the C-54 to Berlin Children, 1948; Out of Space, 1995, in memory of those who died for freedom. Gail S. Halvorsen, Col. USAF Ret. The Berlin Candy Bomber."

To me it was incredible. It wasn't the feeling that the parachute was incredible, but rather the chain of events that it represents.

It spans the time when some felt that the Germans were still the enemy. Then the Soviets became the enemy. The infamous wall went up to lock the people in. We were returned to Tempelhof in 1970 for four years. Uniformed Russians were on the other side of the wall. The wall fell and the Soviet Union came apart. Some areas of re-approachment emerged, such as this space mission. There were joint commercial ventures. We even airlifted food to former Soviet Republics in the early 1990s. Russia opened its borders to Churches from the outside. We were being introduced to our first Russians in St. Petersburg not long before the parachute was also being introduced to its first Russian in the Space Station, Mir.

The incredible part for me was this series of events, interwoven with warm and lasting relationships with wonderful new friends from nations who were former enemies. Most of it was because of two sticks of gum. I have often wondered what my life would have been like if I had chewed all five sticks in that pack of gum before I got to Berlin.

* * * * *

What were the experiences in Germany and Russia like? The German experience has been described. Our Russian experience was special from the standpoint of preconceptions and what was real.

It has been our experience that when life is going along about the way you plan it, something is going to change. You hope the change is a positive one, neutral, or that despite the difficulty it will provide an opportunity to grow. How we react to it is the important thing.

We had just finished a meal of fresh vegetables from the garden. It was a quiet evening in September 1995 and we were finally getting caught up with work on the farm and things generally. We had just gone over the Brigham Young University football schedule for fall. We were deep in the color layout of our first cruise, on a ship scheduled to sail in January when the days get cold and dark. I always said that anticipation is half the fun, and long winters can be a drag.

"Alta," I said, "If it wasn't for those two horses that need to be broke we would be in pretty good shape." We had been given two beautiful Arabian horses by the Forbis's, owners of the Ansata Egyptian Arab Stud Ranch in Mena, Arkansas.

The Berlin Airlift Historical Foundation C-54, a flying museum of the Berlin Airlift, was flown there by the founder and Chief Pilot, President Tim Chopp. I joined the crew in Mena to fly co-pilot part way back to its base in New Jersey. Judith Forbis and her husband were interested in the Airlift, and because of their generosity and the experience I had with the Berlin kids, the horses were ours.

This serene scene was interrupted by a raspy telephone dinger that would wake a corpse. "How you doing?" came the vaguely familiar voice. Sounded like it was coming from just around the corner. After getting reacquainted, we were directly asked how fast we could get to St. Petersburg. "How long would we be needed there?" "Eighteen months" came the uncompromising response. "When?" we shot back. "Last week. We need you as soon as possible and it isn't St. Petersburg, Florida" came the response. Grasping at any straw, I finally got my mind in motion, "We were on opposite sides of the Berlin Wall for four years. They don't like me over there. Better find someone else." Short pause. "I'll check it out," he said.

Although the requesting organizations were totally different, this call was reminiscent of a like call in December 1969 requesting us to go to the Berlin, Tempelhof job. I turned to Alta and, same as then, said, "Honey we're off the hook!" Like 1969, it only took a couple of days before the next call.

"Most of the Russians were never told about the Blockade of Berlin. Leningrad was blockaded for 900 days by the Germans. There is no problem. The job is to train teachers of the youth. The classes have started. The last couple had health problems and had to be sent home. The salary is the same as usual, pay your own expenses. We really need you now. We haven't been able to get anyone else or we wouldn't have called you."

In desperation I played my ace, "I'll be 75 next month and I can't run very fast." No pause. "Will you come?"

"Call us tomorrow," we said and hung up. All kinds of problems seemed to suddenly come up. What about the farm, the horses, our health, the house, and especially the 24 grandkids? We had gone through one of these assignments to England in 1986 and 1987. We had the same problems then, so there must be solutions. A prayer and little sleep that night and the answer was, "yes."

We landed in St. Petersburg on 12 October 1995. We knew about two words of Russian. We found beautiful caring people, eager to learn what we had to say about the mission of Jesus Christ. Some were not interested.

Elder and sister Halvorsen walking across the one kilometer wide Neva River. March 1996. Hermitage just in front of us out of the picture.

Our main jobs were to train teachers, visit the classes at night during the week, and to plan youth activities. We had excellent Russian translators and young American missionaries who also were very good translators. There were about 40 teachers and from 225 to over 300 students. We had five districts, with a coordinator to help us with each district. A fabulous young woman, Natasha Akolushnaya coordinated the five coordinators. We learned to love these pioneers dearly, and at the end of our 18 months we knew that we had left part of our hearts there and had been taught more than we had been teachers.

Our area of responsibility included St. Petersburg and surrounding areas, Vyborg near the Finnish border and to a lesser degree Kalliningrad on the Baltic.

For 18 months we learned to live without an automobile, washer, dryer, television, micro wave, disposal, dishwasher, vacuum cleaner, and other non-essential items. The apartment was warm and comfortable. The public

Elder and Sister Halvorsen in the
Russia St. Petersburg Mission Office.

transportation is very good. The entire Metro underground was without the marks of graffiti. It was a twenty-five-minute walk to get to the closest entry and likely a 20-minute walk to a class on the other end or an equally long trolley ride plus another walk. Ice and snow was hard. We never felt threatened riding the system, even when coming home quite late. To us the extent of the drinking problem was not totally evident on the Metro.

In the beginning the biggest shock for me was at rush hour getting on the Metro or a trolley bus. It wasn't just because we were packed in like sardines and couldn't get our hand up to scratch our nose. The shock came in merging my suit with the uniform fabric of Russian officers and soldiers. Previously we only saw them at some distance across the wall in Berlin or at the checkpoints entering or exiting the autobahn through East Germany. They had been the enemy, and now we were really with them. The longer we looked, the more we found them to be very similar to us.

The hardest part was missing our grandchildren. At home the little ones on their way to our house would often pick and bring us fresh flowers from the

Veterans Day in Russia, May 9th, 1996.
The Hermitage is in the background.

neighbor's yard. Now they knew how we missed them, therefore they also knew we thought it must be very important to be where we were. Maybe some day, when they consider the need to serve one another or former enemies, they may remember. It is our hope, for it has been our joy.

We were discussing the grandchildren one night coming back from visiting a class in Nevskii. Our discussion was terminated when we were forcibly stopped by an attendant at the Metro turnstile. We were trying to put our Metro coins in the slot. The husky matron grabbed us by the arms and pulled us through the wider entry by her booth. All the time she was lecturing us in a very animated voice. We understood not a word. Beyond the barrier we stopped to regroup. I still had my coin in my hand but she didn't seem to want it. She was still shouting something at us from her booth. Was she friend or enemy?

A softer voice in broken English came through, "May I help you?" A well-dressed woman approached us with a warm smile. "You are Americans," she said without asking. "I am Irina Chockmotava. Don't worry. The lady is just telling you that you are too old to have to pay." It had been a challenging lesson earlier that night, but I didn't think it took that much out of us.

Irina was a part-time resident of St. Petersburg, but she was originally from near Murmansk. Her love of life shone from the depths of her warm grey-green eyes. We rode together down the escalator to the bottom of the deep tunnel. She explained that pensioners in Russia didn't have to pay for the Metro, but foreigners in that category did unless they obtained a special card that was not reasonably attainable.

By the time we reached the train platform we were friends. We exchanged addresses, telephone numbers, children data and arranged to go to Church together the next Sunday. Our relationship bloomed and continues. Not all were so helpful, but we found enough like souls to warm us through the two cold, dark winters and for the rest of our lives.

Friend Yuri Lieberman, left; Halvorsen, right. Background: Russian copy of our C-47. Notice the engine covers for cold weather. Also reference page 235 for aircraft.

One like man was Yuri. We met him not long after our arrival. He is a seasoned PhD in the State Office of Climatology. He makes about the equivalent of $100 a month. Sometimes he isn't paid for some months, but he never misses a day of work. He loves his city of St. Petersburg and enjoys sharing it with Americans. We were most fortunate to have him for our guide when he and we were free. It was impossible to pay him for his services. His joy and reward came from serving others. The character strength apparent in his face comes from within and is nurtured by his well-placed values. He is one of the dwindling group of survivors of the terrible 900-day blockade of Leningrad. Nearly one million lost their lives.

Once or twice a month we took the two and a half hour train ride to be with the teachers and classes in Vyborg, not far from the Finnish border. The train coaches in the winter may or may not have operational heaters. Our second winter was not as cold as the first. To pass the time we read, studied or found someone who could dialogue with us in English. We and our Russian tutor were frustrated by our slow learning curve. We tried.

One January day in 1996 on the way to Vyborg (it was about the time our cruise ship was leaving Miami), a fine-looking young man came on the coach with a burst of snow and cold air. He took a sled from under his arm and carefully placed it in the overhead rack. He sat down opposite us on the unyielding and polished hardwood bench. He gathered his young son in his arms. In a few moments we were engrossed in the exchange of who and what everyone was. His name is Alexey, a young pediatrician. His salary was $45 a month.

Dr. Alexey Bolashov and his son Nikita. We first met him on the train to Vyborg.

With his mother and son he was headed for their Dacha in the country. Alexey's wife is a medical student and was at school. His father was at his medical institute. Their openness and friendship were genuine. Their Dacha provided us fresh vegetables in the summer time and some vegetables pickled in vinegar and big glass jars in the winter time.

We never did get accustomed to the idea that we were in the land where, Alexey said, "It wasn't long ago that I couldn't have spoken to you in that train car." The first time we walked into a teacher training session and found a Russian Army officer in uniform it was a momentary shock. Dimitri simply hadn't had time to change his clothes and had come directly from work.

One of our assistants had worked for the KGB. Another was in the Red Army stationed in East Berlin, almost the same time we were in West Berlin. He was with a special forces unit supplied with only two hours of ammunition and other necessities in case they had to cross the wall in response to an international crisis. He said they were considered expendable.

One good friend was a retired Lt. Colonel with service in the Red Army. Waiting for a District meeting to start he asked, "What do you Americans paint on the tanks that take the part of the enemy tanks when you have practice maneuvers in the United States?" I said, "I'm not sure, but my Army buddies have said it was a red star." I asked, "What did you paint on yours?" He said, "We painted a big US and a white star on our enemy tanks." We both had a good laugh, but I was pinching myself to see if this dialogue was just a dream.

The teachers and students in Vyborg were exceptional. We were always eager to be with them. A light snow squeaked with every footstep as we left the train

Marshal Georgi K. Zhukov on horse. The Soviet General who took Berlin. Kremlin.

and hiked to the beautiful new chapel, the first one built by The Church of Jesus Christ of Latter-day Saints in Russia.

As with St. Petersburg, our last visit was the hardest.

* * * * *

On 14 April 1997 we left the St. Petersburg Airport for Berlin. The farewell was one we shall never forget. The 18 months were reluctantly finished, and the memory phase began. As we landed in Berlin we were greeted by Peter and Mercedes Wild, and memories from times gone by rushed back.

That night, for about the 15th time, we slept in the old apartment house from which Mercedes wrote me her famous white chickens letter in November 1948. As you have read, Peter and Mercedes do a great deal to keep the memory of the Airlift alive. One of their many contributions is the airlift of Berlin High School students which comes to Utah and our students go to Berlin. Peter, Mercedes and their students will be with Brent Chambers in Utah again in March 1998 and their 25 students will be settled with host families.

There are other people and other organizations that should likewise be recognized:

Perhaps the person who has done and is doing the most to preserve the memory of the Airlift is Berliner Heinz-Gerd Reese, the Geschaftsfuhrer of the Stiftung "Luftbruckendank." This man and his far-reaching program is fully backed by the Berlin and the German Governments. Scholarships are provided to selected students each year, contests for young people are organized, survivors of those killed on the Airlift are regularly recognized, and Veterans of the Airlift have been included in special observances and anniversaries. By far the largest events sponsored for the Veterans by this organization and the grateful Berliners will be in Berlin in 1998 and 1999. Berlin will host the Veterans' visit.

Left to right: Mercedes Wild; Gail Halvorsen; Dr. Helmut Trotnow; Heinz-Gerd Reese, Peter Wild. Berlin.

Dr. Helmut Trotnow, the Director of the Allied Museum in Berlin, also promotes Berlin Airlift understanding. His museum was established in 1994 to document and present the role of the Western Allies to bring about a democratic society in Germany. The official inauguration will take place in June 1998. The Berlin Airlift will be featured. Dr. Trotnow has plans for

Cutting the ribbon on the Berlin Airlift International Exhibit in Frankfurt, organized by John Provan. My uniform is the one from 1948. Far left is United States Air Force Europe Commander, General Robert Oaks from Provo, Utah. Berlin and Frankfurt dignitaries. On my left is Gerdi and Gerd Rausch. Note: cross reference with page 229 and the paragraph that starts, "Just a few of the old faithfuls—Gerdi and Gerd Rausch, March 1994.

Airlift displays and activities for 1998 and 1999. He has sponsored panel discussions that were broadcast by radio.

One of the most active individuals living in the Frankfurt area, in my view, is John Provan. John plans, develops, collects, and constructs exhibits that display and preserve the Airlift heritage and memories. He is an accomplished historian, writer, and museum curator. He is a key participant with the Frankfurt Historical Museum, with Professor Dr. Koch, in preparing their displays which highlight the Berlin Airlift and the U.S. presence in Germany. Exhibits are to be in place for the special activities planned for 1998 and 1999. John will provide materials from his extensive collections now displayed in a building on Rhein-Main. He was responsible for the very successful Berlin Airlift Exhibit in the Frankfurt International Exhibit Hall which had an extended run starting in March 1994. His energy is exceeded only by his ability to visualize a project and then build it himself. He is ingenious.

One of the great contributors at Rhein-Main has always been the Luftbrucke Chapter of the Airlift/Tanker Association. This Chapter has done the improbable. The Airlift Memorial complex on Rhein-Main is a product of their accomplishments. They have planned and carried out many other projects to support awareness of the Berlin Airlift and some of about 300 humanitarian airlift operations flown out of Rhein-Main since 1947.

Just a few of the old faithfuls who have left their mark are: Gerdi and Gerd Rausch, they have served with distinction from the beginning and are still at it; Col Ray Holden is a past president of the Chapter and did a great deal to create the Rhein-Main Airlift Memorial. He planned well and knew how to locate exhibit aircraft. Col. Tom Hansen Ret. is now back at Rhein-Main as manager of the Base services provided by ITT/FSIC. Tom, with Chapter members, did a great deal to complete the Airlift Memorial project on Rhein-Main. He is a past president of the Chapter, a past president of the Tunner Chapter of the Airlift Tanker Association, and a Director of the Berlin Airlift Veterans Association. The current Chapter president is Colonel Sterling Palmer, the commander of the 626th Air Mobility Support Squadron. Col Palmer is doing great things with the Chapter's help in preparation for 1998 and 1999.

Left to right: name missing; Elder Halvorsen; Sister Halvorsen; John Provan; Peg and Tom Hansen and my talking dummy, right rear as part of my 1948 room mock-up. Rhein Main 1997.

There are two major non-profit organizations in the United States that are dedicated to keeping the memory of the Berlin Airlift alive. They are "The Berlin Airlift Veterans Association," and "The Berlin Airlift Historical Foundation."

The Berlin Airlift Veterans Association (BAVA) was launched by veterans with the help of Galaxy Tours and a set of By-Laws in Las Vegas, Nevada in September 1990. The organization was incorporated in the State of Pennsylvania on January 11, 1991.

Colonel Kenneth Herman, USAF (Retired) was elected president and has been unanimously reelected every term since. His performance has been outstanding as were his pilot skills during his 190 missions as an Aircraft Commander flying the Airlift.

The Association's activities are governed by a 12-member Board of Directors. The By-Laws provided for the commemoration of the service rendered by the Veterans of the Berlin Airlift, for activities to perpetuate the history and significance of the Berlin Airlift, for actions to honor those who lost their lives while serving on the Berlin Airlift, for activities to establish Berlin Airlift Memorials in the United States and other locations and for activities to raise funds for memorials, and for the administration of the Association and future activities.

There have been reunions every year since 1990. The one in Berlin in 1999 will be the largest and most nostalgic of all. In September 1989 the 40th anniversary reunion was held in Frankfurt/Weisbaden, Celle, Fassberg and Berlin, with about 400 members attending. A good Morning America television team joined the reunion in Berlin and flew aboard the "Little Vittles" C-130 to record the commemorative candy drop to the kids at Tempelhof.

BAVA memorial plaques have been placed at: the USAF Museum Memorial Park, Wright-Patterson, Ohio; USAF Academy Memorial Cemetery; Arlington National Cemetery; Berlin Airlift Memorial, Rhein-Main AB, Frankfurt, Germany; and a contribution was made for the license to construct a 1/6th scale replica of the Tempelhof and Rhein-Main Airlift Memorial on Scott AFB, Illinois.

The streets on Lindsey Air Station, Weisbaden, Germany were named for US personnel who lost their lives during the Blockade. These signs were retrieved by BAVA and presented to members of the deceased airmen's families. The leadership of Col. Herman was a key factor.

BAVA is not just a United States organization. British, German, French, and other nationalities work together for the above-stated objectives. A very close relationship exists with the British airmen with whom we were full flying partners during the Airlift operation. But in my view it was the Berliners who were the real heroes of the Berlin Airlift. They never gave up.

The Berlin Airlift Historical Foundation (BAHF) was founded in New Jersey by the current President, Timothy Chopp, in the fall of 1988. Officers working with President Chopp coordinate the efforts of members from around the world. The Foundation is a non-profit, tax exempt, educational and historical organization with the primary objective of preserving the history of the Berlin Airlift.

"The Spirit of Freedom." Berlin or Bust.

The principal tool to accomplish the mission is the "Spirit of Freedom," a Douglas C-54E Berlin Airlift support aircraft which was purchased by the Foundation in December 1992. After extensive renovation by experts and teenagers it became operational in 1994. On the outside it is painted in the 1948 colors of the 48th Troop Carrier Squadron, a very large red lightening bolt on both sides of the fuselage. On the inside it is an exhibit hall on Berlin Airlift history. Historical panels are mounted on the walls, mockups of the types of cargo flown are displayed, a memorial with the pictures of those who lost their lives during the operation, charts and graphs, political background information, cartoons and display cases with models and memorabilia greet eager school children and adults. BAHF has contracted for a flyable C-97, only one of two remaining aircraft. When paid off it will be a museum of the Cold War era.

The "Spirit" has made many appearances at airports near schools and at numerous air shows across the United States. A highly professional, uniformed and well-informed volunteer team fly and conduct interior and exterior tours of this exceptional aircraft.

In 1994, under the expert instruction of Chief Pilot Tim Chopp, I was able to check out as a qualified co-pilot, and in 1994 and 1995 I made a number of flights. Although I have over 4000 hours in that type aircraft I hadn't flown it for 37 years. It was an indescribable thrill coming down the final approach and making that first landing after such a long time. Bill Morrissey of Danville Indiana, possibly the youngest traffic controller on the Berlin Airlift, was aboard. He came on the mike and said something like, "Big Easy Triple Nickel, clear the runway, traffic behind you!" For just a split second it was like we were back in Berlin.

"Spirit" inside fuselage. Flour and coal sacks. Mural of a C-54 approaching Tempelhof. Kids by barbed wire fence below. Rest of walls covered by historic displays.

My flight medical certificate is renewed, and I am excited with a lot of others who are preparing themselves and the old "Spirit of Freedom" to fly to Frankfurt and Berlin for a big celebration in May 1998.

President Tim Chopp was born a long time after the Airlift was over. He is a jet contract pilot who flies business executives to different destinations. To me it is re-

My first flight since 1957 in a C-54. Fun!

markable the interest and knowledge he has of the Berlin Airlift and the fantastic number of quality volunteers he has organized and who make things happen with hard work. Many are young aviation professionals, some just aviation enthusiasts, all want to help. Some are BAVA members such as Fred Hall who is a great mechanic from the days of the Lift. He

The crew of the "Spirit" at the Air show at Scott AFB 7 June, 1997. Man in the middle with white hat has his 1948 Airlift uniform on. On his left is president Tim Chopp and on his left traffic controller Bill Morrissey. A great crew!

has driven countless trips to New Jersey from his home in Baltimore to help breathe the spirit into the "Spirit."

Now back to Berlin on the way home from Russia. The 16th of April 1997 was the anniversary of the 1949 Easter Parade. It was also our 48th wedding anniversary. I had the honor of giving the address that preceded the entry of a mint condition, restored Berlin Airlift C-47 to the Berlin Deutsches Technikmuseum. Prof. Dr. Dr. Holger Steinle and other museum leaders are keen supporters of Berlin Airlift awareness. A new aircraft and space wing will be added to this great old museum. The Easter Parade was made up of US and British aircraft that flew almost 13,000 tons of supplies to Berlin in 24 hours. This was one reason that Stalin capitulated and lifted the blockade on 12 May 1949. We continued to stockpile reserves until 30 Sept. 1949. Some of my words at the Deutsches Technikmuseum event were:

> Berlin was a beacon of hope that became a reality for people in the East. As your great Governing Mayor, Ernst Reuter, declared, "We cannot be bartered, we cannot be negotiated, we cannot be sold—there is only one possibility for all of us: to stand jointly together until this fight has been won."

> The major part of Europe is more at peace now than at any time in centuries. Do we become complacent and say all is well? What dangers lie in complacency and boredom? Will true values be defended or forgotten? How important is our freedom? . . .

What then of the future? I think you will agree with me that our children are our future. Not just our children, but everyone's children. In 1948-1949 I saw gratitude shine in the eyes of boys and girls at the fence surrounding Tempelhof, gratitude for flour to keep them free.

This past 18 months my wife and I have seen gratitude shining in the eyes of Russian children who are very similar to those who were by the fence at Tempelhof. These Russian children are now in very humble circumstance as they strive to learn more about what free agency means. . . .

We know that this facility (museum) will contribute to a better world because of the people and children who will visit here. It will help older ones to remember and younger ones to learn those principles that are worthy of sacrifice.

We were straight from the streets of St. Petersburg. A museum near the city had a Russian copy of an American C-47 that helped break the 900-day German blockade (1941-1944) of Leningrad, now St. Petersburg. Now I stood in Berlin by this American C-47 which had a part in breaking the Russian blockade of Berlin in 1948-1949. We were not far from where I parked my C-54 on the Tempelhof flight line almost exactly 49 years before.

My head was swimming with the time warp. The complex relationships between the British, French, Americans, Germans and the Soviets were all intertwined with intrigue, unusual alliances, suspicion and bright spots. How did we feel?

One thing we knew for sure was that some of our best friends have been drawn from the ranks of those we once thought to be our worst enemies. In Russia we not only witnessed remarkable change in the lives of others but we saw our lives changed as well.

It was a case of cultural shock all over again as we arrived in the United States of America. There is no place in the world like it. Every one of our five children, their spouses and all the grandchildren (24) except one on a mission to Germany, were at the jet way to welcome us home. What a sight! We heard a deplaning passenger say, "Wow, is that all one family?"

The next day on the way to the farm I wondered if the horses would remember me. They were far into the lower pasture. I filled my lungs and yelled, "RAJA!!" Their heads came up, tails in the air. The Arabians were in the lead. They hadn't forgotten.

There is work to do here if I can stay off the phone. In just a few months Berlin will reclaim some tired warriors and hopefully the rejuvenated "Spirit of Freedom."

16

Lessons Learned

We had a reasonable period of time to get the farm in shape then the phone began ringing off the hook. Tim Chopp, President and Chief Pilot of the Berlin Historical Foundation, excitedly came on the line, "Heinz-Gerd Reese, Director of the Stiftung Luftbruckendank in Berlin wants the "Spirit of Freedom," C-54, over Berlin 12 May, 1998 for a special 50th anniversary commemoration for the Berliners. Can you be one of the pilots?" Lightning is fast but I was faster, "Give me the time and place and I'm there," I pleaded. Tim continued, "Meet us at Dover Air Force Base, Delaware for shake down flights. We need to get you and crew checked out for the long haul across the pond. A National Geographic photo team will also participate." At Dover AFB we were briefed by McGuire AFB survival experts on life support systems, exposure suits, 20 man life rafts and the rest of the gear in case the 53 year old Airlift "Spirit of Freedom" got too tired to make it all the way across the North Atlantic.

On 5 May, 1998 the Spirit and professional crew of 15 waved good-bye to wives and girl friends. We lined up on the runway at Floyd Bennett Field in New York City and put the throttles to the wall.

The first stop was Westover AFB, the main support airport for the Airlift, 1948-49, and near Chicopee Massachusetts, former headquarters for Operation Little Vittles. We were met with a lively band, 800 school children and the Chicopee Mayor with a key to the city. Present were some of those who had tied up the parachutes and candy bars those many years ago.

The next stop was Goose Bay, Labrador. Noticeably cooler. Engines sounded great. From there we took off direct to Iceland. As we crossed the southern tip of Greenland we were in awe of the fields

Over the southern tip of Greenland, headed to Iceland.

of icebergs and the grandeur of the landscape itself. Soon it was behind us and the heavy white capped North Atlantic spread out in every direction. Not a pleasant sight if we had to ditch the old girl. The wind was on the nose and very strong at our 7000 foot level.

We had just settled down for the long haul when the oil temperature on number one engine went sky high and the oil pressure started dropping to the red line. "Haul out the life rafts and prepare your exposure suits," Tim shouted. "We may lose number one."

That woke everyone up. After a little professional nursing and a reduction of power Tim managed to stabilize the temperature and pressure at minimal acceptable levels. We felt pretty good that we didn't have to shut her down but the reduced power on number one would extend our flight time and our exposure to the fierce head winds. Things got back to almost normal when suddenly there was smoke in the cockpit. Tim called for the emergency oxygen hoods provided by McGuire AFB and immediately turned off all of our electrical circuits except engine ignition. It wasn't long before the smoke subsided. One at a time Tim brought the electrical systems back on line. The problem very soon became more than evident. The cockpit heater had failed. The cockpit temperature plummeted to outside air temperatures. That wasn't very comfortable, especially around the ankles. However, compared to the alternative (a fire) it wasn't so bad. After hours of suspense we sighted Iceland and landed at Keflavik AFB. The cold had congealed the oil in the oil cooler line and blocked the flow through the cooler causing our problems on number one engine. The nose heater took some special attention to get it back on line. Great crew!

Berlin Airlift Historical Foundation, Founder and Chief Pilot, Tim Chopp after the cockpit heater went out.

The next leg was to Prestwick, Scotland. We had made it across! It was the beginning of a real odyssey. We would be traveling in Europe for 69 days and give 27 airshows distributed in Great Britain, Luxembourg, France, and several visits to Germany. The "Spirit" made every show on time!

The greatest thrill of the trip was our arrival over Berlin. Traffic control suggested we fly over the city low enough so that those Berliners who were there during the blockade could see the aircraft and hear those engines. That sight and sound meant freedom in 1948 and 1949. The British had many different types of aircraft but the C-54 hauled all but a little of the American contribution. Our reception on landing at Tempelhof was unforgettable. Mercedes and Peter were there to greet us and we would renew old times for the several weeks we were there. The Wild's hospitality is incredible! What memorable events were placed in motion with that November 1948 letter from Mercedes.

The days we were at Tempelhof and Schonefeld in Berlin "The Spirit of Freedom" brought thousands of Berliners through the great Airlift exhibits inside her gleaming fuselage. It was immediately evident which Berliners were there during those dark days of 1948-49. Each had a special look about them; elevated emotion, and moist eyes. "Thank you for our freedom!" was repeated time after time to each of our crew. The genuine gratitude was over powering. We were just a few accepting their appreciation on behalf of the 79 who gave their lives and the thousands of air and ground personnel, military and civilian, French, British, German, and American, that made the Airlift work.

Several told the same story:

"I wasn't alive during the Airlift but I am here because of it. My father and mother were not married long before my father was called to the Russian front. They didn't want to have children under those circumstances. Sometime after the war my father and mother found each other again in Berlin, but Stalin threatened to take Berlin and

The "Spirit of Freedom" arriving over Berlin.
The former East Berlin TV tower/restaurant is just below the aircraft.
The reflected cross on the bubble has been called "The Pope's Revenge."

The "Spirit" crew deplaning and being welcomed at Tempelhof.
Gail and Mercedes in the middle. Heinz-Gerd Reese in the far back corner.

blockaded the city. Again my parents postponed the thought of having children under such a threat. The Airlift started and supplies increased every month. On the 16th of April 1949 the Airlift, the British, French and Americans, delivered almost 13,000 tons of supplies to Berlin in 24 hours. Confidence sky-rocketed. That is when my mother looked at my father in a way that he knew they could now start a family. I was conceived that very day and was born after the Blockade was over. I owe my life to the Airlift." At least three gave a very similar account.

Hundreds of older former East Berliners came through the old C-54 and repeated similar feelings. "We prayed for our loved ones in West Berlin and for the success of the Airlift and the safety of your crews," they repeated one after the other.

Inside the fuselage, among the exhibits, a dignified, well-dressed man of 60 years came up to me after fighting to control his emotions. In a subdued tone of voice he said, "50 years ago I was a boy of 10 on my way to school. The clouds were very low with light rain. I could hear the planes landing though I couldn't see them. (The GCA, ground control approach

The crew and the "Spirit" had just delivered the Berlin Airlift commemorative stamp to Tempelhof for the first official cancellation, 26 June, 1998.

radar, operators were the heros that made it possible for us to land in terrible weather.) Suddenly out of the mist came a parachute with a fresh Hershey chocolate bar from America. It landed right at my feet. I knew it was happening but couldn't believe it was for me. It took me a week to eat that candy bar. I hid it day and night. The chocolate was wonderful but it wasn't the chocolate that was most important. What it meant was that someone in America knew I was here, in trouble and needed help. Someone in America cared. That parachute was something more important than candy. It represented hope. Hope that some day we would be free." Then he went on to say something I think significant: "Without hope the soul dies. I could have lived on the thin rations but not without hope." To the Berliners the dried eggs, dried potatoes, powdered milk, coal, and dried carrots were very important but what they represented was more important: Hope. Hope that the free people of the world would not give up the task or forsake them. We see people in our communities who are in deep depression and without hope. They have lost their support base and the ability to function.

Everyone in deep trouble needs an outside source in which to place their hope. For the Berliners it was the Allies. In my difficult times that outside source has been my wife, family, and ultimately my Savior Jesus Christ. Without that help, in tragic times, I could lose hope.

Hours after closing time people were still coming through the "Spirit of Freedom." One man of about 65 approached me under the aircraft wing. It had been dark for an hour. He seemed reluctant to speak. Finally he marshaled the courage. With an apologetic voice and in school English he introduced himself and produced an old envelope from his tattered jacket. His hand shook as he handed it to me. "Look at this please," he said. I carefully removed the contents to find a handkerchief parachute with note attached. It was too dark to read the faint message. The beam of a friend's flashlight revealed, in German, "Please return this parachute to a Military Policeman." And in English, "MP: Take them to

A modern girl in Berlin free from worries of chocolate or gum supplies in the city. 14 May, 1998.

"Little Vittles" für die Kinder von Lt. Halverson.
Bitte seidenen Fallschirm an der M.P. Wache Flugplatz Tempelhof abgeben, da sie wieder gebraucht werden.

MP TAKE THEM TO FLIGHT OPERATIONS

SEPT. 1948   PLEASE.

flight operations, please" It was one of the first parachutes to which I had attached the note. We had run very low on parachutes. Many were returned. This one hadn't been. "Please forgive me," he said. "I just couldn't part with my parachute, my personal symbol of freedom." I made a xerox copy of the handkerchief parachute and left his prize and freedom's symbol with him. Betty and Hal Cunningham from Elverson, PA had sent the handkerchief to me for use in the "Little Vittles" operation. They had written, "Best Wishes" on their handkerchief, below their names.

On 14 May 1998 at Tempelhof we parked the "Spirit" nose to nose with a brand new C-17 transport, an exceptional new airlift aircraft, flown in by Captain Erik Hansen from Charleston AFB South Carolina. Erik was just a lad of about 15 back in 1972 and lived in Berlin with his parents when we were there. He was the same age as one of our sons, and a good friend. His father was in the Air Force assigned to Potsdam, near Berlin.

Chancellor Kohl, President Clinton, Gail Halvorsen and Mercedes Wild in front of the "Spirit" before christening of the C17. See page 247 for the Christening photo.

That day President Clinton, Chancellor Kohl and others would christen the C-17 the "Spirit of Berlin." Mercedes and I were on a platform between the two aircraft and we spoke briefly to the crowd before the ceremony. She got the biggest applause. The next day the two aircraft, the old and the new airlifters, rendezvoused over Ramstein AFB for some historical photos. Erik had the flaps down with reduced power and we had the flaps up with full power in order to fly some kind of formation. The old and the new. What a quantum leap in capability! It would take only about 30 C-17s to do the job of the 225 C-54s that were on the Airlift.

In 1998 and 1999 the wonderful City of Berlin, under the management of Heinz-Gerd Reese, brought back all the Berlin Airlift Veterans that could be found. The City treated us with special attention, food, lodging, gratitude and fun programs. One of the greatest events was the massing of all the Airlift Veterans in the tunnel leading into the historic Olympic Stadium. We then marched in to the acclaim of a wildly

Over Ramstein, the new C-17, now the "Spirit of Berlin," alongside the "Spirit of Freedom," C-54.

cheering, standing, crowd, banners flying and bands playing. What a thrill. Then public expressions of gratitude were showered down on us as we marched to our seats. Enemies during the war had become friends.

In January, 1999 tragedy struck. Alta, the light of my life, suddenly returned to her heavenly home. We only had three months to go to join the celebration our children had planned for our 50th anniversary. It wouldn't happen. Of any good I have done or acclaim I may have received I owe it all to Alta Jolley Halvorsen, a perfect example of the Savior's exhortation to give service before self and to love your neighbor. Alta, my parents and the Church of Jesus Christ of Latter-day Saints gave me the tools I have to meet life's demanding challenges. It is hard to understand why I fall so short.

Berlin Airlift Veterans being welcomed in the Olympic Stadium, Berlin.

Sixty three years ago in the halls of Bear River High School, Garland, Utah, I met a young lady, Lorraine Pace. She was from a remote cattle ranch in Southern Utah. When she showed me a photo of her in chaps, the reins of her saddle horse in one hand and the lead rope of a pack horse in the other, I flipped. The pack horse was loaded with snow from the high La Sal mountains. The snow was destined for a 4th of July ice cream making party at the main ranch house in Sally's Hollow.

Lorraine was the only girl I dated the spring of my senior year at Bear River. Some of those dates were in the old Maxwell (see page 19). The large initials L. P. are on the other door. We talked of marriage when we grew up. Then came Pearl Harbor and the Army Air Corps. We went different ways. Lorraine married. A few years later I met Alta. Alta and I were married almost seven years after that in 1949. Until a few years ago Lorraine and I didn't know if the other was alive or dead. Then she saw me on a television program from Berlin. Her husband had died some 12 years before. Lorraine had moved from the ranch and Moab to Grand Junction, Colorado to Tubac then Amado, Arizona. She wrote. We met. We married. We are starting over where we left off 62 years earlier, rebuilding our lives together. Lorraine rides the two Egyptian Arabians, given me for two sticks of gum, better than I do. We built a house on a bluff overlooking the farm and the Spanish Fork River bottoms, next to the horses and cows.

We watch fox, pheasants, ducks, geese, hawks and the cows calving from our deck. On our walks we laughed at the eager beavers trying to dam up the Spanish Fork River. And then they did it! A real example to all of us about what impossible things can be done if we have a positive attitude. In the winter time we go to Lorraine's place in Arizona. It is replete with wild life.

In May of 1999 General John P. Jumper, at the time Commanding General of the United States Air Force Europe and now Air Force Chief of Staff, asked if I would like to fly on a C-130 supply run to Tirana, Albania. That question got an immediate, "Yes Sir!!" Before departure I obtained some resupply needs for the kids. Besides my gum and candy the Air Force wives clubs added to

Marine helicopter, Gail. Albania, near Kosavar refugee Camp Hope

that, plus a big supply of stuffed animals and teddy bears. The real down to earth gift was a great package of school materials.

On arrival in Albania a Marine Helicopter was waiting to take me to Camp Hope, a Kosovar refugee camp, appropriately named. It was loaded with children. What a reception! The school supplies got less action but were appreciated especially by the teachers. These children had the same bright faces, appreciation, and optimism exhibited by the Berlin kids at the barbed wire fence in 1948. In many cases these kids had lost family members and/or their homes but they were surprisingly upbeat. They had hope because of people in America who knew they were there, knew they were in trouble and promised to stand by them. Hope is still the name of the game.

Kosavar children entering Camp Hope with Col. Halvorsen.

In December 2000 Lorraine and I were invited to Anderson AFB in Guam to participate with the great 36th Airlift Squadron-The Eagle Airlifters, for the Christmas Drop to Natives in the Micronesian Islands. We had worked with the 36th at Yokota AFB in June of 2000. What a wonderful experience flying with that team and their Commander Lt. Col. Randy Kee. We had eight drops on seven islands about 300 miles south of Guam. This was but a small part of the overall effort. The boxes for each parachute weighed about 400 pounds filled with Christmas goodies, clothing, machetes, fishing gear, books and surprises for the little kids. It was a real thrill to watch the precision work of the crew in positioning the aircraft just over the right spot and the loadmaster's release at just the right time. Watching the parachute canopy snap open then come to a full bloom

A 425-pound package of Christmas joy prepares to hit the surf near the beach for the natives of Falalop Island and their children. This remote Micronesian island is 300 miles south of Guam. December 2000.

is exciting. The tethered navigator, John Steckbeck, standing in the open cargo door waving to the recipients replete in his Santa Claus suit was the final Christmas touch!

The drops were usually just off shore and the native's charge from the beach was a joy to behold. Dugout canoes and free swimmers raced to see who could get there first. The prize was taken from the shimmering turquoise waters to the contrasting gleaming white sand. The precious goods were then distributed by the Chief according to need.

These training missions began in the early 1950's by Air Force personnel in aircraft returning from missions with extra rations. The rations were dropped to grateful natives. Air crews wanted to brighten up the lives of those isolated people. The wives' clubs of all the services on Guam now provide much of the gathering of the goods and organizing the annual event. Each year a task force is established and the local merchants provide much of the items assembled. The effects have been far reaching. Mitchell P. Warner reports the following:

At Christmastime 1956, Koisimy Rudolph, a lad of six living on the tiny isolated atoll of Nukuoro watched in amazement as a package fell from the back of a low flying aircraft. The contents were retrieved and divided evenly among the people by the tribal Chief. Koisimy was one of five brothers in a fatherless subsistence farming family. He recalled, "I have very strong, detailed, warm and personal memories of my gifts from that day. I especially remember receiving some pencils, a pencil sharpener and some crayons packed in a small box. These were my own personal items and I treasured them greatly. They were special and I treated them as if they were fragile. At school there were coloring books which I could use. I recall that time as 'The Year That I Colored.' The crayons and sharpener changed my life." With that encouragement Koisimy relentlessly pursued what seemed to be an impossible education. But through hard work and motivation from the air drop he began learning and teaching. First in elementary schools and then the Pohnpei Secondary High School, and then as an elementary teacher on the Parem Island in the Pohnpei lagoon. He was chosen with 25 others in all the islands to attend Suiomi College in Hancock, Michigan. He went on to finish his college work at Bethany College in Lindsborg, Kansas. Koisimy became a teacher, executive director of a bible society in Micronesia, Community College Instructor, and President of the United Micronesian Association and a member of the Advisory Committee of the Kapingamarangi Nukuoro Association.

This is another tale of little things making a difference in lives. In my case, sharing two sticks of gum changed my life and had an impact on the lives of many in Berlin during the blockade. These are examples of what my parents taught me in my youth: ". . . by small and simple things are great things brought to pass." Alma 37:6

After last year's drop a little girl who didn't get her desired Barbie doll wrote that it was OK anyway. She expressed humble gratitude for what was given and was reluctant to ask again for such a special item. In our drop to her island there was a Barbie doll among the goodies with her name, firmly attached.

A special benefit for the Guam trip was being with our host family, Lt Col Brad Jensen, wife Kathy, and their lovely children. They and other Air Force people took exceptional care of us. Brad's father and mother, De Lamar and Mary Jensen, are Alta and my best friends. I went to high school with Mary and Alta went to College with her. Our families have done things together since Alta and I were married in 1949. We have camped together with our children in Europe and the United States. Our son Bob and Brad are best friends. I swore those two into the Air Force the same day in 1982. Memories are still being made!

Part of the Christmas Drop Crew. Left to right: Lorraine Halvorsen, Col. Halvorsen, Kathy Jensen, Lt. Col. Brad Jensen (the local Branch President), and Jacob Jensen, their son.

One of the most exciting calls in my career came one early spring day in 2001. My thoughts were on what to plant in the garden more than how long it took to unload an aircraft on the Berlin Airlift. It was about the fourth ring before I got out of the multicolored spring catalog and found the phone. "Colonel Halvorsen this is Tony Robertson, will you be available about the 20th of June?" I don't often get a call from the Commander of the Air Mobility Command who also is the Commander of the United States Transportation Command.

I didn't know what I had for the 20th but knew in a heartbeat I'd be available. "General, what is it?" I ventured.

"We have just designed and built a new 25 K (25,000 lb.) universal aircraft loader and it needs a name. Mind if we use yours?" It took me a while to believe what I was hearing, first General Robertson and second the loader. It didn't take but a moment after that to express my surprise and astonished acceptance. The General went on, "You know the 50K loader was named for General Tunner. We will be using the 25 K all over the world. There will be over 250 of them."

"It's a good chance to join General Tunner on the flight line again Sir," I quipped light-heartedly.

General Robertson, Gail Halvorsen and the
newly-christened "Halvorsen Loader."

Certificate of Training

Presented to
Colonel Gail S. Halvorsen, USAF, Retired
"Uncle Wiggly Wings"
on successful completion of the 25K Halvorsen Loader
Operator Course
certified this *19th* day of *June 2001*

JERRY V. WALLACE, MSgt, USAF
Loader Operations Manager

MICHAEL T. FRIEDLEIN, Lt Col, USAF
Commander, 436th Aerial Port Squadron

Proof of training for Loader's namesake.

"See you at Dover AFB on the 20th of June. They will have their first loader ready to be christened," concluded the General.

At Dover I had a crash training course on how to operate this fabulous piece of machinery. From over 18 feet in the air to the ground it was a loadmaster's dream. Lorraine was honored to be escorted for the ceremony by Retired Air Force Chief of Staff, General Ronald R. Fogleman. The event marked the beginning of an extensive training program to make good the full potential of this latest edition of essential materials handling equipment (MHE).

Soon after we returned home, the phone was ringing again. The lovely voice of Lila Wilson from Pigeon Forge, Tennessee came through, "Just a reminder Colonel Halvorsen our Celebrate Freedom Week is in August. We want you and Lorraine here the 9th for about a week."

We had been part of the celebration the year before and we wouldn't miss it. Lila continued, "In addition to the seminars and panel discussions Tim Chopp and crew will be there with the "Spirit of Freedom." If you are good he says you can fly it again." That was a convincer but not as moving as Lorraine's response. She had flown with me in the "Spirit" the year before at Pigeon Forge and said, "We're going!"

That little town is incredible. Their programs are aimed at honoring veterans from all the military services with a fabulous parade, food, programs, and entertainment seldom matched. I am firmly convinced that the program should be on National TV. What a true celebration of freedom by heart-warming patriotic folks.

Besides all the other benefits of Pigeon Forge I found myself at the controls of the shiny C-54 taking off again with a great crew aboard. It was good to be alongside Tim Chopp. It was a chance for him to give me the latest on the Foundation's C-97 aircraft, "The Angel of Deliverance." The aircraft will become a Cold War flying museum. On the next flight I was in the back end with hundreds of parachutes for kids eagerly waiting below. My Airlift buddy, Bill Morrissey, was giving me a helpful hand. These well fed American kids had all the candy and gum their dentist-sensitive parents wanted them to have but they seemed just as excited as the kids in Berlin. It must be something about having gum and candy airdropped that makes it taste a lot better. With tongue in cheek we justify these airdrops as training missions in case some city is blockaded again. That is pretty certain given our inability to keep history from repeating itself and a seemingly unchanging human nature. Great time in Pigeon Forge! What a progressive little town. Lila and crew are magnificent.

Training is a major element in every operational unit no matter their mission. Readiness is the key to survival. You can't be ready without training. We were not ready for the events of 11 September 2001. Such an event was unthinkable. However, the quick response of our forces to the refusal of the Taliban to turn over the terrorists is a testimony to the participating unit's preparedness. I have been taught, "If ye are prepared ye shall not fear."

Our tanker fleet got many of our key aircraft in place and our airlifters had the critical men and supplies available to support the war fighting CINCS. What a great mission; feeding the starving Afghans while their source of oppression was being removed. Our professional Navy comrades in arms were in much evidence here as they were in the Berlin Airlift. I was told that the first major Afghan food drop as seen on TV was from "The Spirit of Berlin," the C-17 christened in Berlin and our formation companion over Ramstein!

The Airlift tradition, "We can fly anything anywhere anytime," comes down to us from the days of the Berlin Airlift. Lessons learned there still stand us in good stead. We need modern equipment, replacements for material handling equipment and aircraft that are costly to maintain and well beyond their service life. An active research and development program to ensure we are on the cutting edge of new technology, as it applies to aircraft and these systems, is essential to survival.

This is a new century and it will be a departure from the past. For the first time the home ground has become the battle ground. We must expect to sacrifice in order to ferret out and remove the cowardly terrorists and defend the freedoms we have taken too casually in the past. We are under siege from an unconventional enemy but we are not alone. The Berliners were equal to the task and so are we. In support of their American friends

Parachutes coming down to children of the Amelia Earhart School, Provo, Utah in a previous drop but similar in reaction to the Pigeon Forge drop.

Berlin Mayor Diepgen, General Jumper, President Clinton, Chancellor Kohl, and Gail Halvorsen christening the C-17, "The Spirit of Berlin."

200,000 Berliners marched in the streets of their city as the tragedy of New York and Washington, DC unfolded.

The healing process began but it was not easy. The possibility of canceling the 2002 Winter Olympic Games in Salt Lake City was actively discussed. Three billion viewers world wide would be a prime target and a showcase for terrorists to make a follow-up statement. The threat was pressing and real but the need for nations to come together in peace was the greater. Resolute leaders with cooler, pragmatic heads prevailed and the nearly 80 nations were assured that their participants' safety would not be compromised. The games went on without any significant interference. The games were some of the very best and as they unfolded the sportsmanship and drama added considerably to the healing process.

For the winter we had planned, as usual, on being at our place near Elephant Head, Arizona to be out of the cold and, this year, out of the Olympic crowds. In a controlled environment the TV would bring us the excitement of the event without cold feet. At 81 years old the circulation isn't what it used to be.

Then the phone rang: "This is David Fewster from The Church of Jesus Christ of Latter-day Saints. As a sponsor of the Olympic Games we can choose placard bearers for the German and Great Britain teams. We would like you to lead the German Olympic Team into the Eccles Stadium for the opening and closing ceremonies. Will you do it?" After a pause to recover from the shock, my answer came quickly: "Unbelievable. Once in a lifetime."

I met over 160 members of the German team in the Huntsman Center on the campus of the University of Utah before our march into the stadium. I soon became aware that there were a number of men and women on the team from Berlin. Were some of them grandchildren or great grandchildren of those I helped feed during the blockade of Berlin in 1948 and 1949? The image of that destroyed city under my C-54 wings came back in a flood of other memories. Years later the blood of young Peter Fechter had flowed out with his life—along with his hope for freedom—into the coarse sand at the base of the infamous Wall on the East Berlin side, his call for help unheeded. He and many more had made that ultimate sacrifice in their unsuccessful quest for freedom. Now, behind me, were perhaps athletes whose ancestors also longed to be free for they had lived in former East Berlin and East Germany. And maybe some of these athletes had ancestors who were guards at the Berlin Wall. If so, could one of their relatives have fired the shots that killed Peter Fechter? But now, all stood behind me representing a united Berlin and Germany.

With these thoughts in my mind, my feelings on our entry together into the stadium, which was filled with light, hope, cheering crowds and incredible sound, are beyond my ability to express. To me, this latest adventure represented an incredible climb to previously unimagined

From left to right: Rhona Martin, Great Britain team flag bearer and
Curling medal winner; Steve Young, Great Britain placard bearer and famous BYU
and San Francisco 49ers quarterback; Gail Halvorsen, placard bearer;
and Georg Hackl, German team flag bearer and Luge silver medal winner.

heights, beginning with two sticks of gum given to sweet-starved children at a barbed-wire fence in Berlin 54 years ago!

A fitting closure came 16 days later on 24 February 2002 during the closing ceremony. Georg Hackl, the German team representative, a veteran of five Olympics and a winner of five medals in the Luge competition, handed me the "new" united Germany flag. I placed it in sight of the Olympic flame with the flags of those countries who chose to participate in the Olympic family games of 2002.

As I look back I thank the blockaded children in Berlin for reminding me of the importance of putting principle before pleasure when faced with an important decision. Freedom later was more important to them than the offer of food from the Soviets, the pleasure of food now. In our time and our land the lure of "pleasure drugs" leads many to miss both their present and long-term goals and even steals their ability to retain their freedom, their free agency.

The Berlin children taught me to be more grateful for what ever I have, but most especially for freedom. The children reminded me of the essentiality of hope in human progress from tragedy to light. The Berlin Airlift experience taught me the reality of the Savior's guide to fulfillment. Service before self is also one of the Air Force core values. I only knew one person on the Lift who genuinely was disaffected with flying day and night in every weather condition for the welfare of a former enemy. The rewards of service to the less fortunate can hardly be equaled.

This is the wonderful thing about the Airlift mission. The Airlifters and Tankers are directly in the business of service before self. Earth quakes, floods, fires, critical support for a beleaguered comrade, city, or for a war fighting CINC, Airlifters and Tankers are there. The one common denominator of much of human need and resultant conflict hinges on the crux, the issue of freedom.

Freedom for our country goes back to a group of inspired statesmen. Rex Lee, an accomplished student and teacher of the Constitution, once

said words to the effect that if we took the 50 greatest statesmen this country has ever produced, fully one third of them were present for the drafting of the Declaration of Independence and later, the Constitution. These great men were taken from a population the size of New York! One such statesman was Samuel Adams.

There was a debate between those whose livelihood and comfort depended on loyalty to the king and those who pledged their means, honor and even their lives if necessary for the unknowns of liberty. To those depending on the king Mr. Adams turned and said something like the following:

"If ye love wealth better than liberty, the tranquility of servitude more than the animated

Bronze of Gail Halvorsen presented on his induction into the Airlift/Tanker Hall of Fame, Dallas, Texas November, 1999. Located near Gen. Tunner's bronze at Scott AFB, IL.

contest of freedom; go home from us in peace. We seek not your counsel nor your arms. Stoop down and lick the hands of he that feeds you and may your chains rest lightly on your shoulders and may your posterity forget that ye were ever our countrymen."

Jesus Christ said, "Greater love hath no man than this, that a man lay down his life for his friends." Nathan Hale, Patrick Henry and countless others since have given their lives that we might be free. Thirty one of my Air Force airlifter buddies and thirty nine of my British flying comrades gave their lives for an enemy, who had become friends.

I am grateful for patriots gone before and those patriots today in harms way for they have made it possible for us to drink from wells we haven't dug, and warm ourselves by fires we haven't built. They have given us skies unmarked by the con trails of enemy aircraft, rolling fields of grain unmarked by the treads of enemy tanks, and harbors nesting friendly ships. But now we have experienced the wounding of a proud city on our own soil. Smoke has risen from the ashes of a once magnificent structure that became a tomb for its admiring residents. The sturdy walls of the Pentagon were likewise breached by the act of cowardly assassins. Terrorists will not prevail. Patriots of today and the young patriots of tomorrow will not let it be. As the children of Berlin sacrificed for their tomorrows so today we must be willing to do the same.

God bless those dedicated to winning and safeguarding freedom.

God bless the United States of America!

Photo Credits

U.S. Air force: 10, 11, 23, 34, 39, 40, 44, 52, 58, 60, 61, 62, 67, 68, 81, 85, 94, 97, 112, 115, 119, 121, 123, 124, 126, 128, 129, 132, 138, 140, 143, 145, 146, 150, 161, 164, 174, 175, 184, 185, 187, 189, 190, 191, 193, 198, 200, 201 (bottom), 202 (top), 206, 240, 241, 242, 244

United States Air Force Art Collection: 111

U.S. Army: 38

AP: 236, 237 (top), 238, 247 (bottom)

Airlift/Tanker Association: 250

Brigham University: 197, 199 (top)

Budesbildstelle Bonn: 56

Chicopee Public Library: 156

Wolfgang Chodan: 235 (top)

Curis Earl: 157

Guy Dunn: 37

Landesbildstelle Berlin: 13, 70, 163, 173, 178, 198, 200, 201 (top left)

John Pickering: 147

Tom Rivera: 233 (top and bottom), 234

Ullan Studio, Las Vegas: 159

Eugene Williams: 152

Author: 18, 19, 33, 49, 50, 55, 107, 110, 148, 160, 165, 202 (bottom), 237 (bottom), 239 (top), 249

Endnotes

1. William H. Tunner, *Over the Hump,* (New York: Duell, Sloan & Pierce, 1964), p. 154.
2. *Ibid.*
3. *Ibid.,* p. 172.
4. Lucius D. Clay, *Decision In Germany,* (New York: doubleday and Co., 1950), p. 115.
5. Robert Jackson, *The Berlin Airlift,* (Letchworth, Hertfordshire: Adlard and Son Limited, 1988), p. 67.
6. *Ibid.,* p. 44.
7. *Berlin Airlift: A United States Air Force Europe Summary,* n.d. p. 11.
8. D.M. Giangreco and Robert E. Griffin, *Airbridge to Berlin,* (Novato, CA: Presido Press, 1988), p. 28.
9. *Ibid.*
10. Richard Collier, *Bridge Across the Sky,* (New York: McGraw-Hill, 1978), p. 52.
11. Giangreco and Griffin, *op. cit.,* p. 83.
12. Collier, *op. cit.,* p. 50.
13. Giangreco and Griffin, *op. cit.,* p. 96.
14. Jackson, *op. cit.,* p. 67.
15. Rober D. Launius and Coy F. Cross II, *Military Airlift Command, and the Legacy of the Berlin Airlift,* (Scott AFB: Military Airlift Command, 1989), p. 10.
16. *Ibid.,* p. 11
17. *The World Book Encyclopedia,* Vol. 5, (Chicago, Ill.: Field Enterprises, 1965), p. 193.
18. *Flight Manual USAF Series C-54-Navy R5D,* (USAF T.O. 1 C-54-D1, 1963), p. 72.
19. *Ibid.,* p. 222.
20. Launius and Cross II, *op. cit.,* p. 20.
21. Roger D. Launius, *The Berlin Airlift: Constructive Air Power,* (Wash. D.C.: Air Power History, Spring, 1989), p.13.

22. Jackson, *op. cit.,* Appendix Three.
23. *Ibid.,* p. 55 and *Berlin Airlift, An Account of the British Contribution,* (30 Rockefeller Plaza, NY: British Information Service, 1949), p. 40.
24. Jackson, *op. cit.,* p. 8.
25. John Provan, *Zeppelins, Rhein-Main,* (Frankfurt: Self, 1985), p. 17.
26. Tunner, *op. cit.,* p. 187.
27. Tunner, *op. cit.,* p. 218 and Collier. *op. cit.,* p. 93.
28. Edward A. Morrow, "Berlin," New York Times, (New York: *New York Times,* 16 Oct. 1948).
29. Tunner, *op. cit.,* p. 183.
30. *A Special Study of Operation "Vittles,"* Aviation Operations, (New York: ConnoverMast Publications, April 1949), p. 62.
31. *Flight Manual,* T.O. 1C-54-D1, *op. cit.,* Fig. A2-13.
32. Collier, *op. cit.,* p. 67 and Giangreco and Griffin, *op. cit.,* p. 96.
33. Collier, *op. cit.,* p. 95.
34. Launius and Cross II, *op. cit.,* p. 52.
35. Collier, *op. cit.,* p. 97.
36. *Berlin for Young People,* Informationszentrum, (Berlin: 1988).
37. Cornelius Ryan, *The Last Battle,* (London, England: Collins, 1966), p. 296.
38. Jackson, *op. cit.,* p. 87.
39. Eugene C. Zack, WSPN Radio Broadcast, (Chicopee, Mass.: WSPN News Editor, 21 January, 1949).
40. Collier, *op. cit.,* p. 119.
41. *Air Force Times,* 16 October 1948.
42. *Berlin Airlift, An Account of the British Contribution, op. cit.,* p. 60.
43. *Task Force Times,* (Wiesbaden, Germany: Combined Airlift Task Force, 28 January, 1949), p. 2.
44. *Chicopee News,* Mass., 28 January 1949.
45. Zack, *op. cit.,* 28 January 1949.
46. *New York Herald Tribune,* 10 February 1949.
47. *Luftbrucke Commemoration,* Zentralflughafen-Tempelhof, (Berlin, Germany: Tripartite Program, 12 May 1989).
48. *The Tabulator,* Tempelhof, 735th Support Group, USAFE, Base Newspaper, (Neukoelln, Berlin: Chimelorz, 14 May 1971).

About the Author

Gail Halvorsen was born in Salt Lake City, Utah, and grew up on small farms in Utah and Idaho. He earned a private pilot license under the non-college Civilian Pilot Training Program in September of 1941. Almost concurrently Gail joined the Civil Air Patrol as a pilot. He joined the United States Army Air Corps in June 1942. Fighter pilot training was with the Royal Air Force after which he was returned to the Army Air Corps and was assigned flight duty in foreign transport operations in the South Atlantic Theater. After WWII he flew in the Berlin Airlift where he became known as "Uncle Wiggly Wings," the "Chocolate Flyer" and the "Berlin Candy Bomber." The blockade of Berlin began in June 1948 and ended 12 May 1949. Flights continued until 30 September 1949 to build up reserves.

In 1952 he received his Bachelor and Masters degrees in Aeronautical Engineering from the Air Force Institute of Technology. From 1952 to 1970 he was assigned research and development duties with Air Force Systems Command in aircraft and research and development and operational duties in the Air Force Space Program. The Titan III Space Launch vehicle was one of his special projects.

Next, Halvorsen was assigned as the Commander of Tempelhof Central Airport in Berlin and as the United States Air Force Representative to the city of Berlin. He earned a Masters degree in Counseling and Guidance in 1973 through a Wayne State "On Base" education program.

Gail retired from the Air Force 30 September 1974 with over 8,000 flying hours. In addition to other Air Force decorations he has been awarded the Legion of Merit; Cheney Award 1948-49; Ira Eaker "Fellow" Award by the USAF Chief of Staff, General Ryan for the AFA, 1998; Americanism Award Air Force Sergeants Association 1998 (some previous recipients were Bob Hope and President George Bush); Service Cross to the Order of Merit from the President of Germany 1974; the Freedom Award from the City of Provo; The Distinguished Humanitarian Award from the Institute of German American Relations 1999; and with some other Airlift pilots the Eric Warburg Pries, 1998. (Henry Kissinger was a previous recipient). On

5 February 2004, he was awarded the Freedom Foundation at Valley Forge National Award for Adult Communication of Utah.

For ten years he was the Assistant Dean of Student Life at BYU. Later, he and Alta served a mission for their church in England, 1986–87.

In 1994, he participated in C-130 night resupply drops over Bosnia. From 1995 to 1997, he and Alta served another mission for their church in St. Petersburg, Russia. In 1998, he was a pilot on the Berlin Airlift Historical Foundation C-54, the "Spirit of Freedom," across the North Atlantic for 69 days and 27 air shows in 4 European countries. In May 1999, he flew with a C-130 supply run to Albania and visited Camp Hope, a Kosova refugee camp to deliver candy, toys, and school supplies to the Kosova children at that camp. In 1999, he was inducted into the Airlift/Tanker Hall of Fame, and into the Utah Aviation Hall of Fame in May 2001. In June 2000, he was a guest at Yokota AFB, Japan, for several talks. June 2001 saw the new 25,000-pound aircraft loader named after him. In December 2000 and 2002, he and Loraine flew out of Guam on the annual "Christmas Drop" to natives of several Micronesian Islands. In 2002, Margot Raven wrote *Mercedes and the Chocolate Pilot*. The book is used in elementary schools across the nation in post and cold war studies. In December 2002 and 2003, he and Lorraine flew in the BAHF C-54, *Spirit of Freedom* over Kitty Hawk, with airdrops celebrating the 100th Anniversary of Flight. Since then, Col. Halvorsen and his wife have made many candy drops to schools across the U.S. On August 6, 2003, the Halvorsens opened the New York City NASDAQ Stock Exchange.

Col. Halvorsen belongs to The Church of Jesus Christ of Latter-day Saints and has been a stake president, bishop, high councilman, and served in other callings.

Gail married Alta Jolley of Zion National Park on 16 April 1949. They have 5 children, 24 grandchildren, and 21 great-grandchildren. Three of their grandchildren have attended a school named for Gail in Frankfurt, Germany.

Approaching 50 years of marriage, Alta died in January 1999. Gail is now married to his high school steady from 62 years ago, Lorraine Pace, who has 3 children, 8 grandchildren, and 10 great-grandchildren. They presently live on their farm in Spanish Fork, Utah. Winters are spent at Lorraine's home in Arizona.

Epilogue

As I look back at "Operation Little Vittles" and the years that have followed, there is one human characteristic above all others that gave it birth—the silent gratitude of the children at a barbed wire fence in Berlin, July 1948. They did not beg for chocolate. Flour meant freedom. They would not lower themselves to ask for more. Because not one child begged, thousands received over 21 tons of candy from the sky, or delivered on the ground, over the next 14 months.

Other events are memorable: the excitement as the children chased the parachutes; the letters with heart-given messages; the drawings; the gifts to crew members on the flight line; the assignment in 1970 for four years as commander of Tempelhof Central Airport, a direct result of the Operation; the personal gifts of many descriptions including two Arabian stallions; the personal contact with Peter and Mercedes Wild and Berlin children now grown; and flying with Tim Chopp and crew in *The Spirit of Freedom* since 1994, including the trip to Europe in 1998 for 69 days. As a direct result of that trip, my high school steady of 1939, Lorraine Pace, found me after all those years and now helps me carry on after the death of my beloved Alta. So many spiritual and material rewards.

In man's search for fulfillment and happiness, material rewards pale compared to the importance of gratitude, integrity, and service before self. Gratitude brings unexpected special blessings, communication is facilitated, understanding is accomplished, and progress accelerated. Gratitude, integrity, and service to the unfortunate provide more rewards than all things material. They are the foundation upon which hope is born. They provide the strength by which hope endures.

A victim of the blockade once told me, "Without hope the soul dies." The airlift with its dried eggs, dried potatoes, dried milk, coal, and even chocolate meant hope for freedom. Freedom was more important than a full stomach or a rare treat. It was hope, not the flour, that gave the West

Berliners the strength to carry on. That hope came to full fruition with the fall of the Wall and the reunification of Germany in 1989–90. The Americans, British, French, and Germans prevailed. Air crews, ground crews, and sea crews did the job!

General William Tunner was the airlift genius who made the airlift a resounding success. The heroes of the Berlin Airlift are the 31 Americans and the 39 British who gave their lives to deliver freedom and democracy to a former enemy. Service to others before self was their mission. It is the only true recipe by which full fulfillment may be attained in this life. It is one of the core values of the United States Air Force. Today the Air Mobility Command, in the airlift tradition, launches a mission of mercy every 90 seconds somewhere around the world. The American flag on the aircraft tail is the symbol of hope to those in deep despair from whatever the source of oppression.

With the Compliments
of
The President

To Lorraine and Gail Halvorsen
With best wishes,

Above: Photo with President Bush. Andrews AFB, Washington D.C., September 2004, prior to President Bush's departure to a conference.

Below: Alta and Gail meeting Prince Phillip at Fairford Air Show in England, 26 July 1998.

Above: Delivering Santa Claus in the *Spirit of Freedom* to the kids at Manteo Airport, North Carolina, 17 December 2003. Near Kitty Hawk.

Below: C-54 *Spirit of Freedom* Tim Chopp and Gail prior to take off for flight over Kitty Hawk, North Carolina, 17 December 2003, anniversary of the Wright Brothers' first flight. The third year in a row that they did it.

Above: Ambassador to Germany's wife, Sue Timken (right), holding the book *Mercedes and the Chocolate Pilot* and reading it to German Children in October 2005.

Below: Mural about the Airlift presented to President Reagan in July 1987, Tempelhof Central Airport, Berlin. The President greeted Gail at the presentation of the Mural. Gail is in front, taken in July 2004. He is also in the far left of the mural.

Above: Mercedes Wild and Gail at the Tempelhof Central Airport reception in September 2005 announcing *The Berlin Candy Bomber* and *Mercedes and the Chocolate Pilot* coming out in the German language.

Below: Martin Roenkendorf from Hamburg, Germany, on his visit to the Berlin Candy Bomber in Arizona. They will meet with Martin's father in the Allied Museum, Berlin, on 12 May 2009.

Lieutenant Colonel
Gail Halvorsen

1525 Dove Way
Amado, AZ 85645
USA

Hamburg, 9. February 2009

Dear Mr Halvorsen,

when I was a little kid, (33 years now), my dad always had to tell me bedtime stories. Everytime he asked me, what kind of stories I want to hear. Of course he knew already, I was about to say: something when you were a kid and watched those airplanes at Tempelhof Airfield. And there he was, told this stories over and over again and I glanced at him with big eyes, the way I glanced at airplanes in those days - and still do.

He told me about chocolate bars flying on parachutes and a lot of tiny little side stories. I was amazed but also couldn't believe it back then, that something like the airlift really had happened. When I grew up, I asked my dad again and again to tell me more about it. I've read books, watched several movies and do-cumentaries. And there he is, my hero - Lieutenant Colonel Gail Halvorsen, United States Army - even if I wasn't born yet, when this amazing thing happend. My dad grew up in Berlin and saw those planes and was as fascinated of flying, planes, the airlift and what the american government did for the people of Berlin.

He will turn 75 this year and I have a big surprise for him. We're going to Berlin together and I've booked a flight on a remaining Raisin Bomber, a DC-3, a roundtrip over the roofs of Berlin. I am sure, he will like it. A journey to his own history with awesome memories.

I have a wonderful friend, his name is Marc. He's been working in advertising for years but then decided to start over, writing books about life and all that really matters. He inspires me a lot, especially the way he tries to make his dreams come true. Just recently he's been to San Diego to meet the guys from the Apollo 8 Mission, an evolutionary step in history Marc grew up with. And there I was, thinking about a person I always wanted to meet, the hero of not only my generation but also of my and my families history.

I would so happy to meet you once - just for an hour, chat a little bit about life, flying, the Skymaster, your experiences with the airlift in Berlin. Honestly, there would be my biggest dream come true.

I know, it's really on short notice, but my girlfriend and I decided on short notice to take a break and fly to California for 2 weeks from February 16th to March 2nd. May be you have time for an hour to meet me or us. That would make me so happy.

Best regards from across the ocean,

MARTIN ROENKENDORF

We are in contact and will likely meet with his father in the Allied Museum in Berlin, 12 May 2009.

This was the news as broadcast on WSPR

Our listeners heard this story over WSPR

On Jan. 21st 1949 We thought you might like this copy

A group of Chicopee school children -- who adopted "Operation Little Vittles" as their own pet project -- today were preparing a welcome for the originator of the plan to supply candy and chewing gum to German youngsters.

Founder of "Little Vittles" is Lieutenant Gail S. Halverson, a pilot with the Berlin Air Lift. It was Halverson who first devised the scheme of using handkerchief parachutes to drop the candy bars and chewing gum to the German children, as his "Vittles" plane roared into Templehof Airdrome at Berlin.

Now, Halverson is returning to the United States -- his tour of duty with the Air Lift completed. But before he left Germany, Halverson entrusted the continued operation of "Little Vittles" to his fellow Air Lift pilots.

The flier is scheduled to arrive at Westover Airforce Base sometime tomorrow. And on hand to meet his plane will be the delegation of Chicopee school children -- headed by "Little Vittles" chairman, Miss Mary Connors.

The youngsters have shipped more than eighteen tons of candy bars, chewing gum, and handkerchief parachutes to Germany since the start of the project. Now at peak operation, the "Little Vittles" committee is processing shipments of eight hundred pounds each, which go out every other day.

When Halverson arrives, he'll be taken in tow by the Chicopee youngsters, will visit the fire station donated by the mayor for their headquarters, and will give the children some idea of the importance of their project.

Eugene C. Zack
WSPR News Editor

Twenty-two schools in the Chicopee, MA, area tied up and sent 800 pounds of candy parachutes almost every other day to Gail and his successor, Captain Willy Williams. This source and others made a total of over 21 tons of candy delivered by air, or on the ground, from July 1948 until the end of September 1949.

The following photos depict activities since the last printing of *The Berlin Candy Bomber*.

Above: Gail Halvorsen with his son Bob after flying Gail's REMOS from Oshkosh, Wisconsin, to Spanish Fork, Utah, in 2007.

Below: Gail in a REMOS with chocolate bars for children waiting for him near the LDS Temple in Sacramento, California, 2007.

Above: Gail Halvorsen and Mercedes Wild with German Chancellor Angela Merkel, ILA Air Show, Berlin 2008. They are pictured with General Duncan McNabb (at the time Vice Chief of Staff, USAF), second from right, and General Roger Brady (Commander USAF Europe), far right.

Below: Gail and Lorraine Halvorsen with President George Bush Sr. at the grand opening of the new American Embassy in Berlin, 4 July 2008.

Above: New York City mayor Michael Bloomberg; Gail Halvorsen; and Lars Halter, General Chairman of the General von Steuben Parade in New York City on 20 September 2008. They were discussing plans for the parade.

Below: Parade participants, left to right, Gail Halvorsen; German Ambassador to the United States, Dr. Klaus Scharioth; the Ambassador's wife, Dr. Ulrike Scharioth; Micaela Leon, singer; fellow Grand Marshal Ralf Moller, actor in the popular movie *The Gladiator*; Lars Halter, Chairman; Lars's wife; and Lorraine Halvorsen, Gail's wife. They all led the parade down Fifth Avenue on 20 July 2008.

Above: Gail Halvorsen is wearing the medal of service presented to him by the Europaminister from the state of Hessen, Volker Hoff. The medal was awarded to Gail on the night before the General von Steuben Parade in New York City.

Below: Gail Halvorsen in front of a photo of the *Spirit of Freedom* C-54 that Tim Chopp and his crew (including Gail) flew to Germany in 1998. Gail is at the ILA Air Show in Berlin in May 2008.

Above: Gail Halvorsen with Richard Perlia, the 103-year-old test pilot for Hitler before and during World War II. Richard was selling his books at the ILA Air Show in Berlin, May 2008.

Below: Gail Halvorsen and Annette Cordova, actress, on the City of Los Angeles float in the Rose Bowl Parade on 1 January 2009.

January 23, 2009

Greetings Mr. Robert Halvorsen,

I am very grateful for the opportunity to write to you. My name is Mrs. Doris Galambos and I reside in Sarasota, Florida. I recently met

Lt. Col. Lee F. Kichen, and while conversing with him I learned your father was the "Candy Bomber" in World War II. You have no idea how much this information thrilled my heart! I am originally from Germany and was a little girl during those days.

However, I remember very well when candy was dropped from the airplane. I hope and pray that your dad is still with you. All my life I've wanted to say, "thank you" to the pilot who flew that plane and dropped the candy. I would love to meet him and tell him how thankful we children were for the candy and his kind generosity. This would be a dream come true for me. Therefore, I am asking, is there a chance for me to meet and talk with your dad? Please contact me and let me know if this is possible. I would be very grateful to hear back from you soon.

I thank you for your time Sir.

Sincerely,   *Doris Galambos*

Doris Galambos

Lt. Col Kichen knew my son, a Delta Airline captain, and he gave Mrs. Galambos the airline's address. Gail has spoken with her and sent her a copy of this book. They will meet!

Military Job Description–Major Halvorsen 1959–1960 described by LtCol Wallace E. Bjornson, Director Manned Research, Space Programs

Halvorsen's Current Duty: Military Space Systems AF Ballistic Missile Division (AFBMD), Los Angeles CA. Assigned as the Chief, Dyna Soar Division and responsible for all AFBMD support of the Dyna Soar Program including design engineering of modified Titan Booster, design of special systems, launching arrangements, scheduling, special studies, presentations, and submission of reports as required. The program calls for production of the first large space booster undertaken by the USAF separately from ballistic missile production and requires control of a major contractor effort. Major Halvorsen's work and recommendations were approved by General Schriever, the USAF Scientific Advisory Board, General Curtis LeMay and the Air Staff at the Pentagon and led to the selection of the Dyna Soar configuration.

DEPARTMENT OF THE AIR FORCE
HEADQUARTERS UNITED STATES AIR FORCES IN EUROPE
OFFICE OF THE COMMANDER IN CHIEF
APO NEW YORK 09012

21 DEC 1973

Dear Col Halvorsen

I have just reviewed the Inspection Report of the 7350th Air Base Group, 10-14 December 1973. The ratings achieved by your command are impressive. The Inspector General informed me that his Directorate of Inspection conducted their usual in-depth inspection and found your organization to be the best managed of any they have inspected in the past two years.

My congratulations to you, your officers, noncommissioned officers, and airmen for this outstanding achievement. Best wishes to you and the 7350th Air Base Group for your continued success in the coming year.

Sincerely,

DAVID C. JONES
General   USAF
Commander in Chief

Colonel Gail S. Halvorsen
Commander
7350th Air Base Group
APO 09611
BERLIN

Colonel Halvorsen gives credit to the exceptional officers, airmen (and women), and excellent German civilian workforce for this superior rating.

Huyler's
SINCE 1876

EXECUTIVE OFFICES • 30-30 NORTHERN BOULEVARD, L. I. C. 1, NEW YORK • TEL. IRONSIDES 6-6615

<u>Via Air Mail</u>   November 23rd
                                     1 9 4 8

Lt. G.S. Halvorsen
C-54 PROV GRP 17 ATS
APO 57, c/o Postmaster
New York, N.Y.

Dear Lt. Halvorsen:

Your letter of November 15th addressed to Mr. Swersey has been turned
over to the writer for reply, your letter having crossed his of November 16th and mine of November 12th.

In my letter of the 12th, it was explained that General Clay had issued
a Directive for the handling of future shipments, the arrangements in
Washington being handled by Lt. Col. Ayres. In all probability you have
learned by now additional details as to how the shipments will be handled
upon arrival at Bremerhaven.

We are pleased to advise that another shipment consisting of 54,856 units
of Assorted Candies and Crackers went forward from the N.Y. Port of Embark-
ation on the SS GREENVILLE VICTORY on November 18th. This makes a total
of 100,700 units that have gone forward by steamer through the Army Transport Service. Am positive this routing will afford quicker arrival at
destination and the quantity will give you sufficient units for the Christmas Holidays.

We sincerely hope you are making arrangements to have the 2,960 units
picked up from Capt. DuBose' residence. We understand these are still
there.

The Directive issued by General Clay was for a total of ten (10) tons
against which we have delivered a little over six and one-half (6½) tons.
After this amount has been cleared, we understand further instructions
will be issued by General Clay as to how additional quantities are to be
handled.

No doubt the contents of this letter will be very pleasing to you and would
ask that you keep us informed as to how things are going.

With kindest regards from all, we are

                              Yours very sincerely,
                              HUYLER'S

                              C.H. Clark
                              C.H. CLARK

CHC:W

Lessons Learned from the Best Teachers
Gail S. Halvorsen, 6 April 2010

1. * The desire for freedom is inborn in every human soul, no matter on which side of the border he or she is born. "I do it myself" comes in every language from the lips of most children when at two or three years old they are pushed too fast. Free agency is already at work, but all are not free to exercise it.

2. * Children hold the future of the entire world in their hands—Our children and everyone's children.

3. * Keep your word. Integrity begets hope, faith, trust, peace of mind, and confidence for yourself and others. A West Berliner recipient of a chocolate bar once told me, "Without hope the soul dies." His hope and faith were based on the word of the British, French, and Americans that we would stand by him.

4. * Give service to others if you seek genuine fulfillment. The Dead Sea is dead because it does not give.

5. * Be grateful to others without preconditions, and unplanned rewards will be yours; more important, another person's day will be brightened.

6. * Seek a positive outlook on life, and the world will be manageable, even if difficult. Attitude is not everything but it does affect everything. It determines your success or failure in how you complete the mission and in the world of work. It is more important than grade point average.

7. * Little decisions put your footsteps on the path that will lead you to your final destination, good or bad.

8. * It is never so good or so bad that the existing situation cannot be improved with patience, determination, love, and hard work.

9. * My mother always said, "Perseverance wins!" She was right. Patience and work are again the keys.

10. * A good woman is uniquely powerful, inspirational, and to be prized.

11. * My father taught we should not only endure to the end but also strive to excel through the journey.

12. * Families that work and pray together are the ideal building blocks for a beneficial society.

13. * My scoutmaster said, "Always do your best!" He was right.

14. * If there is a conflict when you make a decision, put principle before pleasure. The Berlin kids did. Freedom sometime in the dim future was more important to them than the pleasure of enough food.

15. * As we travel the roads of life, let us look in the rearview mirror to learn, but not look too long for "what if," "what might have been," how great or bad we were, or how bad someone else was. We may miss the road to what we can become.

16. * God is alive and well. We are all on a path to somewhere on our spaceship "Earth." He has given us a GPS** that will direct us around the mud holes of life and radar** that we may not ice our wings, or hit rocks in that which clouds our vision. If we keep our batteries properly charged, we will make the journey safely back to him.

  * Items that reflect values taught to me by my best teachers and exhibited by the people of West Berlin and the Berlin Airlift air, ground, and sea personnel during the Soviet Blockade of Berlin 1948–49.

** The scriptures, ancient, modern, and the Holy Ghost.

HALVORSEN NEW YORK TRIP REPORT TO GENERAL TUNNER
29 September 1948

To: General Tunner
        Commanding General
        Airlift Task Force (Prov)
        APO 633, US Army

1. After an uneventful trip across the Atlantic in a C-54, I arrived at Westover Air Force Base Saturday morning, 11 September and after checking in with the Public Information Office, I took a train for New York. Mr. Aubray Williams, producer of "We The People" met me at the depot and, through his personal interest and hospitality, made me feel right at home. Sunday afternoon I attended the Dodgers-Giants baseball game as Mr. William's guest.

2. Monday morning I reported to "We the People" and helped prepare the script for the program. Also acted as technical advisor on "Vittles" details. That afternoon we ran through the first rehearsal of the Tuesday evening show. Monday night I attended the musical show, "Inside USA", accompanied by Mr. And Mrs. Williams. Attended two rehearsals of "We the People" Tuesday morning and a dress rehearsal in the afternoon. Early that evening I was made up for the television broadcast and "We the People" went out over the air at 10:PM. A Russian girl by the name of Natasha whose parents were killed in Russia also appeared on the program. Upon learning that I had spent a great deal of time in Heidelberg she asked if I would bring back a package to her girl friend in Heidelberg. The package was a gift of nylon stockings.

3. Wednesday morning, 10:00, I attended a press conference at the Wings Club at the Biltmore Hotel. Reporters and photographers representing the New York Sun, New York Times, Journal American, Herald Tribune, Daily Mirror and the Daily News were present for this conference. That afternoon I received an invitation from the Mutual Broadcasting Company to appear on two broadcasts for that evening. One broadcast was at 4:00PM,"Human Side of the News", and the other was for the 10:00PM,"Mutual Newsreel". I spent all day Thursday at ABC and NBC running over proposed scripts for two television shows Saturday evening. Thursday night I attended the musical show "Show Boat."

4. Friday I acted as Technical Advisor on a half hour Airlift broadcast staring Joe E. Brown and Henry Fonda. I was asked to rewrite the part of the scrip that had to do with radio contacts and GCA procedures. Friday Evening I was contacted by Mr. Swersey, Vice President of the Huyler Candy Company. During dinner Mr. Swersey informed me that he would be glad to supply, through the whole candy industry, 10,000 bars of candy a week. I was also invite out to Mr. Orland King's home and was offered the administrative set up and warehousing facilities of Operation Democracy of which he is the Director. Mr. King is also owner of Huyler Candy Company and he is very much interested in the operation of Little Vittles. He will take care of everything, transportation, supply, etc. Incidentally, Mr. King and Mr. Swersey are Directors of Confectionaries and they have interested the Hershey , Baby Ruth and other popular candy manufacturers in supplying Little Vittles. Mrs. King, former Congresswoman from Arizona, has also taken a personal interest in Little Vittles and is sending 1,000 midget parachute each week. Later that evening I attended the musical show, High Button Shoes, as a guest of Mr. and. Mrs. King.

5. Saturday morning I went on a tour of five different Huyler Candy Companies. Later, I checked the scripts and sets for two television shows over ABC and NBC. That evening I was on an ABC show followed by an NBC show an hour later with Tex McCrary and Air Force pilots who were in New York for the Air Force Day celebrations. Tex, at the end of the show but while we were still on television, ripped off his shirt tail and handed it to me saying, " Here, use this as a parachute." After the broadcast I checked out of New York for Washington.

6. Sunday morning I went over to Bolling Field and checked script for the Air Force Hour. The show was aired at 2:00 PM. Checked with MATS for flight to Westover and was informed that the first plane would depart Monday afternoon. Monday morning I visited the Public Relations Office, Pentagon Building. While there, Major Ralph Slater gave me copies of the wire requesting me to extended my time. Accompanied by Major Slater I went on tour of the Pentagon. Monday noon I again checked with MATS for Westover flights. Caught the plane at Bolling Field and arrived in Westover Monday night. Passenger Section, Westover, told me to report of procession Tuesday morning'

7. Early Tuesday morning I processed as directed and contacted Vittles Operation to see about flying a plane back. Operations informed me that it was possible as they had one already to go. Waited around until late Tuesday afternoon-the plane hadn't finished loading. Checked again that evening and found that the plane would be ready Wednesday morning. Checked in again early Wednesday and was unable to depart as the airplane had no emergency equipment aboard. Checked again in the afternoon and at 10:00 PM, only to discover that they were still working on it!

8. After clearing operations Thursday morning, engineering called and stated the aircraft was out of commission and that it would be from one to five days before it would be ready. After making sure that a crew was available to fly the plane over here, I went back to POE and was placed on a MATS flight as a passenger. I arrive back at Rhein Main Friday morning.

9. Prior to my departure from Westover many of the handkerchiefs and packages of candy had already started to arrive. Contacted Traffic and made arraignments to ship the candy to Germany. Upon arrival at Rhein-Main I found my BOQ stuffed with 1,000 handkerchief chutes and 400 pounds of candy from Brookley Field plus three sacks of personal mail with handkerchiefs and candy.

10, While in New York, I received numerous telephone calls from publicity men asking me to authorize collections for Little Vittles. One call was from an owner of a circus theater. His stunt was to charge handkerchiefs and candy bars as an entrance fee for children. I told the gentleman that their interest was appreciated but that we could not commercialize this operation.

Gail S. Halvorsen
1st Lt. USAF

Foot note: This trip was a result of General Tunner asking me to go to the States in response to the media interest in my operation as well as Operation Vittles.

Gail Halvorsen (center) with President Dieter F. Uchtdorf (left) and Charles W. Dahlquist II (right), Young Men general president and Honorary German General Consul, at the Joseph Smith Memorial Building, 2008, for the 60th Anniversary of the Berlin Airlift luncheon.

Gail Halvorsen with Secretary of Defense Robert Gates, Pentagon, 2008.

Confidential

R.A.F. Form 5012
(for use in U.S.A.)

R.A.F.—TRAINING REPORT

PILOT

School No. 3 B. F. T. S. (at Miami, Oklahoma)

1. Surname HALVORSEN   Christian Names GAIL SEYMOUR

2. Number 19073609   3. Rank AV/C   4. Course No. 19 JUNE/1944 Output

5. Posted from San Antonio   6. Date course commenced 8.12.43 Arrived 6.12.43   7. Date course ended 17.6.44   8. Posted to

9. Ground Examinations	Marks Allotted	Marks Obtained	10. Flying Tests	Marks Allotted	Marks Obtained
(a) Airmanship	300	222	(a) General Flying ...	400	318
(b) Armament	300	215	(b) Applied Flying ...	200	160
(c) Meteorology	100	82	(c) Instrument Flying ...	250	192
(d) Navigation	200	137	(d) Night Flying	100	87
(e) Signals	100	82	(e) Link Trainer	50	40
Total	1,000	738	Total	1,000	797

Order of Merit 41/111   Per Cent. 74   Order of Merit 2/111   Per Cent. 80

11. Assessment of qualities of Character and Leadership	Marks Allotted	Marks Obtained	Order of Merit
	100	81	1 /111

Degree of suitability for further training	0 Not at all suitable	1 Moderately suitable	2 Definitely suitable	3 Extremely suitable
12. For Bomber type aircraft				
13. For Fighter type aircraft				
14. For General Reconnaissance aircraft ...				
15. For Army Co-operation aircraft ...				
16. For Flying Boats				
17. As a Flying Instructor				
18. For Transport Duties			X	

(Mark "X" in appropriate column for each)

FINAL ORDER OF MERIT 3/111

19. If a copy of the O.T.U. report for this pupil is desired, mark here

20. Remarks:—

Has acted as Cadet Officer at this School and shown himself to be energetic, capable and thoroughly reliable. A very sound pilot. Should make an excellent officer.

Date 17 June 1944   Signed M. Roxburgh
Officer Commanding.

B.—Flying Times and Accident Record shown overleaf.)

Gail's Royal Air Force flight record. Gail was the Senior Cadet officer at the British flight school. He received his RAF wings on 17 June 1944.

Gail soloing in his powered parachute on his farm, Spanish Fork, Utah, in 2003.

Acclaimed American Artist, Steve Penley, depicts Gail's chocolate drop in Flowery Branch, Georgia, 2008. The Super Cub was flown by Alan Wayne. Doris Galambos was waiting below.

Gail Halvorsen and Doris Galambos, chocolate parachute drop, Flowery Branch, Georgia, 2009.

2@ MAR 2010

Dear LT. Halvorsen,
I herd in this book
that you gave candy to
kids around the world I
thought you could come
with your plane to
my house to give me
choclate also to my
sister sidney she's 10 years
old I'm 8 years old and
I'm in second grade. I live
in America.
    Your,
    friend Erin

Herigats hill

My Adreess

4022 Dowling Dr.
It's the truck with
green.

Dear Students,

RE: Mercedes and the Chocolate Pilot

Thank you so much for your wonderful letters and drawings! They are of great value to me. What it means is that you are interested in reading and learning about events that make a difference.

It is important to understand how your friends feel. It is even more important to understand why an enemy thinks the way he does about you. If we understand, we can develop peaceful and friendly relationships. That makes a better family, community, and world. To read is one of the best ways to gain understanding. Make it a habit.

I regret that it is not possible for me to answer each of your exceptional letters. Your questions about how the German enemies became friends are important to me. Some asked what I learned from the experience. I have attached sixteen very important lessons that I have learned. They were taught to me by my family, teachers, neighbors, strangers, my church, and the children of Berlin. Mercedes and Peter are two of the most special of the Berlin children. We see each other every few years.

I hope this will answer most of your questions. If you are interested in one special lesson, write to me and I will tell you why I selected that one.

Sincerely,

Gail S. Halvorsen
"The Chocolate Pilot"

A typical reply to students who have read the *Mercedes* book in their "Post and Cold War" studies and then wrote Gail their impressions.

My best thanks for the „Sky-Food",

Rose-Mary Fricke
Berlin-Schöneberg, Gustav-Müller-Platz 1
Berlin, 14ᵗᵉ okt. 1948.

A thank you letter from a Berlin grade-school teacher, Rose-Mary Fricke. Letters from her students are on the following two pages.

FORCE TIMES - OCTOBER 15, 19

Candy Pilot Continues To Get Letters

RHEIN MAIN, OCT. 14 — OF THE HUNDREDS OF THANK-YOU LETTERS RECEIVED BY 1ST LT. GALE HALVORSEN, LITTLE VITTLES "SHOKOLADENFLIEGER" ARE MANY GEMS OF SINCERITY AND WARM HUMOR.

ONE OF HIS LATEST FAN LETTERS CAME FROM A THANKFUL MOTHER, WHO DESCRIBED HOW A CANDY-LADEN PARACHUTE FELL ON THE ROOF OF HER HOME, MIRACULOUSLY PROVIDING A PRESENT FOR HER SON'S OTHERWISE GIFTLESS BIRTHDAY.

"THE OLDEST OF MY SEVEN SONS HAD ON THIS DAY HIS SIXTEENTH BIRTHDAY," THE MOTHER WROTE TO HALVORSEN, "BUT WHEN HE WENT OUT IN THE MORNING WE WERE ALL SAD, BECAUSE WE FELT CERTAIN THIS DAY WOULD BE NO DIFFERENT FROM ANY OTHER.

"BUT HOW HAPPILY EVERYTHING TURNED OUT!

"A PARACHUTE WITH CHOCOLATE LANDED ON OUT ROOF. IT WAS THE FIRST SWEETS FOR THE CHILDREN IN A LONG TIME. MY OLDEST SON, A STUDENT, CAME HOME AT EIGHT O'CLOCK AND I WAS ABLE, AFTER ALL, TO GIVE HIM SOME BIRTHDAY HAPPINESS."

THE GERMAN WOMAN WENT ON TO SAY SHE WOULD GLADLY RETURN THE HANDKERCHIEF PARACHUTE IF NECESSARY, BUT REQUESTED PERMISSION TO KEEP IT AS "A MEMENTO OF THE AIRBRIDGE TO BERLIN."

ANOTHER LETTER WAS FROM AN EIGHT-YEAR-OLD GIRL WHO ENCLOSED EXACT DIRECTIONS FOR FINDING HER HOUSE AND ASKED THAT THE "CHOCOLATE FLIER" TOSS A PARACHUTE HER WAY.

"BUT," SHE ADMONISHED, "DON'T LET MY MOTHER KNOW

Occupation Briefs *Stars & Stripes*

Little Vittles Hits Target On Berliner's Birthday

WIESBADEN, Oct. 17 (Special)— In the hundreds of thank-you letters received by 1st Lt Gale Halvorsen, "Little Vittles Shokoladenflieger," are many gems of sincerity and warm humor.

One of his latest fan letters came from a thankful mother, who described how a candy-laden parachute fell on the roof of her home, miraculously providing a present for her son's otherwise giftless birthday.

"The oldest of my seven sons had on this day his 16th birthday," the mother wrote to Halvorsen, "but when he went out in the morning we were all sad, because we felt certain this day would be no different from any other. But how happily everything turned out.

"A parachute with chocolate landed on our roof. It was the first sweets for the children in a long time. My oldest son, a student, came home at 8 pm and I was able to give him some birthday happiness."

The German woman went on to say she would gladly return the handkerchief parachute if necessary, but requested permission to keep it as "a memento of the air bridge to Berlin."

Another letter was from an 8-year-old girl who enclosed exact directions for finding her house and asked that the "chocolate flier" toss a parachute her way. "But don't let my mother know about this," she said. "She would scold me."

To top off everything, Halvorsen received one proposal in the mail, but he couldn't make out the name and address.

Springfield Daily News Oct. 18, 1948

Direct 'Little Vittles' Campaign

Chicopee, Oct. 18—Officials of the ground force of "Operation Little Vittles," Chicopee Chapter, shown above are, left to right, Mary Reardon, treasurer; Dolores Belcher, vice-president; Mary Connors, president; Laura Chapla, vice-president, and Dorothy Lane, vice-president. These officers will supervise the receiving and processing of candy and parachute materials that will be used to drop candy to the children of Germany.

Carson's project (2007) is an example of many Berlin Airlift displays that have won national awards for young students. Airlift veterans have always assisted the students.

Dear Gail,

   Thank you so much for all of your help.
I'm very happy with the outcome, I won
first place in the regional competition!
This project did teach me allot like giving
kindness to those in need of it eaven if
he is a former enemy, also in my pesonal
life being kinder to my brothers and sister.
Here are a few pictures of my project
                Thanks agian, Carson

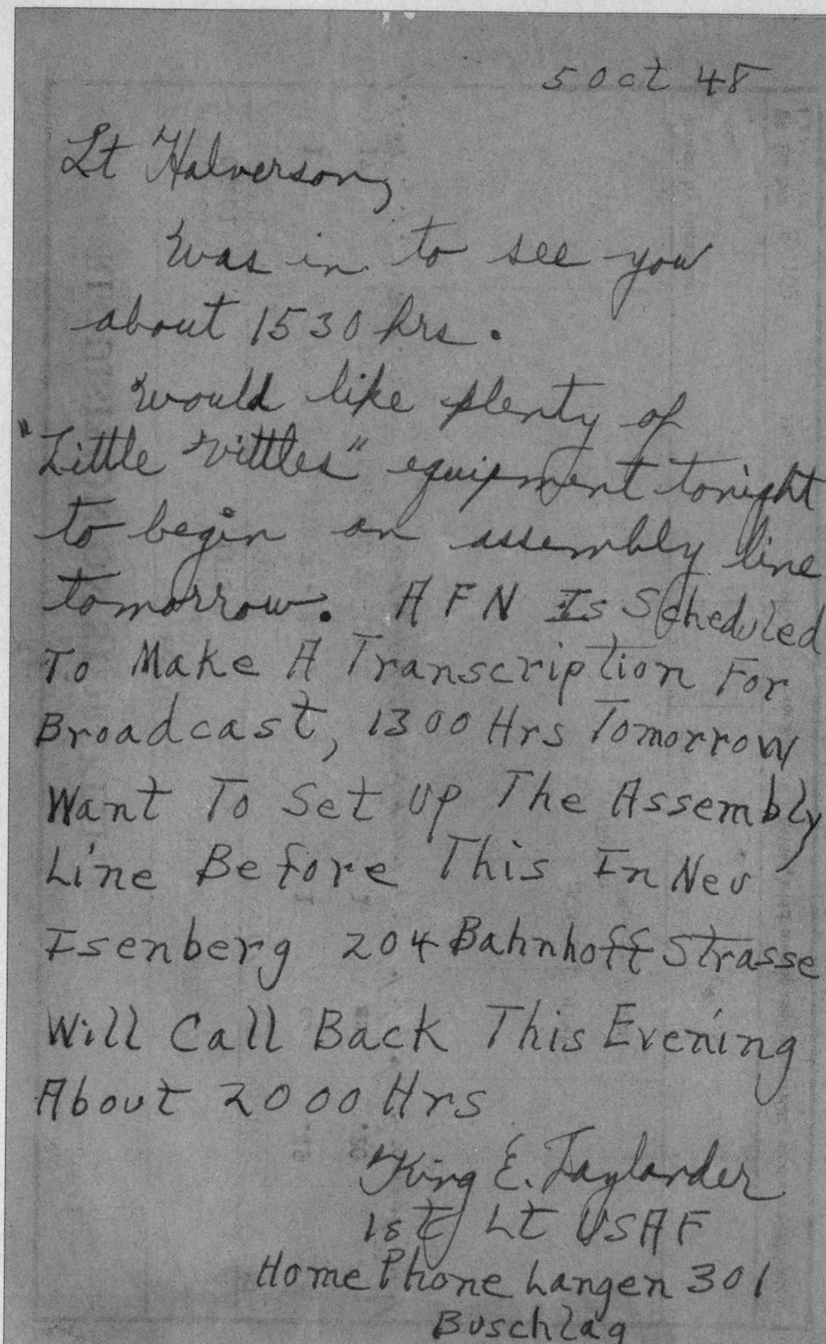

5 Oct 45

Lt Halverson,

Was in to see you about 1530 hrs.

Would like plenty of "Little vittles" equipment tonight to begin an assembly line tomorrow. HFN Is Scheduled To Make A Transcription For Broadcast, 1300 Hrs Tomorrow Want To Set Up The Assembly Line Before This In Neu Isenberg 204 Bahnhoff Strasse

Will Call Back This Evening About 2000 Hrs

King E. Taylarder
1st Lt USAF
Home Phone Langen 301
Buschlag

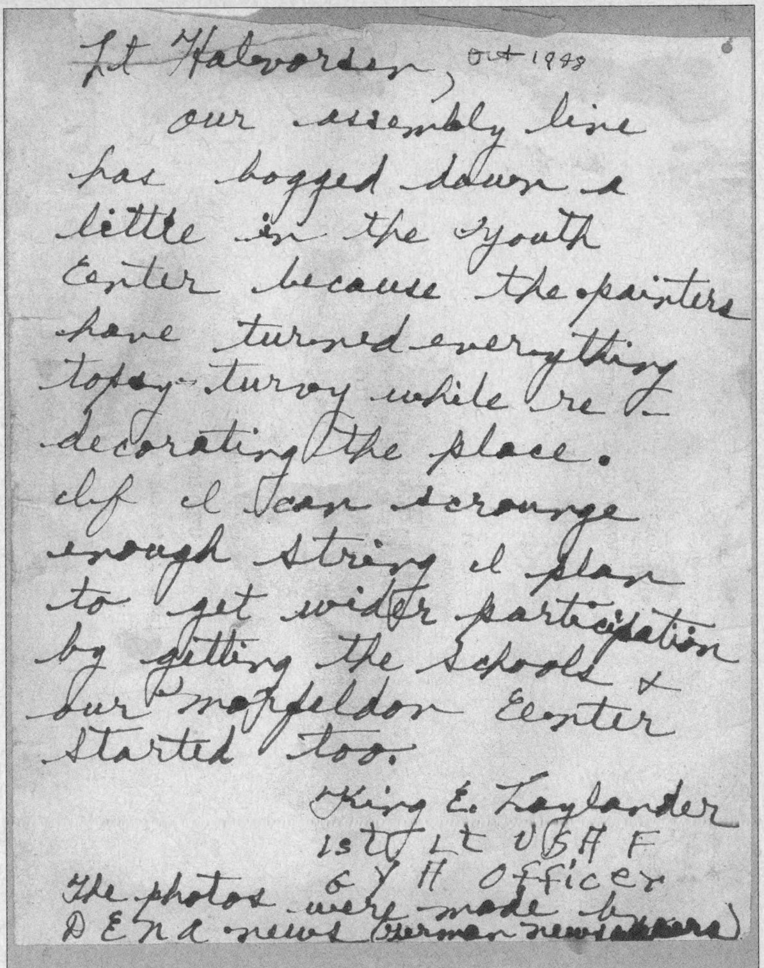

Lt Halvorsen, Oct 1948

our assembly line has bogged down a little in the Youth Center because the painters have turned everything topsy-turvy while re-decorating the place.

If I can scrounge enough string I plan to get wider participation by getting the schools & our mapfeldon Center started too.

King E. Laylander
1st Lt USAF
6 Y H Officer

The photos were made by D E N d news (German newspapers)

Salt Lake Tribune Jan. 16, 1949

'Candy Kid' From Utah Flies Last 'Lift' Trip, Heads Home

FRANKFURT, Germany, Jan. 16 (UP)—The pale-faced children of blockaded Berlin lost their lollipop hero Sunday. The air force is sending Gail Halvorsen home.

The slow talking airlift pilot from Garland, Utah, dropped lollipops from his airplane over Berlin and became the idol of Berlin children.

Since he dropped that first all-day sucker by parachute last July, Halvorsen and his flying buddies have unloaded some 90,000 parachutes loaded with candy.

Flies Last Mission

He did it "just because they were kids."

Last Sunday Halvorsen flew his last airlift mission, completing six months of duty flying the Russian blockade. His turn has come to go home under the rotation policy which limits airlift fliers to six months continuous duty.

"I dropped 2505 parachutes last Sunday—didn't know it was my last trip until I was almost ready to take off," he said. "I just loaded up everything I had."

Two sacks of mail every day arrive at the nearby Wiesbaden air base addressed to Halvorsen from the United States. He got 1400 Christmas cards.

Berliners Hail Hero

Four thousand Berliners, some of them living in the Russian sector, have written Halvorsen to thank him for the candy.

Approximately 30 letters from Berlin residents were handed to Halvorsen every day.

Two American girls have proposed to him.

"Lots of others," many of them U. S. war widows, have hinted at marriage to the good looking, 28-year-old lieutenant. But he just smiles.

"There's a girl back in Salt Lake City I've got to convince on this marriage business," he said. He declined to disclose her name.

Utah Airlift Pilot Returns

FRANKFURT, Germany (AP)—Lt. Gail S. Halvorsen, the American airlift pilot who first parachuted candy to Berlin's blockaded children, left Thursday for home.

The Garland, Utah, airman is being assigned to Brookley Field, Ala., after 125 round trip food flights to Berlin.

Despite his departure, Halvorsen's candy project will be carried on, with Lt. Lawrence L. Casky of Enid, Okla., taking it over.

Halvorsen's return to the United States is part of the rotation plan which keeps a continual flow of fresh men coming in to replace weary airlift fliers.

His plane is expected to arrive at Westover Field, Mass., Friday afternoon.

Office of the Secretary of National Defense, GDR, Harnekop, former East Germany. Atomic Response Control Center, three stories deep in the Bunker. The telephone was a direct line to Moscow. GDR's Leader, Erich Honecker's photo is on the wall. Gail gave an airlift speech on the first level, 2008.

Marilyn Halvorsen Sorensen (Gail's daughter), Gail, and Jenny Oaks Baker, a prominent concert pianist, at the Marriott Center, Provo, Utah, Festival of Freedom, 27 June 2010. Gail is Jenny's former Bishop. Gail led the Pledge of Allegiance, and Jenny performed several wonderful musical numbers. Gail's uniform is an Eisenhower jacket from 1946.

CERTIFICATE OF APPRECIATION
FROM THE UNITED STATES AIR FORCE

TO ALL WHO SHALL SEE THESE PRESENTS, GREETING:
THIS IS TO CERTIFY THAT

MRS GAIL S. HALVORSEN

on the occasion of the retirement of her husband from active duty with the

UNITED STATES AIR FORCE

has earned grateful appreciation for her own unselfish, faithful and devoted service. Her unfailing support and understanding helped to make possible her husband's lasting contribution to the Nation

ON THE FIRST   **DAY OF** SEPTEMBER
ONE THOUSAND NINE HUNDRED AND SEVENTY FOUR

EDMUND A. RAWALKO
Major General, USAF
Commander

CHIEF OF STAFF USAF

---

1 1 JUL 1995

Colonel Gail S. Halvorsen, USAF, Retired
1220 Locust Lane
Provo, Utah 84602

Dear Colonel Halvorsen

    Congratulations! You have been selected as the Air Education and Training Command nominee for the 1995 Elder Statesman of Aviation Award. We have *202-3* forwarded your nomination to the National Aeronautics Association to compete at the national level. Your achievements and contributions to aviation are deserving of this prestigious award. We wish you the best of luck as a finalist.

    We truly appreciate your dedication to your country and the art of aviation and wish you continued success.

Sincerely

BILLY J. BOLES
General, USAF
Commander

Gail and "Sully" Sullenberger exchange books and flight experiences in Danville, California, on 17 July 2010. Sully landed his plane and 155 passengers and crew in the Hudson River when both engines quit. All survived!

"Sully" Sullenberger signs a book for Gail while Bill Anderson, an Airlift pilot, looks on. (Photo courtesy of Christine Saunders.)

Left to right: Bill Anderson, airlift pilot; Gail; Captain Sully Sullenberger; and Danville, California, mayor, Mike Doyle, who is also a Berlin airlift veteran, assistant chaplain. Gail gave two firesides there on 17 July 2010. (Photo courtesy of Christine Saunders.)

On the anniversary of the Air Force, 17 September 1983, the Air Force honored Air Force veterans with a parade at Lackland AFB, Texas. Reviewing the parade are left to right: General Larry Armstrong, Lackland Commander; General Curtis LeMay, the Strategic Air Command legend and Chief of Staff USAF (He also launched the Berlin Airlift in 1948.); General Flynn, fighter ace; General Foster; Col Paul Tibbets, who dropped the first atomic bomb; Col Tex Hill, one of the most famous Flying Tigers in China; Col Gail Halvorsen; and Col Gabreski, fighter ace with 37½ enemy aircraft to his credit. Bob Hope was the master of ceremonies at a dinner in San Antonio where the city honored Air Force veterans the night before the parade.

The Berlin "kids" with Colonel Halvorsen, from left to right: Brunhilde Merrill, Steffani Plumb, Roswitha Barry, Gail, Ilse de Temple, Christa Schneider, Barbara Kuznetzoff, Patrick Weidhaas, and Chris Saunders. Chris organized the full house, Danville fireside. Steffani caught a good number of chocolate bars. She traded some chocolate for parachutes from which she made undergarments. All except Chris were children in Berlin during the Blockade. (Photo courtesy of Dolores Fox Ciardelli/DanvilleExpress.com.)

NEARER MY GOD TO THEE
Gail S. Halvorsen

Soaring through the clouds
I half expect here to see
An angel dining next to me.
A table here, a table there,
or perhaps a place for a rocking chair.

This room is furnished and replete.
The floor is soft for angels' feet.
You've seen the shows and the carpets lined
With a film of cloud that trails behind.

This is it, and first hand now
You see the light in the marbled hall.
The doors are wispy, never slam.
They haven't yet replaced a jam.

For pictures you may raise a call.
but watch those rainbows on the wall.
They change around and hang on straight,
No worry of plaster or adhesive tape.

The Maker of all this must be near,
Some greater presence calms my fears.
How insignificant this machine and man,
In such a great and marvelous plan.

I leave the room, now down the street,
The angels at this lamp post meet
to talk and laugh and play around,
You'd think that life was on the ground,

Till high and free you wandered loose
To watch the spires and taunt the goose,
To feel the breeze and taste the air
That stars and years have heaped up there.

To turn the earth upon it's side,
Then put the nose down in a dive,
To put the gear against the clouds
And leave the heights within their shrouds
That another day may come
And the ascent up once more begun.

Until that day when He will call
And install the wings that never stall!

Written in Natal Brazil in 1946 after flying a Douglas
Dauntless, A-24 dive bomber through the beautiful clouds
over the nearby ocean. Describes my love for the
creations of the Father of us all and my love of flying.

ARMY AIR FORCES
HEADQUARTERS, ATLANTIC DIVISION
AIR TRANSPORT COMMAND
FORT TOTTEN, LONG ISLAND, NEW YORK

IN REPLY REFER
ATLD 201.22

29 APR 1947

SUBJECT: Letter of Appreciation

THRU: Commanding Officer
        1103rd AAF Base Unit, ATLD-ATC
        Morrison Field
        West Palm Beach, Florida

TO: 1st Lieutenant Gail S. Halvorsen
        ASN O-38251
        1103rd AAF Base Unit, ATLD-ATC
        Morrison Field
        West Palm Beach, Florida

1. It is with great pleasure that I extend to you my personal appreciation for the services rendered as Co-Pilot of the C-54 aircraft number 2721, which was engaged by Strategic Air Command to transport Lieutenant Colonel A. F. Reinhardt and his party to Montevideo, Uruguay, for the purpose of establishing prior public relations, logistics support and custom clearance for Army Air Forces personnel participating in inaugural ceremonies at Montevideo.

2. It has been reported to me that you very capably assisted Lieutenant Colonel Reinhardt and his party in obtaining charts and information regarding all the bases visited during the flight. Your knowledge of the Portuguese language was particularly helpful at Natal and Montevideo. As Co-Pilot, you conducted yourself in an outstanding manner throughout the entire mission, which reflects much credit upon yourself and the Air Transport Command.

3. Copies of this correspondence will be made a part of your official 201 file.

WILLIAM H. TUNNER
Maj Gen, USA
Commanding

10 FEB 70 22 16 2

COA996
PTTEZYUW DICE0066 0412159-EEEE--COOK. 10/2/70 259/SQ
ZNY EEEEE
P 102144Z FEB 70 /10
FM DET 1 AFSATELLITECONFCLTY SUNNYVALE CALIF
TO 6596 INSTMNSQ VANDENBERG AFB CALIF
BT   Col Halvorsen   VANDENBERG, AFB RADAR SITE
UNCLAS E F T O SMOT FEB 70. FOR ATTN OF STATION
COMMANDER. SUBJECT: STATION PERFORMANCE ON IRON 6531.
A REVIEW OF RECORDS FROM OPS 6531 REVEALS THAT YOUR LOCATION WAS
THE ONLY DUAL-SIDED STATION TO ACHIEVE 100 PERCENT PERFORMANCE
FOR THE ENTIRE DURATION OF THE FLIGHT TEST.
SUCH EXCELLENT PERFORMANCE CAN ONLY BE ACCOMPLISHED BY EXTRA
EFFORT ON THE PART OF YOUR STATION PERSONNEL AND IS HIGHLY
COMMENDABLE.
PLEASE EXTEND MY HEARTIEST CONGRATULATIONS TO ALL PERSONNEL.
SIGNED C E HUGHES
BT
#0066

FM JEP 43A/HQ USAF WASH DC 131911Z MAY 1949 forwarded to New.
TO UESQ/1ST LT GAIL S HALVORSEN AO 38 251
        125TH TRANSPORT SQD BROOKLEY AFB MOBILE ALA
INFO JEZ/COMMATS ANDREWS AFB CAMP SPRINGS MD
        JEBAB/ATLANTIC DIV MATS WESTOVER AFB MASS
        UESC/CO 1601ST ATG BROOKLEY AFB MOBILE ALA
NNNN   AF GRNC

FROM AFPMP-12-C 16597 PD I AM PLEASED TO INFORM YOU THAT
YOU HAVE BEEN SELECTED AS THE WINNER OF THE CHENEY AWARD
FOR THE YEAR 1948 PD SUBJD AWARD CONSISTS OF A PLAQUE
CMA CERTIFICATE AND $500.00 CHECK PD PRESENTATION OF THIS
AWARD WILL BE HERE IN WASHINGTON WITHIN THE NEXT 30 DAYS
PD WE SHALL INFORM YOU OF THE EXACT DATE AND TIME IN THE
NEAR FUTURE PD PLEASE ACCEPT MY HEARIEST CONGRATULATIONS
PD
CFN AFPMP-12-C 1948 $500.00
                1319427

THE WHITE HOUSE

July 9, 1987

Dear Colonel Halvorsen:

How nice it was to receive your recent message.
Thank you very much for taking the time to let
me know how you feel. It always brightens my
day -- and does wonders for my morale -- to
hear from friends like you. I'm delighted to
know that I can continue to count on your
support.

With my very best wishes,

Sincerely,

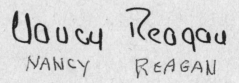

NANCY   REAGAN

Colonel Gail S. Halvorsen, Ret.
78 Northcroft Lane
Newbury, Berkshire   RG13 1BN
England (ON OUR MISSION)

BERLIN AIRLIFT MEMORIAL
Luftbrücke Chapter
The Airlift Association, Inc.
Rhein Main Air Base
6000 Frankfurt/Main 75
West Germany
APO New York 09057
Tel.: (069) 699-6005

Colonel Gail S. Halvorsen (USAF, Retired)   31 May 85
1220 Locust Lane
Provo, Utah 84601

Dear Colonel Halvorsen

We would like to extend to you an invitation to the dedication of the "GAIL S. HALVORSEN AMERICAN ELEMENTARY SCHOOL." This school is our present on-base elementary school which we felt, at a time for remembering events associated with "Operation Vittles," should be named after yourself as being one of the most remembered airmen of the operation, suitably nicknamed the "CANDY BOMBER." The same day, we will dedicate the Junior High School in memory of your commander, Lieutenant General William H. Tunner. The ceremony dedicating both schools will be held at 1400 hours on June 11, 1985 at the school complex. We will, during the ceremony, present a plaque to the school for the schools' exterior with the following inscription:

GAIL S. HALVORSEN
AMERICAN ELEMENTARY SCHOOL

DEDICATED AT RHEIN-MAIN AIR BASE IN HONOR OF COLONEL GAIL S. HALVORSEN--THE "CANDY BOMBER" OF THE BERLIN AIRLIFT. HIS HUMANITARIAN EFFORT ON BEHALF OF THE CHILDREN OF BERLIN TYPIFIES THE AMERICAN AIRMAN'S CONCERN FOR CHILDREN OF THE WORLD.

We look forward to this event and hope that if at all possible, you and your immediate family will join us. We apologize for the late notice but plans could not be confirmed earlier due to the President's European Trip. If you are able to come, please telephone us at 0049-69-699-7080. It is best to phone since the mail may require up to six days. Thank you very much.

Cordially yours

RAYMOND D. HOLDEN
President
Luftbruecke Chapter of the Airlift Association

4 MAR 1974

Dr Joseph L Bishop
President, Weber State College
3750 Harrision Boulevard
Ogden, Utah 84403

Dear Dr Bishop

This is to introduce Colonel Gail S Halvorsen, recently assigned to
Hill AFB as a special assistant to me until he retires on 31 August 1974.
He returns to his native Utah following a four year assignment as Base
Commander, Templehof Central Airport, Berlin, Germany.

Colonel Halvorsen is well known within our "blue suit" circles for his
singular outstanding contributions during the gigantic Berlin Airlift of
the late forties. His impressive career covers the gamut of responsible
operational, managerial, and command assignments. These vary from the
highly technical evaluation of foreign technology in assessing the overall
threat to our national security to his most recent tour in Berlin where he
implemented unusual innovative "people" programs in dealing successfully
with extremely sensitive and potentially explosive conditions in the racial
and social actions areas.

I intend to fully exploit this officer's background and innovative thinking
during the next few months to the benefit of the military and civilian work
force at Hill AFB. I have asked Colonel Halvorsen to undertake a comprehen-
sive review of our social actions and base education programs to help define
our short, mid and long range goals in the affirmative action areas of equal
employment opportunity, upward mobility of minority groups, and improved
communication links between this installation and its surrounding communities.

In this ambitious endeavor, I have asked Colonel Halvorsen to contact members
of your various departments to air views and to determine where your fine
institution may be of assistance. I can predict this gentleman will become
totally involved very quickly and that his contributions will continue in
his role as private citizen long after he retires from active duty.

Colonel Halvorsen will be arranging a visit with you shortly. I know you
will find talking with him a pleasant and refreshing experience.

Sincerely

SIGNED

BRYCE POE II
Major General, USAF
Commander

Too late to make this printing, Gail is scheduled to fly with the Air
Mobility Command C-17 Aircraft Air Evacuation of wounded out
of Afghanistan to Ramstein Air Base in Germany and then on to
Andrews AFB in Washington, DC.